THE IMPERATIVE

━ THE IMPERATIVE

ALPHONSO LINGIS

INDIANA UNIVERSITY PRESS
Bloomington and Indianapolis

This book is a publication of

Indiana University Press
601 North Morton Street
Bloomington, Indiana 47404-3797 USA

www.indiana.edu/~iupress

Telephone orders   800-842-6796
Fax orders   812-855-7931
Orders by e-mail   iuporder@indiana.edu

The paper used in this publication meets the minimum requirements of
American National Standard for Information Sciences—Permanence of
Paper for Printed Library Materials, ANSI Z39.48-1984.

Manufactured in the United States of America

Library of Congress Cataloging-in-Publication Data

Lingis, Alphonso, date
    The imperative / Alphonso Lingis.
      p.   cm. — (Studies in Continental thought)
    ISBN 978-0-253-33442-8 (cloth : alk. paper). —
    ISBN 978-0-253-21231-3 (pbk. : alk. paper)
        1. Commands (Logic) 2. Perception (Philosophy)
    3. Kant, Immanuel, 1724–1804.   I. Title.   II. Series.
    BC199.C5L56   1998
    128—dc21   98-20003

    2   3   4   5   6   13   12   11   10   09   08

CONTENTS

.

ILLUSTRATIONS

The photographs were taken by the author.

THE IMPERATIVE

PREFACE

There are in our cultures today those who in all things seek to set forth their freedom. For them humans are the free animals; freedom is not only distinctive to humans, but is their supreme and sole value. For them civilization is emancipation; the further we go, we extend freedom from want and from labor. With freedom alone they constitute individual identities. One must be free to give birth or not, to live or not. Death itself is no longer to make a mockery of our freedom; though we have to die, we must be free to die when and as we choose.

Industrialization, automation, and robotization require fewer and fewer people as productive workers. The mass production of consumer commodities and free markets require everybody as consumers. They make freedom of choice possible—the freedom to make our individual selection from among the ever-growing number of mass-produced consumer goods laid out along the aisles of shopping malls, the freedom to make our individual selection from the information and infotainment on the electronic highways. Virtual reality technology is on the verge of eliminating for any consumer the constraints distance and the inertia of material reality put on individual freedom. We will touch the remote on our virtual reality equipment and instantaneously surround ourselves with whatever apartment overlooking the Seine or the Baie aux Anges, whatever manor or chateau, beach or mountain, tropical ocean or glacier we choose.

But how many people are there who in everything they think, do, and feel respond to directives! For craftsmen there is a right way to make something and a right way to use each thing. Hang gliders learn from the winds and the thermals and from the materials the right way to make and to fly a hang glider, as the composer learns from the symphony emerging before him which are not yet the right notes.

Explorers of microcosms and macrocosms devote their minds to those microcosms and macrocosms like dancers to the score and calibrate their sense organs and manual skills to their instruments like performers to the keyboard and pedals of a cathedral organ or synthesizer. The more vast and baffling the problem—the formation of galaxies millions of light years from our own and in the first seconds of the cosmic Big Bang, armed conflicts between peoples that have lasted for generations, global warming and the destruction of Earth's ozone shield—the more there arise, exultant and proud, people who find in it a summons for their minds, their feelings, and their skills.

As for performers there are the right feelings to find for every turn in the score of the concerto and dance, there are the right feelings to find for an ancient ritual in a sacred place, for the Colca Canyon, and for an endangered animal species, for condors and lemurs. Every sensualist knows that there is a right way to savor the wine and the smells of a tropical town, a right way to move in the rain forest and see the hummingbird dance and the night come upon the mountain town.

Tact is a brief and modest word, but it designates the right way to speak or to be silent before our adolescent child in his anguish and before the excitement of two people in the nursing home who have fallen in love.

Everyone who has found how to live and live well knows that there will come a time when he or she will have to find the right answer to the question: Is now the time for me to die? And he or she knows there are times when we have to be there to accompany someone who has to die.

The transport of the one who has at length found the song he was born to sing, who one day standing on Himalayan summits or in the white Antarctic night knows that she sees the grand things her eyes were made to see, who has found the intellectual, social, or environmental task that commits in the most exacting fashion all his energies, is the exultation of destiny.

How many people are there who prize only the no-self and a compassion extended to cosmic dimensions! They do not only find imperatives in pressing or remote problems addressed to their minds and in the structure of instruments and organisms given over to their care, but hear summons addressed to their sensibility and sensuality in the desert and the ocean, the summer and the winter, the dawn and the night. These people instinctively turn away from the one who with air conditioning and electric lighting freely chooses his own climate when outside the tropical rain is dancing over the dry dormant earth and over the laughing birds and children. When night comes, they confide themselves to it; insomniacs, Maurice Blanchot wrote, are people who cannot trust and cannot be trusted. For sensuality understands the summons of the sun that as it sets pours its gold on the seas, the summons of the outer regions where the world of work and reason enters into decomposition.

These exultant oblivion-seekers are not isolated individuals. How much there is that is festive in society—champagne that is poured out like water to anyone without asking recompense, dangerous games where limb or life are staked for nothing, voluptuousness and orgasm, the bravery that leaps into the icy river to save the drowning stranger and that under the dictatorship joins the guerrillas!

The one who emerges, not through the force of arms and of propaganda, as the leader of his or her people does not only call forth unto a system of just laws, but also to a land, a climate, a way of building, a way of rejoicing and feasting, a way of remembering the dead, and of dying.

This book speaks of those whose minds find at each moment exacting directives in the structure of the sciences and in the problem, whose hands find imperatives in the materials, the instruments, and the craft, whose hearts find summons in the glaciers and the tropical butterflies given to their care. The book elaborates two theses: it shows sensibility, sensuality, and perception to be not reactions to physical causality nor adjustments to physical pressures, nor free and spontaneous impositions of order on amorphous data, but responses to directives. And, resisting all forms of holism,[1] it holds that the directives we find in the night, the elements, the home, the alien spaces, the carpentry of things, the halos and reflections of things, the faces of fellow humans, and death have to be described separately.

In the philosophy of mind, no one doubts that thought is subject to an imperative; as soon as we think, we find that we must conceive concepts correctly and reason rightly.[2] Thought is obedience. The freedom of thought makes this obedience possible. Thought subjects itself to the order of what is, what was and shall be, what must be and may be. Though our eyes and hands are free to wander unhindered in the environment, they do not shape a drifting mass of tints and tones; things become visible and tangible as tasks and summons for sight and touch.

The working natural scientist subjects his or her theoretical elaborations to observable events. Every theoretical entity he or she constructs remains but hypothetical, an instrument of calculation, until it enables him or her to make predictions which are verified by observation, that is, by perceivable events in a practicable field. The diverse kinds of laws, paradigms, and schemata used to relate observations, the different mathematics and different logics used to formulate observations and laws, and the models used to construct theories respond to the ways nature is ordered.

But the philosophy of mind has failed to recognize the way perception *responds to directives*. The proliferation of new models to understand our relationship with our environments continues to invoke only the two opposites of physical determinism or a freedom exercised in choice and in the positing of values and prescriptions. Genetics, which announces the identification of genetic determination of alcoholism, sexual preference, and character traits, supplies new models for our response to our environment, and reinforces explanation by physical determinism. Cognitive science seeks in information science models for the data processing done by our minds.

The philosophy of mind still maintains the notion that a properly untendentious description of our perceived environment would not mention any directives, that what guides our sensibility and perception as directives is in fact imposed or projected onto our surroundings. The *ought* cannot be derived from the *is*; the account of what is is a description, by an observer whose freedom is nowise compromised, of the environment where everything is produced by causal determinism. One attempts to produce such a description.[3] The focusing of the eyes, the centering of the touch and the nonrandom stroking that perceives things would have to be described as compound reflex reactions. The directives vision and movement find in perceived things would have to be described as clues and information-bits that are in fact projected onto things by interpretation. Reality can only be said to "constrain" our perception, our imagination, our kinesics, but not direct it.[4]

Discourse in terms of means and ends is parallel to the discourse that separates facts from values. For this discourse, it is not that perception sees directives in things and in the levels upon which things are found; it is that once ends are projected or posited by the agent, the intervening things are seen as means, routes, or obstacles.

This kind of account, where perception is compound reflex reaction and projective interpretation, disconnects the representation constructed by the working empirical scientist, whose most speculative thought is subject to the order he finds in nature, from his, and everyone's, perceptual experience. The notion that physics is a genre of literature is the consequence.[5]

This book sets out to show how the movements of perception—both the controlled perception which is scientific observation, and the continual perception which is the scientist's, and our, life—are neither reactions and adjustments nor intentional and teleological acts, but responses. If perception is not a succession of mechanical determinisms, our perception exercises freedom because it obeys directives it finds in the environment.

The philosophy of mind no longer describes the environment as perceived by our sensory-motor organisms as a stream of sensations rippling on the surfaces of our bodies. The perceived field is no longer taken to be a patchwork of tints, a succession of tones, a multitude of pressures. But the phenomenology of perception still recognizes but one kind of percept: things, figures against the background.

This book rejects such reductionism, and describes separately the night, the elements, the sensory levels, the space inhabited, the alien spaces, the carpentry of things, the halos and reflections of things, the sensitive and susceptible surfaces of fellow-animate beings, and their faces. It describes separately the summons the night addresses to us and the directives the elements, the habitat and the alien spaces, the things, the impracticable zones, and our fellow living beings address to us.

The accepted account of sensibility and sensuality is only an account of affective reactions of pleasure and pain in our psychophysiological substance. Some philosophers have even asserted that everything we do is done for pleasure—an assertion which can avoid being obviously false only by, vacuously, identifying our desire to do something with pleasure. The philosophy of mind has failed to recognize the obedience in sensibility and sensuality which every sensualist knows.

Part Two of this book studies how Immanuel Kant isolated the experience of the imperative and how he represented the way it commands our imagination, our perception, and our action. Kant set forth the rational agent as one who is not simply efficacious but exemplary, and a responsible citizen of the universe.

Contemporary developments in our scientific representation of nature, the technological field, and society force us to revise Kant's account of how the imperative for law functions in science. Our criticisms of the way Kant represented the form of the imperative enable us to bring out in relief the force of the imperative.

We then go on to explain how and why we must supply, in place of Kant's account of the medley of sense, a phenomenology of perception which brings out the order and ordinance inherent in the perceived field. The order we put in our scientific representation of the universe has to be connected to the order we find in our observed environment. But the holism and figure-ground presuppositions of the phenomenology of perception have to be discarded. A field of perceived things is not the basic form of our sentient contact with our environment. We must elaborate a phenomenology of the levels upon which things take form, the kinds of space, the sensuous elements, and the night.

Since we must know nature as it is, act in an environment structured as a practicable field, and interact with others, Kant understood that we must take nature, the practicable world, and society as models of how we must integrate ourselves in order to act rationally. But the Kantian notion of model, or "type," has to be criticized and replaced, as well as the Kantian conception of the imagination which has to produce the advance representation of our initiatives.

Kant's distinction between hypothetical and categorical imperatives has to be understood differently. The theory of intentionality and of intentional acts distorts our relationship with our environment. The holistic and universalistic presuppositions of Kant's practical philosophy have to be disengaged and criticized.

We all admit that the organization of a branch of mathematics or natural science commands whoever calculates and whoever observes and argues scientifically. Everyone who speaks as a physicist or a biologist, and everyone who frames questions to put to a physicist or a biologist, recognizes as decrees the determination, within that scientific discipline, of what could count as observations, what standards of accuracy in determining observations are possible, how the words of common language are restricted and refined for use in different scientific disciplines and for practical or technological uses, what could count as an argument in logic, in physics, in history, in literary criticism or in biblical scholarship, in economics, in penology, in jurisprudence, and in military strategy. And there is no natural science without a mind committed to control all its constructions by empirical observation. We also all admit that the axes of the sublime and the base, the essential and the accessory, the triumphant and the degenerate, the noble and the superficial, are set forth in epics and legends, monuments and shrines, statues and songs. We find in them the ordinances that command our affirmations and our reprobations, our hopes and our visions. We also all admit that in the order in effect in the basic forms of association in our society, set forth in its constitution and in the sacrifices of our heroes, the meaning and form of justice are set forth. The Japanese who with a discreet sign invites us to take off our shoes before entering the house, the Brazilian who during Carnaval throws forth his *alegria* and his samba to the foreign visitor also promulgate directives, and for us to respond to them is to enter into association.

But we also find that we are contested by the words of foreigners and of those without scientific culture, and by the nonsense of children, the laughter of adults, and the nonwisdom of the aged. We recognize as imperative the words of the sick and the dying. The silence of the departed and the silenced weighs on what we say and do.

PART ONE — *Directives*

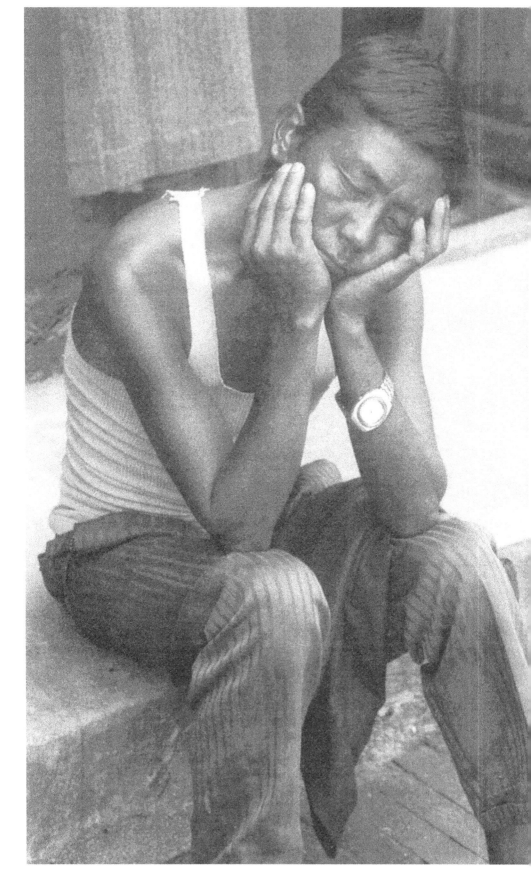

ONE ⬝ *Nightwatch*

As the day comes to an end, the twilight dissolves the surfaces, absorbing their colors, leaving their reflections suspended in space. The luminous transparency in open spaces condenses into beams and phosphorescence. Things lose their separateness. The shadows advance over the colors and the contours that they outlined are lost. Darkness infiltrates the landscape, obliterating its paths and filling up its open planes. Overhead the blue of the atmosphere recedes and the starlights drift over unmeasurable distances.

The electrification of human habitats maintains this twilight and stops the oncoming of the night. Along city streets the shop windows, restaurants, bars, and discos enclose twilight havens where the hard edges of things are softened into glows and reflections.

When the night itself is there, there is no longer anything to see. The cries, murmurs, and rumbles no longer locate separate beings signalling one another or colliding with one another on observable coordinates. Shouts or distant lights do not mark locations in the night but make the whole of the night vibrant. The odors drift. The ground which we feel and which extends indefinitely about us no longer supports things in their places. What we touch adheres to our hands and is no longer the contour of something closed over its own structure and substance. The rain no longer streaks the distance of its fall.

Though there is no longer anything to see, we see and do not see nothingness. We see the darkness. The night is not a black mass that stops our sight on the surfaces of our eyes; our look goes out into the night which is vast and boundless. The sense of sight can be taut and acute in the depths of the dark. The night is not a substance but an event; it pervades a space freed from barriers and horizons. It extends a duration which moves without breaking up into moments; night comes incessantly in a presence which does not mark a residue as past nor outline a different presence to come.

The darkness which softly wipes away the urgencies and the destinations and the hard edges of reality is felt in an enjoyment that conforms to its depths without resistance and that gives itself over to the rumble of the city and the murmur of nature, to the silken, mossy, and liquid substances that caress our bodies, to the odors and savors adrift in their own space. The visible night gives way to a high noon of sounds, odors, and textures.

When we close our doors to forces that may prey on us under the cover of darkness, we redouble the visible night with an auditory night, an olfactory night, a tactile night.

Then as the night abolishes the menaces from the surfaces and back alleys of the landscape, it insinuates the menace of its own disquietude.

The night invades; it is within as well as without. It depersonalizes. The night effaces the identity we had which we had found reflected from faces and responsibilities, effaces the shape and skills we had gauged from mirrors and tools, and effaces the immaturity or maturity we assumed and the gender we maintained. Without our coordinates, our post, and our tasks spread about us, we are not left alone with ourselves. As the night invades, it extinguishes our personality, our efficacy, and our identity. One subsists as a vigilance that watches where there is nothing to watch for.

The night is not nothing; it is real, it is a presence without boundaries, frontiers, or limits. It is without ends, goals, or termination. In insomnia one finds one's existence and one's wakefulness maintained by the incessant oncoming of the night. Insomnia longs for sleep from which the day will awaken it. Insomnia suffers from not being able to put an end to itself, not being able to die. To act, to cast forth a project, is to take hold of an end. It is the end we take hold of that can make our movement determinate. Insomnia is existence divested of every form of project, existence as indeterminate endurance.

Insomnia is a wakefulness that suffers from not being able to awaken, to be born. To be born is to take place, to occupy a place that is one's own. The "I" is a standpoint, a point of departure.

Descartes, seated by his fire, abolishes the world by universal methodic doubt, then posits the existence of his *I* as a firm and unshakable ground, and sets out to ensure a world about himself. Consciousness is this power to establish a *here*, a starting point. It is initiative, awakening to. . . . It is the power to interrupt, to create a blank slate. It is to turn to the past as though it were effaced by methodic doubt, and construct it, starting from being here now.

The nocturnal vigilance is a wakefulness that cannot commence, cannot awaken as a consciousness. Insomnia suffers from being unable to interrupt the night, or itself. More than the impossibility of goals, ends, the impossibility of terminating and determining, it suffers the impossibility of commencing.

An anonymous vigilance subsists in the heart of the night, a wakefulness that the incessant oncoming of the night maintains. The night watches.

Insomnia senses a night beyond the night that interrupts and preserves the day. It senses the cosmic night which the practicable day does not interrupt or put an end to.

There is a willfulness that is determined to seize hold of the life in which one finds oneself born and harness all its energies into giving oneself form, identity, and significance. Willfulness stakes out paths and directions, takes hold of ends, stabilizes and maintains a practicable field. For it, insomnia is a suffering that inexplicably befalls it, and which one's willful initiatives—swallowing a drink or a pill—can put an end to, in order to flee the night into a sleep that harbors and restores one's energies for another day.

Yet we know the night not just as something to be pushed away with artificial electric twilights or eluded by sleep. Each of us knows how the night itself summons us.

Insomnia is also a spell that one accepts and obeys, recognizing the summons to aimlessly wander the night, to exist as the pulse of anonymous awareness where the night watches and is for itself. It obeys this summons in the seductive fatalism that recognizes a destiny.

Do we not also know moments when the night summons us in the high noon of a world? In the day agitated by the orders shouted by and to others and stamped on things, one listens to oneself. One hearkens to one's inner garrulousness assessing prospects and ambitions, and one's consciousness is a mirror in which one evaluates the images of one's shape and skills that are cast on others. But when one hearkens to the wakefulness of sensibility in the inner night of one's organism, one can sense the summons of the night itself.

TWO — *The Elements*

The Sensuous Depths

We awaken immersed in a plenum. Feeling spreads into a tangible medium and into warmth or cold. Smell drifts in a dank or scented space. Hearing stirs in the bustle of the day or the rustling of the night. The eyes open and are flooded by the light or find themselves adrift in darkness. The look that springs forth is sustained by the radiance or the dark. The sensuous elements are not there as a multiplicity that has to be collected or as data that have to be identified, but as depths without surfaces or boundaries.[1]

Visual space is not pure transparency; it is filled with light, intense or somber, crystalline or mellow, serene or lugubrious. If the light seems neutral when we look at things, that is because its color is without surfaces and our eyes do not go to encounter it like an object. Our gaze is immersed in it and sees with its cast, sees the colors of things that surface as contrasts with the tone of the light. The directions in which the light, advancing across the planes and probing the hollows, conducts our gaze lead to things and to open vistas and to horizons, seas, and skies. Each time we look for illuminated things, our gaze refracts off their surfaces into the luminous openness. The light is sometimes so dazzling that we can see nothing through it. Its radiance fills and thickens the space such that the surfaces of gleaming or shadowy things at a distance are dissolved in it.

Our hearing is not just a recording of sounds, noises, and words, with silences between them. For hearing to awaken is to listen in to the rumble of the city or the murmur of nature, from which sounds emerge and back into which they sink. At the concert hall our listening lets go of the static of whispered conversation and coughs to settle into the undifferentiated vibrancy of the symphonic field where the melody will begin to move. A voice takes up the vibrant currents of the air and sends its intonations into them.

To awaken to the heat, damp, or cold is not to feel these as surfaces laid on the contours of our body. Sultriness or aridity extends space about us. The cold is an unbounded zone open about our mobile body; the torrid expanse spreads amorphous directions for languid movement.

Our awakening is terrestrial; we feel the stability of the ground, even when we try to imagine ourselves trying to get on our feet on a sphere whirling through empty space at twelve thousand miles an hour. The ground is not—save for astronauts and for the imagination of astronomers—the planet, an object which viewed from the distance is spherical. We do not feel ourselves on a platform supported by nothing but feel a reservoir of support extending indefinitely in depth. The ground is not there as the sum-total of particles of dirt and rocks we have seen. Once we have made contact with terra firma the force of the ground extends indefinitely before our steps. The ground is there when we assume a posture and support ourselves upright to move and when we no longer position ourselves and abandon our limbs and organs to its repose.

To go to sleep is to entrust oneself to the immemorial repose of the terrestrial.[2] It is to let go of the layout of tasks and urgencies, to turn in one's bed and hold on to the pillow as the condensation of repose and support. Because our sensibility maintains contact with the ground in and by sleep, the great black bird that rises and falls and turns into a handful of ashes does not soar in directions that are only those of our respiration and sexual stirrings, and our dreams do not circulate in the paths of practicable fields but hover over the ground and are terrestrial.

When we lose contact with the ground, we find ourselves not in empty space but in wind and open sea. At the concert we find ourselves moving in a sonorous expanse whose density surges and rolls. The mountains that loom over the mists, the moon that draws us up from the darkened landscape, and the shadows into which fleeting visions beckon draw us into zones of mercurial elements. There are also apparitions in dreams that do not safeguard our sleep but, like omens caught sight of in ruined sanctuaries, summon us into spaces dense with nonterrestrial forces.

The elements are sensuous realities; they are not perceptible frameworks, dimensions, or intelligible structures. The elemental qualities are not properties of underlying substrates. Not contained within surfaces or boundaries, the cold, the dark, the gloom, the savage, the sustaining, the luminous, and the exultant extend in depth indefinitely. They are not terms, not nouns, but free-floating adjectives.

The elements are there by incessant oncoming. Their presence does not indicate a source from which they come. The illumination about us dissolves all traces of its own past tones. The light which opens the horizons obturates with its radiance the horizons of its future. Beyond its presence, its future is not a framework of consistency and coherence that assures the present but is the realm of chance and fortune. The light is there as by grace. The ground rises in incessant presence without evincing the universality and necessity of laws that would found it nor the abyss in which it would be contingently suspended. It extends its support before us without retaining upon itself, like an object becoming more consistent as we turn about it, the accumulating force of its past support, and it is there without guarantees for the future. Sonority floats in waves of presence which rise to shut out the distant rumble of waves to come and the echoes of its past. The ardor into which the voluptuous sensuality advances is there without its oncoming tide having been seen from a distance and without its endurance being measurable; it is there as the element of adventure where nothing was anticipated nor is promised.

Sensuality

The elements are not a multiplicity of discrete things successively perceived in their places from vantage points and collated; they are not sensed by a perception which identifies surface patterns. The elements are not given as a medley of information-bits, sensations that have sense and are signs given for us to organize and interpret. The sensibility for the elements is not the passive recording of a multiplicity of elementary sense data. It is not apprehension which makes contact with the contours of a substance, nor comprehension which takes hold of something consistent and coherent. It is not a movement that casts our synergic forces toward some object-objective present across a distance. Sensuality is not intentionality, is not a movement aiming at something exterior, transcendent, a movement that objectifies; it is not identification of a diversity with an ideal identity term; it is not imposition of form nor attribution of meaning.

Sensuality is a movement of involution in a medium. One finds the light by immersion, one is in atmosphere, in sonority, in redolence or in stench, in warmth or in cold. One feels the supporting element of the ground rising up within one's posture and within one's orgasmic prostration and in one's sleep where dreams hover. The elements manifest themselves adverbially, qualifying our movements and our composure. Liquidity is there by giving play to the hand that is immersed in it, by yielding before and sustaining the thrust of the swimmer. The light manifests its radiance by buoying up the gaze that is set free in it. The terrestrial manifests its sustaining force to the mobility of the one who stands upright and advances, and manifests its repose to the one who abandons his postural tension to it.

The element is not a means, not an intermediary. Sensing is a movement which ends with the given, which envisions no future and no possibility, ends in light, warmth, ardor, resonance, earth. Its involution, not an initiative but a conformity with what supports and sustains, a conformity with the sensuous medium, was identified by Emmanuel Levinas as enjoyment.[3]

Life has been understood negatively, when it is needs and lacks suffered in a material system that were taken to agitate it and move it toward outside resources. The force of life has been taken to be the force of these negativities. Life was taken to posit a constellation of entities in the void as its objectives, to be consumed. The movement in the self, by which an organism is for-itself, was taken to be an anxiety that recoils to negate the nothingness of needs and lacks. (This concept is verified in modern society, where overpopulation and the political management of appropriation makes life in the deprived labor for the needs of life, and where the human engineering of marketing implants ever more needs and ever more wants in the appropriators.)

Natural and nascent life finds itself immersed from the first in the superabundance of the elements, in boundless light, in terrestrial warmth, in resonating depths. Vitality is reborn in pleasure, contented with the ephemeral and gratuitous splendor of the twilight over the industrial zones of the city, with the repose of the warm flank of a hillside among the lazy buzzing of iridescent flies, with a drink of spring water come upon by chance in the shade, contented with its contentment that forgets the cares that brought one here and the death to come.

Needs and wants are not the essence of life; they are partial and superficial, accidents that befall the plenitude of an organism which is alive for itself in its sensuality. The ego that arises as an awareness of needs and wants, the self that forms as the cramp knotted over this negativity, is intermittent and shallow. Sentient life is not a succession of initiatives driven by need and want and aiming at objectives. Life is not the recurrence of need and satisfaction, eating and getting hungry again and drinking and getting thirsty again, in an enterprise that is gradually losing its reserve, in an anxiety repeatedly postponing death.

The care for reality is not at bottom an anxiety, which makes our life an apprehension of things and beings because it is apprehensive of nothingness. To be born is not to be cast into the imminence of nothingness but to find oneself in a sustaining medium. The perception of things does not arise out of a universal methodic doubt and its contact with the terrestrial is not a quest for certainty that is a quest for assurance.

The movement that senses the elements is not the movement of need or want, the movement of an emptiness that seeks, in the distance, a content; sensuality finds itself in a gratuitous abundance. To be alive is to enjoy the light, enjoy the support of the ground, the open paths and the buoyancy of the air.

There is enjoyment even in the repugnance that shrinks back from the lugubrious light and the rank and fetid zones. There is a complacency in the melancholy and moroseness that feel the gloom of the skies and the misery of barren time. Nausea does not succeed in preventing the rancid spell of decomposition from invading one; revulsion is already caught in the mire; horror is a fascination. These excremental feelings draw their momentum from their involution in the medium of decomposition. Filled with it as with a content, there is indulgence and contentment in them. Abhorrence and loathing with gulping breath and flared nostrils savor the taste and smell of evil until it sweats from all one's pores. One enjoys one's abhorrence and one's loathing, and enjoys with them.

Life lives on sensation; the elements are a nourishing medium. Enjoyment is savoring what one assimilates and that in which one is assimilated. There are intermittent and superficial hungers that are sated in the eating, and there is an appetite that comes in the eating, savoring without consuming. Prior to the practical perception that draws out a practicable layout and pursues objectives, there is the appetite for the elements. The light is not just transparency which the gaze slips through on its way to distant surfaces; our gaze delights in the vivacity of the light itself. It assimilates in its languor the soft depths of the dark. The sonority is not just a succession of sense data which the hearing identifies as signals and information-bits; the ears are contented with the resonance of realm beyond realm as with a content. The touch lets go of things to relish the terrestrial and solar warmth. The earth extends its indefinite expanses before the steps of the nomad who is not scouting for any retreat, moved by his appetite for open roads and uncharted deserts. Erotic sensuality is not a hunger, a lack that pines for some absent organ, some object-"a" from which it was castrated (Lacan). It surges in a vitality that lacks nothing, is fed and sheltered and contented, a vitality that greets the earth, the skies, the day and the night with the ardor of kisses and caresses.

The Sensual Ego

We enjoy the desert air and the monsoon, and we enjoy our enjoyment. The movement of immersion in the elements turns upon itself. The eyes that are delighted with the light enjoy seeing, the lungs enjoy savoring the good air, the vitality caressed by the warmth of the day revels in its contentment, the gait sustained by the ground enjoys walking buoyantly. A home is not only a locked building full of implements and stocked to satisfy needs; it is a zone of tranquillity and warmth and a precinct of intimacy recessed from the uncharted expanses of the alien. We are contented with enjoying our home.

Life savors its appetites, which are not negativities, agitations arising out of lacks and suffering; they are contents, they fill up life. Life is nourished by its own tastes. The widow fills her life by enjoying the day, the sunlight, taking a walk, enjoying the smell and damp of the springtime earth, enjoying the air, enjoying the appetite for life that the plenitude of the day sustains.

Existing is not just being-there, in the contingency known by anxiety, finding oneself here by extending a field of objectives out there. A living being, immersed in the elements, arises in the discontinuity of a new pleasure. Immersed in the superabundant plenitude of the elements, a sensual life is itself an excess and a superabundance, a life that is good to live.

The inner movement in enjoyment, by which the sensuality affected with the elements is affected with its own savoring of the elements, is the first eddy of ipseity. The movement that diagrams a self, the as-for-me, is not an intuition but an intensification. The ego is a pleasure. A life that finds itself in the elements does not differentiate itself by consuming what it lacks and closing in upon itself. Its contentment overflows the content and is broadcast back to the elements. In the warm radiance of the day, in the serenity of the fields and hills and silver abysses of the skies, how good to be alive! How fresh it feels! How refreshing is this silence! How calm the evening is! The ego ex-ists not in the affirmative mode, a self-positing position, but in the exclamatory mode.

The ego is not an incorporeal entity that forms in the emptiness of needs, wants, and intentions. It is not suspended on the recognition of others, a signifier in discourse and in the grammar of kinship, economic, and political codes. It does not take form on the shape of recognizable skills, body-armor, and uniforms. It also does not first arise with the postural schema that maintains itself in a field of objectives and emanates a "body image" about itself—that first form of reflection, Maurice Merleau-Ponty said.[4] The primary ego is not that of a body positing and positioning itself; it is the exclamation of a body in abandon exposing itself. The eddies of egoism form in the taste for enjoyment by which our skillful and armed body becomes sensual flesh. The ego is the nakedness of our body. This nakedness is not lived as vulnerability and in timidity and precautions, but, beneath its garb and its armor, as sensuality of life exposing itself to the elements, enjoying its exposure.

Things, that is, substances that have contours that contain their properties, can be apprehended, detached, and possessed. We identify ourselves and maintain our identity in the midst of things. The elements which extend no horizons of objectives, which pass into no stock that can be recalled, do not lend themselves to appropriation. One cannot make oneself something separate and consolidate oneself by appropriating the light, by making private property and depriving others of the atmosphere, by monopolizing the warmth, by expropriating the things distributed over the ground of their support. The light that invades the eyes depersonalizes and the anonymity of light illuminates in one's eyes; one sees as eyes of flesh see. The forest murmurs and the rumble of the city invade one's ears that hear as hearing hears. The ground that rises up into one's posture depersonalizes; one stands as trees stand, one walks as terrestrial life walks, and one rests as terrestrial life rests and as rocks and sands rest.

The primary sense of the self is not a movement that reflects itself and maintains itself by containing and consolidating or synopsizing a multiplicity of elementary sense data. Essentially exclamatory, it is a movement of involution that intensifies and releases its energies into the elements in which the sensual body is immersed. How calm the dawn is! How fresh it feels! How pungent it smells!—the zest and the savor vitalizing one's spiraling sensuality are cast forth again indefinitely into the depths of the dawn. Pleasure forms in multiple and ephemeral eddies of enjoyment. Sensual pleasures which throw forth the exclamations of their superabundance to the elements cast forth their eddies of involution elsewhere on the naked substance of the body. The elements are unfragmented and fathomless; in the sensual body immersed in them eddies of egoism differentiate, diversify, discharge, and dissipate. The sensual body is not one through a postural axis that maintains itself but through the labyrinth of pleasures that intersect and lose themselves in one another.

Sensuality is vulnerable and mortal from the start. But this susceptibility is not the vertiginous sense of the contingency of all being, an intuition into the nothingness in which all being would be perilously adrift, and which could be foreseen as a real possibility just beyond the thin screen of the actual being. The contingency of the sensuous element is in the very fullness and abundance of the present, which plugs up the horizons, the future. Coming from nowhere, going nowhere, it is here in incessant oncoming. It is not here as though grudgingly parceled out by the malevolence of nothingness, but as gratuity and grace. Fortuity and goodness of the light, the play of iridescent color, the resplendence of tones, the liquidity of the swelling forces!

Pleasure is exposed not only to the withdrawal of the element it enjoys

but to the excesses of its torrential oncoming. The naked flesh is susceptible to being wounded and rent and pained by the force of the sensuous
element. In pain one is backed up into oneself, mired in oneself, in-oneself;
pain announces the end of sensibility not through a conversion into nothingness, annihilation, but at the limit of prostration, conversion into passivity, materialization. It is in the force of the elements and not in their
inconsistency that our death already touches us and the sensual body knows
its mortality.

Common Enjoyment

Modern epistemology contrasted the public existence of words with the
private and ineffable existence of sensations. Another's mind would be composed of states and intentions accessible to itself alone; another's body will
be exhaustively explored by the outside initiatives of observation and au-
topsy without finding any evidence of mental states other than those of the
outside observer himself. Yet the surges of sensibility and sensuality in its
movements are the very evidence of a body. What is more unmistakable
than the radiant vision in the eyes of a child awakened in the car and shown
the sea dancing in the sun? What is more evident than the warmth of feeling that awakens to the hands that draw off the covers and to the kiss with
which we touch his face? In the darkness of the crowded bus, we feel the
warmth of the body of the passenger next to us and the shiftings that stir
from within. We do not make contact with his sensibility through some
visible surfaces we see, some sounds we hear, and for which we find evidence that the other sees and hears them too. With no quasi-determinate
sense of what it is the other sees and hears, we are awake with the sense of
another sensibility in the dark parallel to our own. The albatrosses soaring
around the planet, the minnows weaving through the seaweed are rays of
vision that materialize momentarily for our eyes; the caterpillars bobbing
along the tomato leaves, the octopods advancing across the coral reefs are
probings of feeling palpating the tangible which we ourselves are fingering.

Imperative Pleasure

When modern philosophy depicted the whole of the outside environment
as decomposable into elementary data possessing only the "primary properties" of extension and duration, each existing in exclusive occupancy of
a point p and an instant t—determining them by negation—it found itself
constrained to conceive of life as a spontaneous, self-activating force. But
enjoyment is not just a spontaneous initiative of a life which nourishes

itself from the outside and turns upon itself as upon an end in itself. Sensuality is awakened from the outside. The luminosity more vast than any panorama that the light outlines in it, the vibrancy that prolongs itself outside the city and beyond the murmur of nature, the darkness more abysmal than the night from which the day dawns and into which it confides itself—summons the sensuality. There is not mastery but obedience in pleasure.

Do we not find offensive the one who, when the landscapes fade out before the epiphany of the cosmic light, puts shades over his eyes so that he can read his texts or decipher the alleged text of the spectacle of a world; do we not turn away from the hubris of the one who persists in that hour to myopically engineer his layout of implements and gear? We turn away, as from a disordered and distempered organism, from the one who pulls the blinds of his windows against the glory of high noon to crawl into his bed and cover his head with blankets, only to then offend the night with his fidgety agitations under the glare of incandescent wires. We avert our eyes, as from someone leprous, from the one who is rigid and cold in the midst of the languorous immensity of the summer. We quickly move out of earshot from the one who prattles shallowness under the vaults of the Hagia Sophia in whose stones the gravity of Byzantine glory has come to rest. Do we not avert our steps from the one whose ears are scabbed with a Walkman when the winter arrives tinkling in on snowflakes, when the petals of the cherry trees of the Silver Pavilion of Kyoto fall in frail music, when the down of white birds intones the skies over Irian Jaya? We shudder before the temerity of the one who stalks resolutely after his prey through the day when the light and the green waves of springtime themselves are dancing. We flee from the contumacy of the one who looks with dry eyes and arid soul over his affairs when the spring rains return all things to their oceanic origins. Do we not smell violence and violation in the desiccating sarcasms of the one who holds on to his mast when the whole landscape streams, undulates, rushes into the dawns beyond dawn, the aurora borealis beyond every north or south pole?

Beyond the practicable and unpracticable vistas through which the nomadism of life charts its own vital space, is it not summoned to the terrestrial, the oceanic, the ardent, the lambent, the night beyond night that no life charts or lays claim to?

Our sensibility is drawn into these depths beyond the profiles of things, summoned by them. Do not our visionary eyes, which are not stopped on the lustrous things which the light of day illuminates, obey another imperative in the light—the imperative to be a *lumen naturale*, a solar incandescence which squanders almost all of its light in the darkness without bringing any things within its reach? Is not our stand which enjoys the support of the earth also subjected to its order, to support itself and to repose? Does not the vertigo over the abyss that descends and descends without end obey not the imperative of the depth to maintain surfaces, but another imperative that depth promotes and is: to deepen? Does not the hearing that hears not the particular songs, cries, and noises of the landscape but the vibrancy beyond the corridors of a world, obey the imperative addressed to hearing that it become vibrant? Is there not in the ground, dampness, atmosphere, and light in which we are immersed the imperative that life live in becoming support, becoming oceanic, becoming aerial, spiritual, lambent?

To withdraw from the illuminated surfaces and contours is to give ourselves over to the night, to be drawn not by the insistence of the body but by an elemental imperative. Sleep is not an extinction of consciousness produced by the nothingness of the night which engulfs all things, but a summons come from the repose of the earth, reservoir of confidence, and from the night beyond night.

The sensuous involution in the elements makes our eyes luminous, our hands warm, our posture supportive, our voice voluble and spiritual and our face ardent. In the involution of enjoyment is generated the gratuitous and excess energies that seek release in exultation. Enjoyment is freedom; in the enjoyment of the radiance of the spring day and the warmth of the ground, we forget our cares, our cravings, and our objectives; we forget our losses and our compensations and we let go of what holds us. Every enjoyment is a death: a dying we know, not as the Heideggerian anxiety knows it—being hurled from being into nothingness—and not as pain knows it— a being mired in oneself and backed up into oneself by the passage into passivity—but as dissolution into the beginningless, endless, and fathomless plenum of the elements.

THREE ⟶ *The Levels*

As we approach an outdoor café in the night, we see a volume of amber-hued glow. When we enter it, our gaze is filled with the light. We begin to make out forms discolored with an amber wash, like fish seen through troubled waters. After some moments, the luminous haze neutralizes and the faces of people emerge in the hues of their own complexions. The tone of the light has become a level about which the colors of things and faces surface according to the intensity and density of their contrast with this level. The light ceases to function as a radiance in which we are immersed; we begin to look not at it but with it and according to it. Our gaze follows the light as it penetrates open spaces, outlines contours, stops on surfaces, and comes upon things it finds and does not make visible.

We enter a concert hall and find ourselves enveloped by the confused hubbub of the crowd and the rumble of the orchestra tuning. The conductor lowers his baton, the opening notes of the music begin, and our hearing finds the key and the volume level of the music. The shuffling and coughing of the audience recede; we hear the pitch, volume, and density of the notes as they rise and fall from the level. The level is given by sounding the dominant at the start. The hearing that remains anchored to it is not a sensory memory which reproduces this sound at each moment of the composition (which would make of each note heard a chord). It is a listening-according-to which orients the listening to the successive notes and chords. The musical characteristics particularize and individuate the succession of sounds as emergences and divergences from the dominant.

We enter a room where a reception is in progress and the babel that fills our ears makes us think it would be impossible to carry on a conversation there. But then we find ourselves facing someone, and our hearing adjusts to the noise level and we find ourselves picking out effortlessly what she is saying. We hear the call of the night owl rising in the whir of the wind. We listen to the droning of a bee and the murmur of the meadow ceases to throb gently on all sides and within us to become a plane along which the buzzing stops and starts again.

When we set out to feel something, our extending hand locates the level of the tangible, which it makes contact with not as an objective but as a directive, imposing the pressure, sweep, and periodicity of the movement that will distinguish the grain of the wood, the fur of an animal, or the Braille letters on the surface of the page.

The light shows itself in its hue and shimmering intensity; it begins to function as illumination and to lead us to things when we enter it. The level of the music is audible and extends the melody before us when we tune into it. The level of the tangible has to be found by the hand. The levels are sensory data that do not occupy a here and a now to the exclusion of other data. They do not simply extend into the space and time of a sensorial field; they extend that field. The odorous and the olfactory are not so many discrete events that make an impact on our sensory surfaces; the smell and taste open upon an odorous medium and a savorous medium and adjust to the level in which in the pungent night our sense of smell can find the perfume of a woman and our taste discern the tang of spring water.

The levels extend directions of support for a movement of vision, hearing, and touch that does not simply get displaced in spasms provoked by the impact of successive stimuli. The light extends an expanse in which things can be seen, extends a wave of duration in which distant things are things we have seen receding into a past and are objectives we shall see. The dominant extends the musical space and duration in which the melody will rise and descend, approach and drift off, expand and contract, in which a melodic initiative will be concluded. In the field of the tangible nothing materializes in the now; each tangible thing forms on a level along which its pattern and grain and resistance can be extended—a level which is also a wave of duration, and a tangible thing is as much a temporal formation as is a melody. In the perceived environment waves of duration are not segments marked out on an empty linear dimension of time prior to the intuition of any content; duration extends as levels of passing and approaching visibility, resonance, and substance along which movements of our look, our listening, and our touch are directed.

The environment does not extend in an empty geometrical space whose infinite dimensions are conceived by a formula or intuited a priori. Its levels are not the Euclidean dimensions of space and the linear dimension of time on which Kant and Hegel locate the here-and-now given *this*. The levels which open a sensible field before our perception are not a framework or the organization according to which things are distributed. By conceiving the perceptual field as the background behind a figure, Edmund Husserl's phenomenology conceives it as a multiplicity of possible figures and misses the functioning of levels. For him inner and outer horizons are ordered sequences of potential figures. The levels are not the system of connections or relationships, such as the spatiotemporal or causal or conditioning relationships specified within the scientific representation of objectivity. The levels are not the network of instrumental couplings Martin Heidegger took to constitute the primary layout of the environment as a practicable field.

The layout of levels is not a network of vectors of signification, where from the first each sensation-complex signifies or refers to other sensation-complexes for a sensibility that is intentional or comprehending. It is not a set of universal and necessary laws of which the things perception locates would be the instantiations.

A level is neither a purely intelligible order, nor a positive form given to a pure a priori intuition; it is a sensory phenomenon. A level is neither a content grasped in a perception nor a form imposed on an amorphous matter of sensation; it is that with which or according to which we perceive. It is not an object formed nor an organization elaborated among objects but an ordinance taken up and followed through.

The levels of our practicable field, but also those of the unpracticable domains, the landscapes, the visions, the spheres of musicality, the oneiric and the erotic fields, the vistas through which our nomadic vitality wanders, are not suspended in void nor in the empty immanence in which our representational faculty a priori would extend the pure form of exteriority. They take form in a vital medium, in light, in the air, in warmth, in the tangible density of exteriority, on the ground, in the night, and in the night beyond night.

The Reliefs

The particulars we see, hear, touch, smell, and taste are salients, contours, contrasts, inceptions and terminations that take form on the levels. The musical functions of a sound do not inhere in it as properties; a C-flat of itself is neither high nor low, thick nor thin, near nor far, lilting nor emphatic. A sound gets its particularizing characteristics—pitch, volume, closeness or remoteness, intensity, attack or terminating force—from the sonorous level from which it diverges, that of the party noise or of the key of the sonata. A color acquires its compactness, vibrancy, localization or diffusion, and inviting or obstructing function from the level of the light and from the general tone of the field which it punctuates. A roughness, sleek-ness, or tackiness is not a multiplicity of pressure points with tactile void between them; it is a rhythmic pattern which rises in relief from the level of the tangible at which the touching hand maintains its pressure and across which it moves.

The music can resound on the surfaces of the drums and in the throats of the trumpets and saxophones; it can pervade the space before us; it can reverberate in our ears; or it can rumble in our bodies not as something specifically acoustic but as visceral stridency, a harmonious quiescence, or a vital throbbing. The eyes are drawn to the red of the roses in the hospital room where it figures as a specific accent in the diffused chromatic atmo-sphere of the room. As the gaze settles on it, the red condenses a spiraled volume. As the eyes narrow their focus on it, the red intensifies and out-lines flakes of surface, the contours of the petals. But even as it surfaces as a property inherent in a thing, the red also plays across the room; the red of the roses intensifies the green of the leaves, bleaches the whiteness of the sheets of the bed, and rouges the cheeks of the sick friend. The whole room became more vibrant when the roses were brought in. As our gaze, seduced, now travels around the coils of the petals, it is drawn inward, into the inner substance of the petals and into the brooding crimson darkness of the core. The red proves translucent, the surface-red makes surface the smoothness and elasticity of the petals and their fleshy thickness. If we remain with it long enough, the red no longer keeps its distance, invades our eyes, and is felt as a sultry ardor that spreads throughout our sensibility.

The red would not be the red it is were it not for the light which it invades and with which it contrasts, were it not for the leaves it greens and the sheets it whitens. In condensing and intensifying on the petals, it be-comes tangible, and this red would not be the red it is did it not mold surfaces with a certain grain and elasticity and quilt depth with a particular spongy density. A color that would be just in a now, that would not have made itself felt a moment before as a solicitation in the tonal atmosphere, and that would not hold the gaze along a certain duration, would not be visible at all.

Painters know that colors are not given as opaque points or patches in-ertly held in their contours; they have an experimental knowledge of what a touch of color does—it bulges out or hollows out space, thins it or makes it dense, intensifies or fades a constellation of other colors, stabilizes or sends movement across planes and distances. A color is not an instanta-neous impact in a dimension of empty time already extended; it presents a present, swells out or contracts a pulse of time, makes it diaphanous or dense; it emerges out of an atmosphere or separates progressively from another color, sends forth a wave which brings other colors into relief and solicits their approach, lays open a field of possibility, and thus materializes a wave of duration.[1] A tone is not an event localized in a line of time already extended. It extends a specific kind of duration in a space it opens; its attack and its after-effects materialize a pulse of duration in a musical space whose scope and volume show through the visual shape of the concert hall which it interferes with and which does not define it. The sensory flux does not present itself as so many space-time points successively filled and emptied and filled again, but as a sphere in which points pivot, edges extend levels, spaces open paths, colors intensify themselves by playing across a field, tones thicken and approach and thin out and recede and send their overtones into one another.

The sensible is not there as the affirmed, the posited, as so many univocal and exclusionary occupancies of positions on the axes of space and time, so many terminations of the interrogation that is in our vacant and volatile looks. The sensible itself exists, Maurice Merleau-Ponty says, in the interrogative mode.[2] The sensible that we encounter when we look, listen, smell, and touch is not an answer to a questioning that is only in us, is not a plenum that fills in a blank opened by us, a positum that is the affirmative answer to our inquiries. The sensible is there as the surfacing of a depth, a crest on a wave that pursues its way. Our eyes touch lightly over the things, just enough to recognize on them the functions the program of our everyday concerns have put on them, but when we look beneath this human function to their sensible natures our eyes discover in the color, our ears in the resonance, not something that is just what it is here and now, without mystery, but something like a quest they join, a tone on its way calling forth echoes and responses—a red come from its own past, responding not to our question but to its own, seeking its redness beyond the moment and elsewhere, water seeking its liquidity in the sunlight rippling across the cypresses in the back of the garden. If, after so many years of looking at colors and listening to tones, they still continue to stir ever anew our curiosity, it is because we do not stand before them as well-appointed judges who demand yes-or-no answers to questions we have an indefatigable capacity to formulate; it is because we find ourselves, despite our own interests and our own answers, incessantly intrigued by the wanderings and mute wonderings, the intimations and divagations of which colors and tones are the materializations.

A sensory entity is a particular that can veer into a level. In some of Anton Webern's dodecaphonic compositions the twelve tones are first played in an order which constitutes a melody; as they are repeated, additional notes rise and fall about each of them. The tones which figured as particulars with which a melody rose and fell, advanced and returned, begin to figure simultaneously as keys about which micromelodies circulate. When the vase of red roses is brought into the hospital room, at first the uniform whiteness of the walls and sheets intensifies the redness of the roses which glows in the coils of the petals. But after awhile the redness of the roses functions as the color-level against which our arms appear pallid and the faces of visitors vibrant. The sensorial is a medium in which any point turns into a pivot, any edge into a level, any surface into a plane, any space between things into a path.

We should not say that, with time, a point does not maintain itself as something toward which the movement of sight advances and upon which it stops, but rather that it turns into a pivot with which the movement of sight orients itself. For there is not first a line of time, as there is not first a layout of empty space, in which sensory patches appear. The endurance of a tone or a color is not a reproduction of a particular in the succession of particular instants of time, and the perception that follows it is not a recall that superimposes upon the particular appearance in the now its particular appearances in a succession of past nows. It is the tone, by extending itself into a level along which other tones rise and fall, that extends duration in a musical space. It is the red of the roses, by inaugurating a new level in visibility along which the crisp whiteness of the sheets, the pallor of the hands, the bright complexions of visitors occur as events soliciting the vision to advance, that extends a wave of duration in the field of the visible. A level is the sensory content of a figure that does not cease to hold the movement of perception when that movement lets go of the contours of that figure; it is a visible that extends unobserved, a sonority that is no longer listened to but that prolongs itself along with the sounds and the silences, a substantiality no longer palpated but that subtends the reliefs and the contours felt—an objective before us that becomes a directive weighing on us.

Sensing is not a passive recording of impressions which would then be mentally organized; the sensibility in our organism is inseparable from its motility. If paper, silk, and balsa wood are just laid on our belly or hand, we feel only vague and indecisive pressures. In order to feel sizes, shapes, weights, and textures, we have to mobilize our fingers as one prehensile organ, support our hand movements with a positioning of our posture, and move across the surface and contours of the solid or through the air or water. To feel the sharpness of a blade, we have to move our finger across it, with the appropriate pressure and rate of movement which we pick up from the blade. The movements that feel the grain of the wood or the nap of the fur are neither desultory and spasmodic nor preprogrammed and willful; they organize as they proceed, with a pacing that is induced in them from the level of the tangible.

To see the water, our eyes do not fix on where it is, do not fix on the pool; our look is led by the light which precedes it and guides it and is led by the movement of the water which makes visible the zigzags of the tiles and the sheets of light within it and sends flashing ripples across the screen of cypresses at the back of the garden.[3] It is each time with a specific focusing and movement of the eyes rubbing across it and with a sustaining postural schema of the body that we see red, yellow, or green. We see yellow with a tightening up, green with a sliding up-and-down movement in the muscle tonus. Red is rending, yellow is stinging, blue and green induce rest and concentration. Green accelerates and red slows down movements outward. The body opens to see blue and green, contracts to view red and yellow.[4] When our body movements are concentrated on putting back together a typewriter we are repairing, the music subsides into an agitation that pulls on us without exhibiting a musical development; when though we keep silent our larynx muscles shape the surging music, when we dance to it, then the phrases, timbre, and cadences sound out. Touching, seeing, hearing, savoring, and feeling are not reactions and not spontaneous initiatives, but are conducted moves.

The Upright Field

The field of perception is not extended like the geometrical space in which science locates its objects. It extends upward and downward, from close to far, to the right and to the left.

Up and down mean nothing in geometrical space, nor in the universe considered objectively—unless we imagine an observer standing on a fixed platform in space. They are also not determined by the position of the images of things on our retinas; when we tilt our heads, the door frame, whose retinal image is now oblique, remains upright.

When we look into an inclined mirror in the shoe store, at first we see the walls and floor and us ourselves leaning at an angle; but after a few moments the scene acquires the normal up-down level and we see ourselves standing upright again. Clinical psychologist G. M. Stratton contrived eyeglasses that reverse the retinal images. He then at first saw a visual field upside-down; then fragmented with some patches right-side up, and finally after a week of wearing them he saw things right-side-up again in their normal upward or downward positions in the visual field.[5]

Is then the up-down axis a relationship which the mind inserts among

mental images adrift in psychic space? But the judgment the subject wearing the eyeglasses makes that the floor is really below and the ceiling above
is not enough to make him see the things arrayed in their normal orientation. Knowing, as we do, that our body has not tilted does not make us see
upright the image of ourselves in that shoe-store mirror inclined at an angle.
In Stratton's experiment, as in our experience with the shoe-store mirror,
what realigns the visual layout about us is the effective engagement of our
practical powers with the things they handle.

Certain cardinal visual things—the sink, the floor, the walls and the
door—extend not only surfaces across which the eyes can circulate but a
level along which multiple practical operations are possible. They solicit
our movements and govern our postures. In the measure that we handle
these things, the up-down orientation of their manipulatable forms extends
into their visual appearances that the mirror had tilted or Stratton's eyeglasses had reversed and reorients them. When we cease to view the image
of ourselves in the mirror against the background of the room outside the
mirror and look at our shoes in the mirror as we pace back and forth, this
space the mirror shows in which we find we can function, can walk without tipping over, appears visually upright. In the course of the week as
Stratton wore the eyeglasses, first the doors, the floor, the tables, and sink
he locates as he moves and acts begin to appear visually upright again, and
then constellations of objects about these things line up with them. The
visual appearances of the things to which he turns line up again along the
upward and footward directions of his practical movements.

The dominant up-down axis that emerges in the field is parallel to the
axis of our upright posture. What aligns visual appearances along this up-
down axis is not the statistical frequency of this parallelism. The vertical
position of our heads is not the most frequent one with which we view
things. Things remain upright when we lean over. The up-down axis which
orients the visual appearances of things persists as our body parts bow and
when our bodies, letting go of their tasks, lie prone.[6] But the up-down axis
is the level of our most effective action. The upright posture is the posture
with which our multiple body powers are most available for the principal
things our body deals with and upon which it anchors itself.[7] In the free-
standing position our two arms and legs are equally available to approach
and handle things; our sensibility is symmetrically turned to the things
before us. Movements in any direction are possible and ready.

The level along which multiple practical operations on accessible things
are possible solicits a corresponding axis in our posture, which then aligns
the visual appearances according to up and down. We enter an airplane,
seat ourselves, adjust our position and movements to the practicable area

about us, arrange the things we will occupy ourselves with during the flight—correspondence, a half-finished novel. The plane takes off; we look out the window, relating ourselves to the city below, putting ourselves down there with our car and our friends, trying to see our lover stretching out to us; we feel ourselves being tilted back as the floor of the plane lists. Then the surface of earth slips back from our prehension, we can no longer make out its posts and occupations, its equipment; it becomes vague and inconsistent. We turn back to our papers, get occupied with our lunch, the cabin floor and ceiling become horizontal and the things align according to the vertical; when we glance at the window it is earth's surface that sways across it.

The level of orientation is also the level of reality; the landscape seen the first day through Stratton's eyeglasses appears not only overturned but strange and inconsistent. The aspect a person, and the room, show in a tilted mirror in the shoe store is not only disconnected from the upright things seen outside the mirror; the tilted forms in the mirror also appear less real. After an accident, the gathered crowd the victim lying prone on the ground sees does not only appear unrecognizable—caricatural faces perched over poles covered with fabric, hands flailing like tentacles—but appears as aberrations of reality. A face in a photograph turned upside-down turns into patterns of color on a surface. It is when our position is lined up along the level of our most effective sensory-motor interaction with the things and the landscape that they settle into the consistency and subsistence of reality.

Even before the apparition and placing of any object, the perceptual field opens in depth as soon as our eyes open, as soon as our sensibility awakens and stirs. Even lying inertly on the bed with eyes closed, our perception is not reduced to pressures felt on our own surfaces; when no movement extends our sensibility outward to reach for things, the surfaces of our bodies cease to form a frontier between an inner space and an outer environment, leaving an undifferentiated voluminosity extending indefinitely in depth. When we sit on a bench on the edge of a look-out point over the valleys and stop locating landmarks or envisioning objectives, the planes lose their differentiation, the colors cease to congeal surfaces and become atmospheric, and we see distance extending about us. When we cease locating the sounds on the surfaces of the drums and in the throats of saxophones and trumpets, the music advances and recedes from us within a depth of musical space. When we feel, the tangible is not just what pressures our surfaces are in contact with; from the first we sense a depth of the tangible and extend our hands into it.

We do not perceive forms that overlap in the frontal plane, and then calculate the distances between them on the flat projection an eye located overhead would see. We see in a depth of reality which recedes from us. The close-far axis is not a dimension in the metric sense, extending discrete locations that are occupied by a succession of images of different sizes. It is a level our sensory-motor bodies find when they extend themselves, a range of the visible our gaze finds itself conducted across, a gradient of reality upon which our postures, gestures, and initiatives apply themselves. Down the close-far axis reliefs exposed to the adequate exploration of our powers harbor each a thickness of content and crowd back other content, and thus appear as real things.

The field extended by the up-down and close-far levels functions as a level of rest, across which movements pull at or break free from our prehensions.

The particular movements we make toward things that move or stabilize are made possible by the movement our sensory-motor powers make to maintain themselves on the levels that extend and maintain a field. If, seated in the compartment of a train and waiting for the departure, we get absorbed in what someone is doing over in the adjacent train, then when one of the trains starts to pull out, it will be ours we experience as pulling us away from the scene or person we are holding on to with multiple interests. But if, when we entered our compartment, we settled into our seat, are now arranging our papers or starting a conversation with our fellow-passengers, then it is the adjacent train we see backing out across the side window. Later, engrossed in our reading or in conversation, it is the trees that lean over and file across the window of the train and not the car that pitches as the train mounts the hills.

As we move our movement is not an augmentation or diminution of the distance between perceived things and our bodies as perceived figures on the map on the landscape, a displacement indifferently attributable to either. When we stop before a stable thing, the rest is not the constancy of the positions of the perceived figure of our body and of that thing relative to one another on the map of the landscape, a constancy indifferently attributable to either of our relative positions or to the landscape. The levels are not seen like the lines of a diagram, and we do not look at our bodies moving across a field. The levels address our posture and are sensed in its stability and orientation. We sense the movement of our bodies become functional by advancing toward things which stabilize on or slip across those levels. The levels hold things upright and in place. Things at rest share the stability of the field. Things in movement—a leaf falling, a cart rolling down a hill—break from the levels and their movement is internal to them; they strain or break away from our hold on them.

The Coherence and Consistency of the Field

When we see we join a level of the visible, and monocular images, visual memories, and ideas represented by diagrams float disconnected from it. "If," Merleau-Ponty writes, "during the process of reflection, I cease to hear sounds, then suddenly become receptive to them again, they appear to me to be already there, and I pick up a thread which I had dropped but which is unbroken."[8] Once we hear something, we are henceforth open to a level of resounding reality; every subsequent sound and silence will be a crest or a trough along this level. The silence on the auditory plane is not that of the purely negative silence of the thought so absorbed in its tasks that it is closed to sensory receptivity.

The consistency and coherence of a level is not that of a continuity of real sounds succeeding real sounds and real visual patterns continually given. It is not that what is really visible maintains its visibility and becomes more clear and distinct as we look; memories and obsessive ideas can well be more consistent and sharply outlined than indecisive colors and fleeting patterns that form on the level of the visible. The consistency and coherence of a level is also not that of certain traits perceived in every audible or visual pattern. The visual is not constituted ex post facto, by an understanding that judges certain images incompatible with the rest, and therefore illusions, memories, or figments of the imagination.

A perceivable *style* is a distinctive kind of coherence. To recognize someone's gait in his successive steps that adjust to the terrain is not to identify some factor that remains the same in a series where other factors are different; it is to perceive each step displacing and departing from the form of the prior one and open to variation in turn. As we recognize a page of an author by the style, we recognize a friend by the style of his conversation, his gesturing, his way of entering into a group, of taking decisions or procrastinating. The style maintains a coherence we catch on to, which varies within a certain range without our being able to predict exactly what turn it will take. We recognize at once what does not belong to this style— sentences, postures, initiatives, and emotions that we perceive as not really his but imported from elsewhere.

Similarly, we recognize the visible, the audible, and the tangible by the way with which they diversely unfold the field. The purely negative silence of a thought closed to sensory receptivity does not have the bearing with which silences insert themselves in a conversation, a sonata, or a thunderstorm. Monocular images, mirages, and diagrams of ideas do not move with the style of the visible. The style of the tangible we recognize even in light and fleeting touches.

This coherence of the visible, this consistency of the audible level is not comprehended in a representation; it is given, we encounter it, we catch on to it. There is not a logic in the levels we perceive which our minds have the capacity to possess in advance in their formulas, but there is a style to the diverse levels which our bodies are competent to catch on to.

For our sentient and mobile bodies are fields in which each phase and each part catches on to the style of the others. In our bodies a particular movement forms neither as a simple reaction to a present stimulation nor as a pure invention; it forms as a variation of a prior movement, and it subsists as a schema that will be varied in turn. Every step inaugurates a gait; every displacement a gesture.

A posture, a gesture, and an operation form as each position and displacement of one limb of our bodies is picked up by and transposed upon the others. The buoyant style of the step initiated by the legs gets picked up by the swinging arms, by the scanning glance of the eyes. Through a transverse propagation of kinetic styles across its limbs and members our body holds together in movement. And its sensibility integrates as it advances, by not the visual qualia but something of the style of filling space that got picked on the eyes getting transferred and transposed onto the other senses.[9] Our sensitive-motile bodies are substances in which every particular position and initiative gets generalized, stylized, and engenders variants of itself.

Our bodies perceive and move in a field. In stylizing, their positions and initiatives pick up the style of the field, catch on to its levels and follow its directives.

Levels of Coexistence

Our awakening to a field is not a succession of discrete acts that are so many spontaneous initiatives. We do not open our eyes, capture a flake of the visible, and then start again to capture another. With the first step a gait is launched; upon opening our eyes our look slides onto the misty or crisp level of the visible morning. Our awakening stylizes itself at once. The level of the visible is a directive that advances by unfolding its gradations and variations. Each move of the look varies the prior one and launches further variations. The look slides back and forth, seeing the visible from reversed and displaced directions. Each look takes form as one of a certain range of ways of looking, equivalent and interchangeable.

Our look is not a singular initiative that catches hold of a flake of the visible materializing uniquely from it, vanishing when the look shifts. It awakens in a variant of a looking that finds itself launched on an indefinite prolongation. We awaken to the level of the visible that sleep had not lost sight of; we awaken to see what we had been looking at the night before, picking up a thread that had been dropped but is unbroken. In awakening we rejoin an immemorial seeing.

When we come upon another carnal being moving along the levels of the visible and the tangible where we are moving, we sense that sentient body seeing and touching as we see and touch. We do not find ourselves in a private universe. The environment, open to indefinite variants of the seeing, touching, hearing with which we are moving in it, is from the first open to a seeing, touching, and hearing that went on before we awakened, can go on on the levels beyond what we see, touch, and hear, and will go on after we return to sleep. The ground supports and the skies are open to movements other than our own.

When our right hand touches our left, it makes contact with the level which directs the pressure and the pace of its movement that makes the pulp and rough texture thinly strewn with hairs of that left hand palpable. But at the same time the right hand feels rising up in our left hand a movement of feeling to meet it, and feels that movement of feeling as a variant of its own movement. When our hand takes hold of the hand of a child or a feeble person to guide it to the handrail of the listing ship, the movement of feeling and the diagram of force of our hand merges into that of the child or feeble person. We feel our sensibility displace itself into the other and to be a variant of that of the other. The other's body is not first a material mass stationed before us and exposed to our inspection and its sentient life not a hypothesis we form in our mind to explain its movements. From the first we find ourselves accompanied, in our movements down the levels of the field, by other sensibilities, other sentient bodies.

We awaken to the rays of light, the expanses of the ground, the clouds and the skies alive with a multiple, anonymous, and moving sensibility. We can never make into a real possibility the notion that as soon as we turn away from the tree it lapses into the inaccessible metaphysical apeiron of the Kantian in-itself. The tree falling in the depths of the rain-forest night is heard by innumerable animal ears of which our own are an ephemeral variant. The deep-sea coral reefs and the Antarctic icescapes are not visions our own eyes create; they are reliefs on levels of visibility visible in general.

Imperative Levels

The levels are not a framework of a field we find already there as soon as we awaken. They emerge from the sensory elements, as directives that summon. By following them, a field unfolds.

It is not with a conceptual apprehension of the system and the laws, nor through an active collating of a discrete multiplicity of data, but with our postural agility and tractability that we know the way the visible, the sonorous, the tangible, and the olfactory unfold and develop. This knowledge is not a program we format moment by moment for our nervous circuitry and musculature; it is a style of synergic mobilization of our sensibility that is induced from the styles of the visible, the tangible, and the sonorous. For a style is not something that we conceive but something we catch on to and that captivates us. The continuation onward of the level summons and guides us from beyond. The layout of a field is not a system of directions, but of directives.

Our gaze sweeps across the environs but the views that form are not desultory; our eyes are led by the light down the paths that lead to things. Vision is, Merleau-Ponty says, an inspired exegesis.[10] The visible reliefs and contours separate of themselves from the perspectival deformations, the appearances made unstable by the distances, dimmed by the intervening medium, the reflections off other things or splashed over them by the light, the monocular images and the mirages. The purely negative silence of a thought closed to sensory receptivity separates from the silences inserted in a conversation, a sonata, or a thunderstorm.

The intersensorial field is not a system given ready-made and a priori intuited as the spatiotemporal framework and the system of laws which engenders its instantiations, nor is it constructed like a hypothesis out of the particularities of our own visual field and those of others. The correspondence of levels, their coherence and consistency, summon us as a directive. This directive is received not on our conceptual understanding and reason, is not first an imperative to conceive for each sensible pattern a universal and necessary category, is not first an imperative for our reason to connect up the objects we conceptually recognize with universal and necessary laws. It is received on our sensory-motor bodies, as bodies we have to anchor on the levels down which our vision, our touch, our listening move. This directive weighs on us, finalizing our perception toward perceiving a field and not a chaos of drifting and bobbling patterns. Obedience to the levels precedes and makes possible any initiative, any freedom, of sensibility and movement.

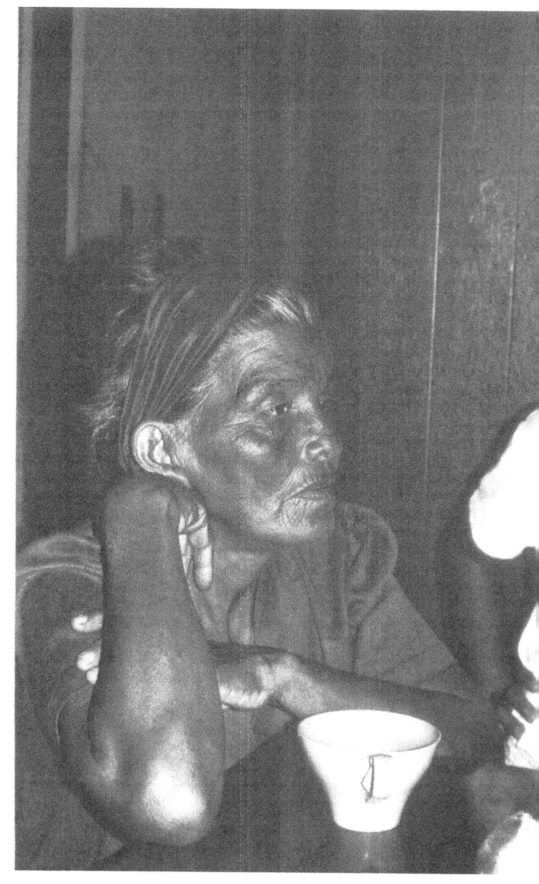

FOUR ➤ *The Intimate and the Alien*

*J*ust arrived in the old colonial city, we watch the cobblestone streets and the centuries-old houses parade before our eyes, a spectacle suspended in the tropical sunlight. We stop before a low stone building with blind facade and august studded-wood door. A plaque informs us that this was the Palace of the Conquistador, built in 1502. We see that it is now a hotel. We step inside the timber-ceilinged entrance hall, are led up the majestic staircase to the upper floor, and admire, like a set in some historical movie, the great oak table under the chandelier.

Then we take a room. The spectacle of the lofty room and its colonial furnishings now thickens with the smells of old wood and damp stone and of the fabrics of the bed cover and draperies, and with the tangible density of their substances. The spectacle becomes real. From its window the street extends to the main square and, to the left, to the cathedral. Established now in this haven of reality, we can begin to envision the layout of the city, of the country, and of the country beyond it we had left to come here.

The levels of the field do not simply move along with us, like a framework attached to our bodies. If we are just passing through a city, it drifts in a sensory flux. When we stop there, we catch on to the level at which the sun-bleached or foggy city becomes visible; when we have set up our tents, we catch on to the level at which the shadowless ice cliffs under Antarctic white-out and the desert in a sandstorm become tangible. When we make this place our home base, our look advances down the directions of the light and we see the level at which the touch must maintain its pressure and movement. What resounds from afar already leads our look to the distance. The levels of warmth and humidity extend along the levels of the visible and the tangible.

The home base is that zone of intimacy where the levels are within one another, and we within them. The warmth and the cold are not out of kilter from the tangible; the sonorous does not, like Chinese court music rising from the instruments in the hands of sneaker-shod adolescents in the high school auditorium, disconnect from the visible. Whatever takes form in the intimacy of the home has intersensorial consistency. Unlike statues observed in museums and meals being prepared on the television screen in far-off cities, whatever takes form can be seen and touched and smelt. To inhabit a home base is to feel ourselves anchored in reality and it in us.

The coherence of the levels, this way they have of corresponding to one another as they extend from a focus, is not something we can depict in a representation or plot with equations. Their correspondence is not given once and for all; it is caught on to when we find our sensitivity shifting continuously from the level of vision to the level of the tangible and the resounding. Our sensibility for the diverse levels integrates itself in assuming a posture, with which we can move along the level of the tangible, and the level of the tangible also reveals the reliefs and contours of the visible. To establish a home base is to take up a position. To maintain a home base is to take up positions and postures.

A home is a zone of warmth and tranquillity, a condensation in the elements. It is given in enjoyment. We can feel at home—in the tropics, in the desert, in the mountains—before laying out a field of tasks there, or before setting out to form a representation of the outlying environment. We can feel at home somewhere as soon as we arrive. Isabelle Eberhardt felt at home in the deserts of Africa as soon as she got there, felt she had finally come home, though she had not yet surveyed the routes that would make it practicable and had no idea what she could take over to make a living there or what she might do there.[1] She was to become a nomad, establishing each time a place of retreat in the desert, and most often leaving it never to cross that way again.

The home base is a pole of repose and departure. The zone of the intimate is a pole of warmth and tranquillity that we keep sight of as we advance into the stretches of the alien and that our nomadic wanderings gravitate back to.

To repose is to let our mobile posture dissolve and give ourselves over to the supporting rest of the ground. The ground is the reservoir of support and it maintains our powers composed for us. The zone of intimacy to which we return is the here maintained by the ground where we sleep and awaken. Sleep is not simply the result of exhaustion; exhaustion produces sleeplessness. Sleep comes when repose and confidence are there.

Repose and sleep break the continuity of the flow of consciousness and make awakening possible, break the continuity of vital processes and make initiatives possible. Repose establishes a position for awakening to things and fields and for commencements. From the door of our home we go forth into an environment stabilized and real.

The outlying regions of the alien are expanses where the levels come apart. The seashore we step out of the car to contemplate is a spectacle; the fishermen are forms, without the smell, the voices. They thus appear at a distance, disconnected from the roadway we are following. The landscape drifts like a scene or a vision. The intense cold settled on the plains separates us from the level of the vision extending paths where things are to be seen. The opening chords of *Boris Godounov* unfold an ancient epic landscape disconnected from the hall of the Chamber of the Supreme Soviet in the Kremlin, where the orchestra of factory workers are pounding on pigskin drums and sawing with bows on catgut.

The levels have a way of separating. There is a seduction to the visible, a way it has of inviting us to follow the ways the patterns emerge and dissolve, a seduction to the audible, and, absorbed in the rhythm and cadence of the conversation, we find ourselves losing sight of our appearance, our clothes and the diagrams of our gestures, losing sight of the seedy club and its derelict habitués. The vibrant smells of an Italian restaurant area and a Bangkok alley where women are stirring steaming woks captivate us and leave our eyes drifting. The levels separating lead onward to the outer regions of the alien.

But the home summons us. The longing for a home is not derived from an idea or ideal contrived by infantile insecurities or unsettled thought. The establishing of a home for ourselves is not just an initiative of our own. We cannot willfully make just anywhere a home.

Welcome, hospitality, is expressed in Spanish, *Mi casa es su casa.* It makes the streets that drifted by as a spectacle real. She or he who makes the place we visit our home is someone who shows us how it looks from her or his house, how it smells, how it sounds. Hospitality consists in the gentleness of a smile, of discreet gestures, language reduced to a sort of animal murmur, a tone of voice that invites us to speak, or be silent. The words of hospitality help us to savor the tranquillity of the garden, the softly moving shadows, the murmur of nature, the streaming of the pond fountain.

The one who addresses to us the summons to come dwell here, with him, is the agency of a summons that is in the place itself: this is a good place to live. It invites human dwelling. This is what he knows who has discovered the wooded slope where a clearing welcomes the other animals in search of sun and opens forth upon the forested hills and the clouds where birds circle, and who sets out to build a cabin, saying, "Don't you see, someone should live here!"—not to displace what is there, but to dwell with the birds and other animals and skies. The agency of welcome and summons could well be other animals. The summons could come from plants.[2]

The diver who descends into the coral seas abandons the breast and crawl strokes she had learned to cover distance at the surface of a pool or lake, and drifts with the currents, using her finned feet as fish steer with their fins. Though she is returning to the warm oceans from which all life, and she too, came, she is only a visitor, freed from the upright posture and surface-strokes, freed from all appropriation. And yet, in the rapture of the deep, we find we can be at home, here with the coral fish, the octopus, the gorgonians. We can be at home in outer space in nights spent with sleeping bags on mountaintops and deserts.

But the alien and the exotic also summon us imperatively. The open roads, the oceanic, the stormy skies summon us. We know the summons of music that soars off to ancient courts, or the shadows that summon us to the realm of spirits and death. We go forth to outlying regions of the alien with the prostheses our sciences have devised to enable us to see with the eyes of eagles and wasps, the sonar echolocation of bats and the sixth sense of fish, the magnetic or cosmic sense of migratory birds and insects, the sensitivity of single cells or single molecules in those bats and fish. The millimeter-wide gardens in which protozoa range and for which technology has devised for us microscopes summon us; the great orbits of the planets and the comets for which technology has devised for us detached honeycomb eyes in space capsules summon us, as they had the Babylonians, the Nazca, and the Aztecs.

FIVE ~ *Things*

*T*hings take form in the light, on the plains of the visible, supported in
their places by the ground. Our look stops on a bleached, gnarled log
on the sands by the sea. We come upon a face carved in a rock set upright
in the midst of the forest in the Guatemalan mountains. The visible surfaces contoured by shadow recede into depth where they close in upon
themselves. In the density and grain of the surfaces, the substance of the
log or the rock looks palpable and its position stabilized by its weight. We
sense the muffled resonance contained within it.

Our look is refracted from the log or the rock to the layout about it as to
a multiplicity of sites to which it turns other faces. About its stability, the
sands cease to be glitter and the forest undercover ceases to be shadow
flowing under our feet to acquire the stability of sites—they become a hollow on the beach where driftwood from the sea comes to rest, a clearing in
the forest where an immemorial shrine broods and waits. Our gaze is refracted to outlying tufts of salt grass about the log or to the bases of trees
standing about the carved rock as to vantage points from which other faces
of the log or the carved rock are visible, and our look already goes there to
envision the thing from their positions. Before we move to go occupy successively those viewpoints, our look, refracted from those sites back to the
log or carved rock, senses the outlines of the faces it turns to those tufts of
salt grass or to the overarching trees.

We do not only see the log or the carved rock with the levels—with the
sunlight dancing over it or probing it through the shadowy forest, with the
verticality and repose of the field—but with the other things which occupy
viewpoints about it. When we look at the banyan before us, our vision
catches on to its profile visible to the temple, to the hills gathered about it,
the river moving below it, and the clouds hovering above it. These other

things, visible and real and possible locations for our look, guarantee for
this tree the reality of all the sides now turned away from our gaze.

When in the glitter and shadow of sands or forest undergrowth flowing
under our feet we come upon the log or the carved rock, it looks like it was
there before this moment and will continue to be there while we walk around
it and after we move on. In presenting itself it also presents how it will go
on being, how it was already. Its presence extends behind and before itself
a level of time extending a past and a future that anticipated and confirm
this presence. When we look at what presented itself, our look is refracted
back to its past and future and catch sight of how it looked and will look.[1]

The log or the carved rock presents itself not as a momentary sensory
pattern suspended on the end of our look but as something crystallized in
a layout of viewpoints occupied by other things; it presents itself not in a
discrete instant but in a presence turned to past and future phases of duration. It situates itself not in a pattern formed on our sensory surfaces, but in
a field of things whose reality is visible and palpable, a field of things whose
presence is held on the levels of past and future time.

Things finalize our sensibility and make it into perception.

The Cohesion of Things

In the reliefs and contrasts that pattern the visible, a depth surfaces. Perception is a synesthetic per-ception.[2] In the transparency or muddiness of
colors, we see the density and inner composition of substances. We see the
homogeneity of its matter in the brilliance of the silver tray; we see the heterogeneous composition of the wood with its dull sheen. We see the hardness of the blade of an axe, the softness of the sawdust. We see the flexibility
of the willow branches and the stiffness of the oak; we see the fluidity of
water, the stickiness of molasses. We see the ductile nature of the copper
glowing with heat in the forge; we see the weight of a block of cast iron
sinking into the sand. We see the hardness and brittleness of the glass and
we see its crystalline sound ringing off the splinters of the dropped win-
dow-pane. At the bus stop, we do not just hear sounds loose in space but
see the barking on the jaws of the dog and the rumble on the tires of the
bus. We hear the softness, liquidity, and turgidity of resounding things; we
hear insinuating movements of the hum of the raw wind or soft breeze; in
the shattering we hear something brittle and massive, in the thud something dense and resilient; we hear the hardness and unevenness of the road
in the rattle of a carriage. It is difficult for us to determine with precision
the pitch of the voices of our friends; with their voices and in them we hear

the diction, the warmth or aloofness, the harshness or frivolity, the probings or waverings of their substantial presence.

Each expanse of color hardens space, extends in depth. Our look does not stop on a surface; the surface-color and grain lead the look inside. The density, solidity, and inner composition of the wood surface in the color we see. The movement of the eyes communicates transversely across our whole motility: this brown looks solid and smooth to the touch. To look we turn our head, adjust our posture, center our surfaces and our motor availability to gather up together murmurs, contours, and textures in the patterned colors. The sensory thresholds of our backs rise to become less receptive to the breeze as our faces turn to something that galvanizes our attention.

At the furniture store we see a lot of tables, and think, separately, of picking out one that is the right size, the right shape, then the right color; then we consider in turn their solidity, their durability, how easy to clean they are. We view them as planes of color, then as extensions of hardness and shininess, like the cut-outs of a stage decor. The reality, the consistency and materiality of tables are not yet in them. When we leave the furniture store, they float like images before our eyes. The reality itself, the table, we recognize when it is in our study anchoring our position seated before it as we view our tasks laid out over it. There it is not just a color and a shape and a hardness our minds assemble and identify with a concept. Before our glance the color is immersed in the density, in the grain and way of holding light and the inner composition, in the way of supporting the sobriety of our tasks or the relaxation of our lunch shared with a friend. It is our habitual posture bent over it, writing letters, reading books, laying out meals, locating our practical positions by it as soon as we enter the room, that addresses the table and knows what it is. The table itself is not so many impressions imprinted on our surfaces nor the sum of its functional uses; it is contained in itself, exists beyond all we could ever itemize off it.

The Real Characteristics of Things

A perceived thing is not simply an amalgamation or a synthesis of the appearances it shows in the course of our exploration of it. A thing has its real color, weight, sound, its real warmth or coldness, its real shape and size, its own bulk, its real right-side-up, its real stability or its movement. As we look about us, colors are obscured in poor lighting, or when seen through an intervening medium or from a distance; shapes are perspectively deformed; there are monocular images and illusions—the real is not the sta-

tistically most frequent percept. There are many people whose real complexion, facial expressions, and behavior we know but rarely see because
we maintain a distance from them such that they appear as automatons or
thin patterns. With most things whose utility we are familiar with, our
glance and our touch pass over them only enough to pick practical clues
off them. But we recognize the real characteristics of things when we look.
They show the thing itself and are there when it is there.

Maurice Merleau-Ponty relates the way perceived appearances are given
with the way the phases of a perceiving movement are given.[3] We do not
sense the movement of our hands that reach out as a succession of distinct
positions occupied. Reaching for something, our hands catch on to the
terminal position from the first and sense their movements as phases of the
diagram of an approach to it. Likewise, our eyes focus to see something, at
a distance or close-up, and the shiftings of the glance are not separate re-
bounds from surfaces encountered, but phases of an approach to the thing.

When our eyes are focused on something at a distance, we have monocular images of close-up things. They adumbrate the visible consistency
of those things that will be there when we shift our focus. The thing then
seen with focused eyes is not composed of those monocular images, which
are thin and inconsistent and vanish when the thing is seen. The colors
obscured by the poor lighting, the surfaces set at an angle before us, the
sounds confused by the medium, thinned out by the distance, and the real
colors, shapes, and sounds do not form a simple succession of discrete
appearances. The real features and the perspectival variants and distortions
are not appraised separately and compared. The paper in shadow, which
reflects onto the retina light the wave-length of grey, is not overlaid with a
mental image of white projected out of memory; the paper does not appear
as paper of a lighter shade of grey than the grey physically produced: it
appears as white paper seen in dim light. The real contours, texture, resonance, weight, and temperature are there when the thing itself is there in
an optimum exhibition of its overall design, its details, the availability to
exploration of its diverse sensory aspects, and enough of its setting so that
its behavior is perceivable. The real colors and shapes are those of the thing
and show the thing; the others are transitional and transitory; they lead to
the real colors and shapes and yield before them.

By shifting back and forth, we locate the right viewing position before a
painting in a gallery, where the canvas exhibits simultaneously its detail
and overall design, its mood and its representational effect. From the wrong
distance we see not the lighting within the scene depicted, but the lighting
of the gallery under which the colors and shapes are smears of clay on the

canvas. The portrait or landscape we see is not composed out of those daubs of color; they are absorbed into it and vanish as it emerges.

In its maneuverings perception locates the viewpoint from which the integral thing exhibits its own properties. The aspect the complexion of a friend has when seen from too far away is seen as a complexion rendered indeterminate by the distance; the aspect the complexion has when our head is up against his or her chest is seen as a complexion rendered loose and vague by the wrong viewing position.

The qualitative features of a thing reveal its nature and reality more than do its quantitative features. In the real colors and weight and resonance and warmth, we perceive the consistency of a real thing. We see that our ballpoint pen is black under the gleaming light the sun reflects off it. The constancy of the black is not the persistence of a certain hue; this blackness is not the black of a sample of pigment on the palette or of one of the color-samples the paint store supplies us with. The black of the ballpoint functions to keep visible under the reflections and varying lighting the smoothness of the surface, the homogeneous substance of the plastic, the consistency and solidity of the cylinder.

Our perception discerns the real weight of a thing when it is held under water, just as our eyes distinguish the real color of the paper when it is seen in shadow and see the snow in the troughs as white seen through blue shadow. The real weight of something is felt when we lift it alone with our most agile parts, our hands. The weight a thing has is felt to be constant whether it is laid on top of our hand or lifted with one finger, whether we lift it with one hand or both, whether we lift it with our hands or feet or teeth, and whether it is laid on our stomach or our forehead which we normally rarely or never use to feel the weights of things. It could not be that some unconscious faculty in us is making instantaneous calculations that ten pounds felt on one square inch of hand muscle is equivalent to one-fourth of a pound felt on each of forty square inches of stomach. We do not know the muscle systems of our bodies as an engineer knows the dimensions, mass, and elasticity of the parts of a machine he has constructed. How would this mind know what formula to use when the thing is put on a part of our body we never use to feel weights—our forehead, the back of the calves of our legs? The weight of the thing felt with different muscle systems is not an impression of mass being compared—just as we do not first see a succession of different images of a man who stands at different positions from us and then select one as the right size. Through the strain on the particular muscle system used, the whole body aims at the weight the thing itself has, the weight which is revealed when the body lifts it with

its hands[4]—just as the sense of the color and form of patterns seen in monocular vision are given as transitory allusions to the color and form of the
thing seen in binocular vision.

Through indecisive contacts, our hand catches on to the level of the
tangible, contracts the specific pressure, rhythm, periodicity of the stroke
in which the real texture of linen or fur, the grain of wood, or the stickiness
of paint is revealed. Our hand that feels does not feel its own rubbery roughness and muscular tensions but the smoothness or tackiness, the contours
and grain of some thing.

We feel the real warmth or coldness of things through the medium that
varies. Ice cream feels as cold on a warm day as on a cold day; a person feels
as warm when felt under the bedcovers and in the water of a pool.

Each thing has its own resonance; we hear the real sound of a person
through the blanket that muffles or the telephone that distorts his or her
voice. For it is the person or thing we listen for and not a tone. We hear
brittleness, hardness, transparency in the real crystal ring of the glass.

Consider coming upon something for the first time: we open a package
that arrived in the mail, and take out a chunk of lava sent by a friend. We
seek to see its shape, its texture and substance, its colors. We turn it about,
hold it at varying distances and positions, in normal light. It itself guides us
to the position before us at which its internal composition and overall form,
its terrestrial nature, and its congealed forces are manifest. Though its colors when more intensely illuminated or narrowly inspected may appear
more vibrant, this position—on a shelf under the window with other rocks,
in which it stands before us as an integral thing—will be for us the one that
reveals the colors it itself has, the colors that function not as gleams of hue
in a purely visual space but as the colors of its contours and pits, the colors
that materialize and make surface its granular compactness, its weight, its
petrified flow.

Perceived things have their own orientations, shapes and sizes, stability
and movement.

Things have their own tops and bottoms. There is one orientation in
which a thing appears with a maximum of articulation and with the force
of reality; it is the orientation in which it is most available to our sensory-
motor powers.[5] The wine glass that is upright requires no unbalance of the
reaching hand to grasp it and fill it. The floor lamp is right-end-up not
when our glance at it reinforces a mental image most frequently given but
when our glance finds its switch and its light oriented along the direction
that makes their functions most accessible.

We recognize our friends at great distances, before we can see the contours of their faces and the color of their complexions and hair, by the

posture and gait. We recognize someone not by the outlines, by running our eyes around the contours of his or her head and trunk, but by the inner lines of posture. To recognize a person is to recognize a typical way of addressing tasks, of envisioning landscapes, of advancing hesitantly and cautiously or ironically, of plunging exuberantly down the paths to us. Someone we know is someone we relate to posturally, someone we walk in step with, someone who maintains a certain style of positioning himself or herself and gesticulating in conversation and with whom we take up a corresponding position as we talk. When we view someone the wrong way, when we look down upon him or her from the head of the hospital bed, the expressive pattern of eyes and smiling mouth we look for does not take, and if we keep looking down on them we end up seeing a material mass with a pink teeth-filled gash on top and two wet spheres rolling in their sockets below. Not only the sense, the recognizability, of the face is abolished with its normal orientation, but its reality; we have before us something strange and unreal. We tilt our heads to view a face in a photograph in the right orientation; otherwise it disintegrates into black and grey splotches on paper.

Things too induce in us an appropriate posture and itinerary of discovery. When we approach a great fir on the crest of the mountain, we stand tall and our eyes travel upwards to the clouds and the eagles; when we approach a willow our gaze sweeps in languid arcs across the banks of fine branches rippling over the lake. When we come upon a fallen tree, we have difficulty seeing that it is a willow or a pine or even a tree; it appears as a thicket about a log, in a confused layout inviting closer scrutiny. Not only is its sense, its recognizability, one with its right orientation, but also its reality. A lamp turned upside down has lost some of its consistency and looks more like a stage prop than a piece of furniture.[6]

What we see are not patterns on a two-dimensional plane before us, but things which bulge out toward us and crowd one another, and whose density and richness of visibility are only possible if they stagger out in depth before us.[7] Each thing we see which advances some of its visibility toward us can be a thing only if other sides of its visible thickness veer back into depth, offering us progressively less clearly articulated expanses of themselves. This is what Cézanne came to understand when he discovered that one cannot paint a real apple by enclosing it with a univocal contour, as though the vision of a real apple were that of an expanse of red bounded by a round edge, and when he approximated it by a number of broken arcs between which the look is vibrated, in a movement toward possibilities.

Each real thing has its normal or right position in the outlying environment about us—a position which it occupies with its reality. A person is recognizably real at the right distance; when our eyes are up against his or her face it decomposes into a material mass, and when he or she recedes too far into the depth he or she becomes an automaton and an image. The person is there when we can effectively deal with him or her, when we can see him or her fully and clearly, hear what he or she says, shake his or her hand. A pen is a pen within a certain range before our eyes, positioned for our hand for which it is more than a visual pattern.

We see as round the plate seen from an angle, see as rectangular the side walls of the house. The real shape is that revealed when the plate or the wall is set before us such that our gaze can readily travel over all its expanse and see the details on one side as well as the other. The dinner plate seen obliquely with the painted Chinese patterns unequally spread out before our gaze on its slopes is seen to not now display the real shape it has. We do not see the side wall of the house as a lozenge, but as a wall fading off and losing articulation as it veers into depth, pulling its real shape from our grasp.

The real size of a perceptual thing is the size revealed when the details are clear and the overall form is visible, and also its behavior in its setting is visible. Something huge exceeds the powers of our body to see at once its grain and texture, its overall shape, as well as its setting. When something is small, we can see its details, its overall shape, and its setting, and still it does not occupy all our powers of vision in the field.

To see the real thing that really moves is not to see what it is, what properties it has, and then to see it occupying successive positions or augmenting its distance from a fixed point. We have a very vivid vision of movement when we see a laborer hurling rocks into a truck, without our eyes gauging the successive positions of his arms relative to some fixed point. The most intensive perception of movement makes impossible the taking note of the successive positions of its field, or its relationship to a fixed point. When we move a pencil quickly across a page on which we have marked a point, the pencil pulls at our eyes as a moving stroke, but at no instant do we see it now over the point. If we slow down the movement of the pencil so as to be able to hold fixed the point, the pencil haunts the space but the movement is no longer in it.[8] In a field without stationary points we can see a figure, a car in the night or an eel in the depths of the open sea, in movement in the streaming of its color and shape. The movement is not gauged by the position of the figure relative to the rim of our own visual field, which itself is not expressly visible nor fixed; the figure itself slides, creeps, flutters, soars. The movement of a moving thing is in that thing, in the continuity, discontinuity, or periodicity with which its details and design merge or mutate. A hummingbird flitting across the garden is a glittering tumult in the sunlight; an eel moving through the waves is a rhythmic undulation of elastic density and hue. The stability of a glass, an armchair, or a boulder is perceived in them before any analytic inspection of their distinguishable properties, and the ground, as the level of rest, is there before any location of stable landmarks.

The Identity and Reality of Things

When we see a *grapefruit*, this identity is not something conceived at once like a concept; it is not an invariant found in all the various aspects; it is not a law or principle like triangularity found in all triangles. We see it by looking, by looking at the way this compartmented cross-section of shiny pale yellow-green involves—makes visible—a certain sense of pulpiness, a certain juiciness, even a certain clear and homogeneous taste. What we see does not have that tomato look, that pear granularness, that mango feel. The yellow-green is the yellow-green it is because it is condensed in this pulp, makes visible this contained liquidity, emanates this clear and tangy savor. The identity or essence of the grapefruit is in this shiny yellow-green, this pulpiness felt or chewed, in this taste and acrid smell. We do not really have a concept of a grapefruit. Perhaps we see enough to attach a name to it from the start, but what a grapefruit really is and means is something that we understand in touching, smelling, chewing, savoring, without ever ending at something like the definitive key to it.

A perceived thing is real in being explorable—not a profile given and more not given, to be filled in by drawing on memory images and concepts, but instead details which, as soon as they are caught on to, lead our gaze into inner levels about which more details will form, to an overall design that coordinates and unfolds facets, to a behavior in an immediate setting that extends beyond it and into the future. This being still outside our grasp, contained in itself, not yet converted into data or information or impressions contained within ourselves, makes a thing appear to have a reality of its own.

We cannot doubt that we are seeing a really red scarf without doubting that we are really seeing; we cannot doubt that there was a whisper in the night without doubting that we really heard. The doubt that works in perception is not a subjective operation that maintains the perceiving act certain and demotes the perceived to a succession of images all immanent of a transcendental reality that is only conjectural. To doubt whether what we see really has a curved edge to it is to replace the present perception with one that reveals the thing more clearly.

On a muddy path we see ahead what looks like a broad flat stone; the sheen of grey light contains a sense of hardness and solidity. It addresses not only the focus of our eyes in the muddy indeterminism of the field, but from the first our whole effort to see our way across the field. It is not simply present; it is at a distance which is also the distance of a future; it emerges as a smooth, firm spot to step on. As the stone comes to occupy our visual powers more fully its real size and density, already visible in the first view, become more and more determinate. There are not successive images of different sizes; each perceived contour merges into the next. If, suddenly, we see that what we took to be a flat rock is a patch of sunlight over the mud, it is not that we project a different identity-term into the same data. There is not simply a change in the organization of the data, or in the hypothetical identity-term of which they would have been taken as signs, but a mutation in the grain, density, and inner patterning of the intersensorial appearance. Now that our sensory-motor powers have come more fully to grips with this section of the path, we can no longer see in the aspect of the patch of light the features that made us see it a moment before as a flat stone.

How Our Bodies Know Things

To feel the tangible, the smooth, the sticky, or the bristly, our touching hand has to move across a substance with a certain pressure, a certain pacing and periodicity, a certain scope of movement. Our look too, in order to see the red of the silk dress, has to focus and move across its expanse with a certain pressure and scope and periodicity. We do not see the dull moss-green of the leaves with the same movement of the look that makes the ardent red of the rose visible. It is in swaying with the melody, rocking with the rhythm, or being jarred by the clatter that we hear it.

The sizes and shapes of things are captured actively; it is in dilating the scope of our look or our grip, eventually filling out the whole field—that is, approaching the limit of what our look or our hearing can hold together before us—that the bigness of something seen or the full-bodiedness of a sound becomes manifest. In the equilibrium of our look traveling about the rim of the plate the circular comes to be before us. In experiencing the length of the wall becoming less clearly articulated for us we feel that end of it pulling away from the hold we have on it and, oriented away from us, receding into distance. It is our maximal hold on it—when its form and grain are clear and distinct for us, when we feel ourselves centered on it—that distinguishes the normal, true, or right appearance of a thing from its variants, from shapes turned to the side, from round or rectangular planes set askew, from things of comparable size staggered out over a distance, from white sheets of paper scattered in the dim light of the hall.

From the first, not a patch of color or a pressure but some thing touched our sensibility; from the first, both eyes respond to converge on it, our fingers close upon it as one organ, our body shifts to center its sensitive surfaces on it. A color, a tone, a texture are not data impressed on the passive surfaces of our receptor organs; when our hands know hardness and our gaze the moon's light, they pick up and communicate with a certain way the external thing has of molding space and extending a duration. Hardness and softness, roughness and smoothness, moonlight and sunlight then present themselves in our recollection not as opaque sensory quale, but as certain kinds of symbioses, specific ways the outside has of invading us and specific ways we have of meeting this invasion.[9] As our whole sensibility converges, the presence and apparition of something appears normal, right and true, and its upright or overturned, close or far, left or right position stabilizes. Our perception tends to an optimum state when our body in all its powers is geared into the setting, centered on something, when there is an inner sense of equilibrium and efficacious adjustment. Our body takes hold of the levels of the field on which things materialize. Our perception tends to the position before things in which the thing it envisions shows the color, weight, temperature, size, shape, and orientation which are its own.

Our body does one thing at a time, Gestalt physiologist Kurt Goldstein wrote;[10] it also perceives one thing at a time—a figure against the ground of the rest. Our sensibility is positioned—is postured—on things as on objectives. To understand the integration of the sensibility—its comprehensive hold on things and its comprehending grasp of their contexts—we have to elucidate the nature of our body's postural schema.

Our body does not tend to a state of rest but maintains a state of tension, expressed in its typical thresholds of excitability, and a state of motility available for its typical tasks in each specific kind of environment. Our body's stance at any moment is not simply the resultant of the positions of the parts, each determined by the force of gravity and the outside pressures and internal tensions; the orienting axis of force of the whole positions each of the parts. The internal vectors of its functional integration of its parts and powers are oriented so as to apply its force to the objective of the moment. This internal diagram of oriented force maintains itself because a shift of position of any energized part induces a systematic redistribution of the positions of the others. The postural axis of someone standing on a chair to unscrew the globe of a ceiling fixture and replace a burnt-out light bulb is continually being adjusted in response to the task; a movement of the hand induces a corresponding shifting of the trunk and tightening of one leg, bending of the other.

Our posture then could not be the result of a program in the circuitry of the central nervous system, and the equilibrating and disequilibrating move-ments are not guided by a mental representation of the body's actual posi-tion. The present diagram of our hand's move contains in itself the schema for a series of functionally equivalent moves, and contains also the schema for the corresponding moves of the supporting trunk and limbs. A new gesture or move does not arise as a spontaneous invention, but as an actu-alization of one of the variants contained in the typical diagrams of organi-zation the body has contracted. In our body every movement is a diagram for equivalent movements, and every diagram engenders a range of variant movements.

Since every seeing of a color is done with a movement of our look, every feeling of a roughness or a resistance done with a movement of our hand, every hearing of a distinct sound done with a movement of our head that turns to center the ears upon it, our postural schema is also the unifying organizer of the sensory organs and surfaces. When, collapsed on the bed, we let our posture dissolve and our legs and arms settle as the force of gravity determines, we eventually no longer sense things but rather sense an undifferentiated atmosphere or medium in which we are immersed.

The apprehension of an exterior objective, as something soliciting the synergic hold of the sensibility, dynamically orients our postural schema. By converging our sensory surfaces on an objective, sensory properties con-solidate and a transcendent and intersensorial—that is, real—thing takes form. Conversely, to contract a motor diagram in our postural schema is already to envision things.[11]

The level of excitability of our whole sensibility, its fatigue, its distrac-tion, or its disintegration, affects the functioning of sight; the contours and color intensity of a lemon become more visible in the measure that it be-comes for the awakened hand more palpable and for smell and taste more distinctively pungent. There is in our body an immanent knowledge of how to center, how to position itself, how to take hold of things such that they are given and manifest in their intersensorial essence. There is in our body a knowledge of a lemon—a competency, a praktognosis, a knowledge of how to deal with such a thing, how to station itself before it, how to apply itself to it—such that the sensible essence of the lemon, its way of being, is communicated to our body's own visible, tangible, sonorous reality.

Our sensibility picks up how a lemon holds together, how it occupies its position—something like its posture. What makes sensory patterns be perceived as things are not outlines that circumscribe masses of sense data but inner lines of force which position substances and with which they move.

In the dim light of the end of the day we recognize our aunt coming down the sidewalk several blocks away, at a distance too far to see the contours of her face or the hue of her complexion: we recognize the walk. Our acquaintances are those we stroll with, work with, look at things with. In perceiving them we do not look at their outlines and scrutinize their colors; our postures pick up their gait, their rhythms. We do not sit erect as the other lounges; our postures and the scope and periodicity of our gestures correspond.

The sense and recognizability of things too do not lie in conceptual categories in which we mentally place them but in their positions and orientations which our postures address. We do not grasp something like its inner law or program in recognizing a lemon, but we see how it holds together in its environment. To recognize a lemon in that lump of rubbery yellow there is to see the distinctive way this yellow occupies its space, holds and reflects the light, shades off in depth as its contours recede, to see how this yellow makes the inner substance surface, makes visible the pulpiness and the homogeneous sourness condensed there. As a cloud passes over the sun and the light dims over it, the shift in its color will induce a corresponding shift in its tangible density. A lemon is a dynamic gestalt; its features are in an active relation with the features of the environment and shifts in one feature induce corresponding shifts in others.

We recognize, in the yard sale, the coat rack by the solidity of its separate stand and the armchair by the squat position with which it offers a hollow. We see the application in the soft caterpillar flopping up the vegetation, we recognize the hare in the distant furry blur by the bound, we see the keen attentiveness in the careening of the swallows circling in the sky. We recognize the elms in the streets of the old town by the arches their limbs rise to one another to form, under foliage that dapples the sky; we recognize the oaks in winter by the way their rigid branches fill in and occupy their spaces. We recognize the mansion by the way it holds itself inflexible among the oak trees on the hill; we recognize the hovel by the way it leans against the adjacent shanties and crouches under the blazing tropical sun. We recognize the path by the way it advances up the hill pushed to one side by the trees and creeping around clumps of bushes, recognize the humble repose of the old bridge under the shade at a turn in the river. We see the walls and towers of Angkor Wat push up and link arms under the protective limbs of the jungle trees.

Our Bodies Know Themselves in Things

As we do not have a conceptual grasp of the essence of a real thing, we do not have a conceptual grasp of the program that would regulate the position and focus of our limbs and organs. It is through its postural schema that our body has, when poised on a stool to pound in a nail, a sense of

where its legs and feet are and what adjustments in their angle and position
to make. The postural schema is a dynamic Gestalt that distributes the
positions of our limbs, regulates the orientation of our forces, the conver-
gence of our organs, the levels of our sensory thresholds. It is a schema of
transverse coordination induced by a movement oriented toward a thing or
a layout of things as toward a task.

To see a real thing is to sense how to position our forces before it; to see
something is to know how to approach it and explore it. The sight of another person calls up within us the corresponding postural diagram that
would position us in the form we see the other maintaining. Our postural
schema is not sensed in a separate kinesthetic diagram; each shift in posture means for us another set of faces the things turn to us.

What psychologists have improperly named the "body image" is not
formed by an act of imagination when we detach our perception from things;
it emanates from our mobilized posture and extends across it. As we walk
through the library we have a sense of the visible shape which we fill out in
its corridors; as we stretch our legs under the table we have a sense of how
their spread looks. When a psychologist projects a videotape of people in
silhouette walking across the landscape, we find we can pick out ourselves
from among them by the gait. As we walk we cannot look at our gait, even
in a mirror, for the observing eye itself which has redirected itself interferes
with the gaze that accompanied our walk down the street and alters our
natural gait. But since we can recognize our way of walking when projected
on the screen, we had while walking an immanent sense of the way our gait
looks from the outside. As we walk through a small office or an open plain,
we have a quasi-vision of ourselves as seen from a witness eye that encompasses that room or that plain. Our hand that touches a solid or elastic
mass and that is a vector of force and feeling spreads about itself a latent
sense of its pulp tangible from the outside. While maintaining our momentum of preoccupied hurry through the streets, we get a sense of the thickness and thrust of our limbs as they would be felt by others who would
brush against us or crowd us. As we speak we have a sense of the sonority
of our own voices as they would be heard by an ear not cupped against our
mouths and recording the momentary vibrations, but at the distance others
take from us to hear our utterances spreading out in whole sentences. It is
sometimes said that our own bodies have no perceived weight, but when
we move to be embraced and held by another or walk across the seedling
grass and climb the ladder we have a sense of the weight of our bodies as
they would be felt by others and by the grass and the wood.

The more our attention is absorbed in our task and our feeling absorbed
in the orientation and rhythm of our forces, the more determinate is this

perception of the sides and outer contours of a thing that we form. Our "body image" is not simply the patches of our surfaces we are actually seeing and the floating after-images of those we have seen and remember. It is the outer aspect, quasi-visible to ourselves, of our body as it would be seen by someone viewing it from a distance sufficient to see the whole posture, the tangible aspect of our body as it would be felt by someone within range to feel it freely, the sonority of our utterances as they would be heard from the outside.

When we see our own body parts as perceptible forms, we have already a motor diagram of how to move them. It is hard to touch one hand with the other and deal with it as an inert and palpable thing; a corresponding motor intention rises up in the hand touched. When we look at ourselves in a mirror, we feel our cigarette burning against the fingers in the mirror. When we are trying to pronounce the phonemes of a foreign language or sing a new song, we listen to the sounds we are emitting and can thus pronounce them again, as though the audible pattern heard converts of itself into a motor diagram for our organs of vocalization. When one of our hands goes to stroke or poke at the other it advances as an agile vector of force and feeling, but the sense of the tangible mass it is for that other hand thickens about it, while in the substance of the touched hand a mobile vector of feeling stirs.

When we look at the visible substance of another's hand, we sense there inner lines of force and feeling. We do not see these nor mentally diagram them, but sense them directly with the dexterity of our hand. Our postural orientation directed on others is directed by them. Through just seeing someone seated on a stool, bench, or couch, our body finds spontaneously the posture corresponding to hers as we go to join her. An infant who, at fifteen days, smiles at the sight of his mother's smile has not yet seen what his own face looks like and will never see the benevolence in the mind of the mother. He then does not set up in his mind an explicit relationship between the arc he sees in visual space, the muscular configuration in his mother's body schema, and the sentiment of benevolence produced in her mind—and then between a sentiment of benevolence he produces in himself, a muscular innervation, and the resultant arc on his face as a visible surface. From the first the outward aspect of his mother induces a motor schema in the infant. In perceiving the outer forms of the others, we capture in our postural schema the corresponding inner lines of their postures and movements. And in contracting inner motor diagrams we quasi-perceive the corresponding visible, tangible, and audible outer form of ourselves turned to the distance where others stand.

Our "body image" is not an image formed in the privacy of our own imagination; its visible, tangible, and audible shape is held in the gaze, touch, and hearing of others. We sense, when we look at another, the inner axes of force with which his or her body assembles and mobilizes its forces and we sense about the axes of our forces the visual form he or she sees of us. In sensing in and with another's positions and moves the focusing of their vision and sensibility, the whole range of the visible, tangible, and audible shifts and refocuses, and we see our visibility with their eyes, feel our tangibility with their hands, hear our voice with their ears. To look is to become visible, to touch is to become tangible, to hear is to become audible.

Likewise, in perceiving the outer forms of things we capture in our postural schema the inner lines of their tensions and orientations. And in contracting inner motor diagrams we quasi-perceive the visible, tangible, and audible form of ourselves turned to them. When we look at the sequoias, our eyes follow the upward thrust of their towering trunks touching the sky and their sparse branches fingering the mists. We comprehend this uprightness of their life not with a concept-generating faculty of our mind but with the uprighting aspiration in our vertebrate organism which they awaken. Our postural axis turned up before them emanates about itself a body image which is shaped not as the visual form our body would turn to a fellow-human standing at normal human viewing-distance but as our body looks to the sequoias. As we advance in a tunnel with a flashlight, we follow the beam of light that advances along the walls and the tracks before us and have a quasi-visual body image of ourselves as seen by the tunnel upon whose rocks the sheets of light flash like light-reflections on their eyes. For our eyes to dance in the dew sparkling across the canyon that the dawn is opening before us is to feel the quasi-visual form of ourselves as seen by the multiple eyes of the canyon. To see the weight of the fieldstones in a plot of land we are digging up for a garden is to feel the diagram of a grip forming in our postural schema, and the weightless force in our arms now emanates about itself an immanent sense of the weight of our limbs which a fieldstone would feel as it struggles with our force. To listen to another is already to know how to pronounce what he or she says; the motor diagrams for speaking in our throat and chest capture the audible patterns he or she presents before us, and when we activate those motor diagrams to repeat and continue what he or she said, the shaping and resonating of our breath through our chest, throat, and mouth emanate about our breath an immanent sense of how our vocalizations sound to the other. As we sing while walking through the forest and shout to the mountain cliffs we hear how we sound to the murmuring trees and in the great ear of the mountain.

It is our own ligneous substance uprighting our posture that perceives the sequoias, it is the compacted ferric substance of the bodybuilder's musculature that knows the inner essence of the steel, it is the breath driving the lungs of the runner and the blood pounding in his veins and the sweat glistening on his chest that know the coursing of the winds, the advance of the rain clouds, and the power of the sun. It is the clay of our own body, dust that shall return to dust, that knows the earth and knows itself as terrestrial. It is the liquid crystals of our eyes that are turned to the stars as to eyes of the night.

Perception is ordered by the ordinances things realize, and we as perceivers realize what we are through the styles of postural integration they induce in us and in the images they project back on us of the way we look, hear, and feel to them.

The Imperatives in Things

The consistency and coherence of a table precede the analytic perception that itemizes its features and the shapes we can see of it and record in different perspectives. It stands there, consolidated in its external reality, and holds our bodies centered on it, anchors a range of points of view about it, and orders the approaches to it with which we inspect its characteristics and behaviors. The inner ordinance which makes the grapefruit coagulate with its rubbery rind, its dense dull yellow, its loose inner pulp, its acrid smell and sour savor, its own size and shape regulates our handling of it and perceptual exploration of it. It regulates the segregation of appearances, qualifying some of them as distortions due to the odd perspective, the interposed medium, the dim light. On the side wall of the house the details are not evenly spread out before our gaze; the wall itself induces the eyes to reposition such that it is viewed parallel with the frontal plane of the face, and the present appearance is not seen as a lozenge but as a rectangular wall seen askew.

The key, the inner formula of a mango, a willow tree, or a flat smooth stone, is never grasped; the real thing is before our perception as a task for an exploration. But the real thing is not the sum of all that we have recorded of it; it closes in upon itself, remains exterior, always beyond all that our perceptual samplings have turned up of it, not a given but an external ordinance. A perceived thing is a pole which draws the convergent surfaces and organs of our bodies like a telos, a task. The reality of things is not given in our perception, but orders it as an imperative.

If, after so many years of making our way among things, looking at them and handling them, they can still, in moments when we stop in our tracks and contemplate them, withdraw from us as so many congealed enigmas, it is because we do not stand before them as well-appointed judges who affirm what is put forth there and supply out of ourselves whatever rationale events could have for transpiring as they did and whatever conclusions we might want to find in the closure of things. It is because we find ourselves, despite our own stock of concepts and our taxonomies, continually implicated in things that are trying out their reality in indecisive and inconclusive appearances, their opaque colors and bulk and resonance besetting the space they occupy with the gravity of a question beset by questions to follow, their essences consistent and coherent evidences that elude formulation.

Our sensory-motor coordination is ordered by things whose reality is not posited there, filling in the blank opened by a question that we put, but tries itself out in diverse perspectives, diverse elements, with provisional and inconclusive responses that put further questions to us. To perceive is to find ourselves not supplied with sense data or objects but subjected in each thing to a reality in the interrogative mode, whose consistency and coherence weighs on us with the weight of an imperative. The imperatives in things, the imperatives things are, do not order us with an imperative for a universal and necessary form of response our thought would program for our sensibility; they order the diagrams and variations of our postural schema and exploratory manipulations. A thing is there not as a given and not as a possibility or a hypothesis but as an imperative.[12]

The Order in the Environment

A thing arises as a relief on the levels of the site which extends about it and harbors other things, to which this thing turns its lateral sides; these outlying things invite us as standpoints from which those sides can be seen. Our gaze sweeps across the environs but the views that form are not desultory; our eyes are led by the light down the paths that lead to things. To reach the other sides of a thing before us, we have to displace ourselves to those other standpoints in the landscape the other things mark out for us. The levels extend the layout as a system where the things witness one another and each contributes to the consistency and coherence of all. It is the consistency and coherence of the whole room we sense when we sense the constancy of the white of the sheets of paper scattered across the desk and floor. The thing ordering the direction of our perception leads us to the consistency and coherence of the levels; the levels, which we can reach only by subjecting ourselves to them, conduct us to things.

Things have to not exhibit all their sides and aspects, have to compress them behind the faces they turn to us, have to tilt back their sides in depth, have to not occupy all the field, because they have to coexist in a field with one another, and that field has to coexist with the fields of other possible things. Each perceived thing is a task and a means toward locating the next thing.

When someone glides into the seminar room with an electric purple face and clad in sequinned disco clothes, he appears unreal, an apparition, disconnected from the basement solidity of the rows of austere desks, a black hole in the flat fluorescent lighting that leaves no shadows and no mystery in the room. We do not perceive him as someone who has a personality, a character, a history in a world; he appears as a role, as so many surface-effects. The cobra that we see in the office building from the first appears unreal; it appears to be adrift over the polished floor and wall and not to be inching across it. What is seen as a mirage is a puddle of water that shimmers over the road ahead, whose boundaries we cannot locate with precision in terms of the edges of the road and which does not lend itself to showing further details of itself as we shift from one side to the other on the sites of the landscape which maintains the layout of things about us.

We can doubt the appearance any thing shows, but we do so in the name of a more consistent, more coherent appearance another viewing position in the perceived landscape promises us. It is the continual transitions by which a field of vision evolves into the next and opens a tangible and anchors a sonorous field that make all of them so many views upon reality, and it is this coherence and consistency of the reality that sustain the reality of the things that rise in relief in it.

The reality of the field of perception itself is not open to doubt; every other order of entities we set up, by science or by metaphysics, could not be more real than a field of perceived things, since everything science posits has to be verified by empirical observation, that is, by looking again in the perceived field, and since the conceptual order out of which we deduce or posit entities can derive its ontological index only from the reality of the ordered environment in which things are perceivable.

Our belief in the reality of any particular thing we perceive is not the result of a process of verification; from the first the table carries with it the evidence of reality and the cobra in the office building hovers over the floor; the appearances sort out by themselves as we advance. The second look dissipates the illusion, without having to be itself warranted by our verifying the connections that coherently and consistently tie what it sees into the landscape. It is because we perceive the table with its own size and shape that we expect the things about it to have sizes and shapes compossible with the table, and not the reverse. Our field of perception is inhabited by a

play of colors, noises, and fleeting tactile patterns which we cannot fit pre-
cisely into the context of the clearly perceived things, yet which we immediately place in the field of real things and do not confuse with our day-
dreams. There are things about us which we count on while only skimming
over them, and we seek to identify them only if one day we sense they are
gone—the furnishings of our home, the main paths of our daily activities,
the trees that line those paths, the implements we use, and the landscapes
we enjoy.

Merleau-Ponty says we are familiar with the ordinance of the perceived
reality as we are familiar with the style a person maintains throughout his
or her requirements, approaches, solicitations, claims, demands, and laugh-
ters.[13] As we awaken it is not by recognizing things seen before, but by
recognizing the way the visible field unfolds that we know we are no longer
dreaming. Once we have heard something, we catch on to the style with
which reality extends its murmurs, cries, and reverberations. Once we have
taken hold of reality, we catch on to the way perceived reality will never
cease to surround our positions, our perceptions, our initiatives, even our
hallucinations and our dreams. For perceivable reality is still the background
over which the schizophrenic elaborates his obsessions; perceivable reality
is still the distant horizon out of which the dreamer composes his visions
and with which his peripheral and anonymous sensibility still maintains
contact, such that when he awakens he recognizes the paths of perceivable
reality he had lost sight of.

It is not with a conceptual apprehension of the system and the laws but
with our postural agility and tractability that we know the way landscapes
develop and unfold, that we know how, in general, to station ourselves
before Flemish primitive, impressionist, or cubist paintings to see the views
they compose, know how to station ourselves before real tables and how to
look at aquarium fish and a Japanese meal to really see them. This knowledge is not a program we format moment by moment for our nervous circuitry and musculature; it is a schema of synergic mobilization of our sensory-motor powers that is induced from the way the levels fit together and
the things take form on them. For a style is not something that we conceive
but something we catch on to and that captivates us.

The directives with which the field of perception extends are not given
in perceptual presentation nor in conceptual representation. Our environment that unfolds coherently is not a text we understand; its ordinance is
not a set of universal and necessary laws from which we can deduce the
particular things. We cannot derive the position and structure of the things
emerging in the course of perceivable reality out of a blueprint our theory
can represent. The layout of our environment is not a Euclidean space; a

particular thing is not an instance of a law, the value of a variable which satisfies the formula. The ordinance in our environment is not grasped through a systematic formulation of laws we devise; it directs us in the coherence and consistency with which the landscapes converge and pass into one another when our sensory-motor movements comply with the ordinance in their levels.

As we turn toward a thing we do see sketched out on the side it turns to us prefigurations of its other sides and we see about it the other things whose consistency witnesses those other sides, but to reach those other sides we have to displace ourselves to see this thing from the standpoints the surrounding things fix for us, and in the time the displacement takes the side we have now left behind may discolor, bulge, shrivel, or disintegrate. Our very exploratory movements about it leave their marks on it. It would take an indefinite stretch of time to make each of its sides face us— and each thing the course of perceived reality presents disintegrates in the course of time. A thing is before us as a task and a reality embedded in the subsistence of the environment inasmuch as it is closed in itself and harbors secrets and surprises. The levels and the layout which maintain it are presented not as a framework surveyed but as directives pursued.

The levels and the layout are then not an order perceived or conceived, but an ordinance. Perception obeys an imperative to anchor ourselves on the consistency and coherence, the reality, of the environment. This is not a determinism; we can see without inevitably seeing things and without necessarily seeing a coherent environment. We can see monocular images and not binocular visions of things; our eyes can get caught up in phantasms and pre-things, in the caricatural doubles and mirages the sensible levels and planes also engender. Our look can record only the contours and finish our desires and our obsessions, our loves and our hatreds have put on the nodes in the fabric of sensible reality; our eyes and our hands can touch only the shapings culture and industry have left on the levels of the environment. We can take refuge from the planes of sensible reality in a dream-space; we can drag fragments of things into a delirious space without levels and consistent dimensions; we can, as in advanced states of melancholia, settle in the realm of death.[14]

The imperative in the environment of things is not received on our conceptual understanding and reason; it is not first an imperative to conceive for each sensible pattern a universal and necessary category, is not first an imperative for our reason to connect up the objects we conceptually recognize with universal and necessary laws. The imperative in our environment is received, not on our understanding in conflict with our sensuality, but on our postural schema which integrates our sensibility and mobilizes our motor forces. It is received on our sensory-motor bodies as bodies we have to center upon things that orient our movements, bodies we have to anchor on the levels down which our vision, our touch, our listening move, on which we station ourselves and move in the heart of reality. It orders our competence. This imperative weighs on us, finalizing our perception toward a perceiving of things and not of a medley of sense, toward a perceiving of the environment as a layout and not a chaos. The environment itself, the coherence and the consistency of reality, the style of all styles, weighs on us as an imperative. The environment is as an imperative.

Obedience is mental and physical action that is directed by something general which we can represent to ourselves. An order that is presented to us has to be inwardly represented in order that it become the effective directive of our action. But inasmuch as it is represented by our own mental power, it is a program that we give ourselves. Obedience exists only inasmuch as we acknowledge not only the form of the order formulated in the representation, but its imperative force. This force affects us, afflicts us; we find ourselves subject to it. Kant called respect the sentiment of the imperative force of orders formulated, and first of all the force of the imperative for order. Perception is not a representation, constitutive of things out of sense data; it is respect for things and respect for our environment.

Imperative Fields

We easily pass from "site" to "perceived field" to "world" and "reality." We speak of "the visible" and "the sonorous" and "the tangible." Do we really perceive in "the world?" Is reality the ordered totality of things?

Things take form in the light, on the contours of the visible, supported in their places by the ground. There is not first an a priori intuition of the space-time extension which distributes things in a "world." It is the thing, intersensorial and real, which emerges on the nexus of levels, that refracts our gaze upon other sites occupied by other things about it and anchors the layout of a site. It is by the experience of the continuous transition from one site to the next that the general terms "perceived field" and "world" acquire their significance. But the consistency and coherence of the "world" is not given; it is as an imperative.

In fact there is also an imperative fragmentation of reality in our perception. The things each summon us into their own settings, and each summons us to forget the rest and devote ourselves to it.

Our glance is not a continuous survey; it drops the thread it was following, the path it was exploring, and turns elsewhere. While washing the dishes, our glance strays out the window and is drawn to a nuthatch circling a tree trunk. No longer absorbed in the leavings to be brushed off the plates being transferred from the sink to the rack, our gaze is shifted to the nuthatch, and joins it in its inspection of the bark, stopping to bore through it to an insect whose feeble vibrations it has registered. The site the nuthatch is so attentively exploring closes in on itself; the sink and the plates stacked on the rack are now as invisible to us as they are to the nuthatch. In shifting from one perceptual layout to another, we shift from one tempo and rhythm of duration to another. When we get lost in following the nuthatch so attentive to the bark and the minute echoes of burrowing insects, and then return to the dishes in the sink, we have the same sense of abruptly dropping from one wave of duration to another that we have when the baroque symphony has come to an end and we slip out during the applause to get to the last subway, or when the all-night shadow-play performance of the Ramayana comes to an end and we awkwardly fit ourselves back into the tour-group schedule.

Strolling along the beach, eyes adrift in the azure light, the sea in waves meanders across our field of vision and sands flow in glitter under our feet. Then, crossing a rise, our eyes are drawn to a bleached gnarled log whose contours curve back upon themselves and whose visible surfaces are packed with the grainy density of its substance, its weight, and its muffled inner resonance. Our gaze is refracted to the outlying tufts of salt grass in the hollow which stabilize as its site, containing so many viewpoints turned to it. The hollow where a piece of driftwood from the sea has come to rest closes in upon itself, a refuge for the driftwood and for our body too; the undulating seascape of azure breezes and glittering sandy flow halts at the rims of this hollow, as the open sea is obliterated from the stable workspace of a reader seated in his cabin on board ship.

A thing is not simply the set of internal relations with all the other things. It pushes back the other things and clamors for all our attention. It is not simply a relay for a movement that stakes out directions and paths beyond it. It is also a terminus for our perception. Things are ends and not means only. The tasks they present to us designate themselves as what is to be accomplished.

Perception which aims for things also sinks into things. Perception has been too much conceived as an apprehension, a movement of the sensory-motor organism outward which returns to itself, an exploration that enriches itself with content assimilated and forms grasped. Our gaze emanates from our eyes and sinks into the depths of things, and also passes between things to dissipate in the distance. It turns into sensuality and enjoyment.

A visitor brings a vase of jasmine into our hospital room. The elegant spray of the stems, the coils of the petals lure our eyes, which travel up and about them. The fervent white of the flesh of the petals draws our eyes to catch on to the way the petals condense and occupy space. But soon our gaze softens, and sinks into the balmy insistence of their substance, in the involution of enjoyment. Our gaze is contented with this plenum, and forgets the outlying room with its pathways and other things to see and explore. Time loses the sense of a progression into a future and extends into an endurance. It can happen that the cumulus white of the jasmine extends into a fathomless depth and perception becomes a specific kind of warmth and pleasure, as when we abandon ourselves to the bliss of the sky or the glimmering light in the blue of the sea.

When we go out for a walk, our look is not continually *interested*, surveying the environment for landmarks and objectives. Even when we are on our way somewhere, for something, once launched we shift into just enjoying—or just enduring—the walk or the ride. Our gaze that passes beyond things is not situating them on coordinates. It sweeps across things, drawn to the distances where it fuses into the tone and mists of the space. Walking down the sidewalks our gaze enjoys the clarity of the winter light and the sparkle of the frost along the long shadows cast by the low sun. Walking through the forest in autumn, our look does not grasp on to and circumscribe patterns, but dances through the spangled patches of light and shadow. Walking in the mountains or by the sea, our gaze retains hardly any forms or information and dissolves into the blue rhythms of the mountains against the pale sky, into the haze over the sea, feeling the pleasure of their substance buoying it up and away. On the Greyhound bus, our sensibility sinks into enduring the desolation of the plains; on the subway, our sensibility, with a kind of spiteful complacency, gives itself over to feeling the grubby squalor of mass transportation. The perception of things, the apprehension of their content and the circumscription of their forms, is not an appropriation of them, but an expropriation of our forces into them, and ends in enjoyment.

six — *Intimate and Alien Things*

A home is a haven of serenity, a condensation in the elements. We enjoy our home. Enjoyment rests in this zone. This enjoyment is also a movement of retreat and recollection, a taking a distance and establishing a distance, a collecting of ourselves, our thoughts, our feelings, and our forces. A home is a zone in the depths of elemental reality where reality is at rest, a zone which is established and maintained as point of departure and point of return. From a home base we view the environment as a field of things. Recollection makes representation possible.

When we are just passing through a town, we experience a stream of images, patterns, spectacles along a line of time. Then one day we make ourselves a home there. We establish a geography where we can find things and do things. We lay out a Main Street—the path from our home base to our place of work. We establish lateral routes, to the grocery, the laundry, the post office, and to the place where our heart yearns after someone. Beyond, there extend the alien regions of the unexplored, marked, on the horizon, by the next towns and the far-off cities we have gotten to and returned from. When we represent the town for ourselves, we represent it as it extends from our door. (To locate things marked in any other geography—that of the city street or state road map, or the geological map—we have to transpose them onto the coordinates of the geography we inhabit.)

Recollection makes initiative possible. Action presupposes a prior constitution of a point of departure fixed in the environment. Our home is the commencement of activities which are forays outside in view of appropriation.

Our mind is not a modular unit in our bodies that has the innate power to take a distance from the whole environment, retreat into itself, and then form a representation of that environment. While we are running or on a roller-coaster in a fairground, we cannot take a distance from the environment, survey it, and form a representation of it. Nobody can work out an epistemological theory while sprinting through the Stock Exchange Building. Philosophers require a place of recollection, whether, like Michel Foucault, a carrel in the Bibliothèque Nationale, or, like Jean-Paul Sartre, the upper floor of the Café Flore, or, like Friedrich Nietzsche, a table in the Piazza San Marco from dawn until ten, when the tourists wake up.

Things with Which We Are at Home

Things are not just patterns projected in space before us or streaming by; they take form in the place we inhabit. They await us in our home and along the paths extended from our door.

Things are durable substances. They hold together of themselves and maintain themselves over time. Things are solids.

They are forms. The clearly delimited contours that constitute a piece of reality as a thing mark out the way it is separate from or detachable from other things.[1] The substance of a thing is graspable; the substance is what lends itself to be detached and removed. What offers no surfaces to take hold of—air, heat, warmth, light, ground—is not a thing. What offers a form but is not detachable—a mountain range, the clouds, the moon—is, Henri Wallon said, an "ultra-thing."[2] Wallon discovered that children who draw houses, people, cars, and trees in relative proportion to one another do not know how big to draw the moon in relation to these things. The moon and the clouds follow us as we walk; they are movables, but not removables.

Its form is the way a substance is closed upon itself, and holds our hand and eyes that reach out for it. Because a thing's form, its closed surfaces, make of it something that is in itself, it is also graspable and detachable and transportable, at our disposal. Through its form, a thing is both in itself and for us.

Things are attractions; they draw our perceptual movements to themselves and hold them. They are not simply relays toward other things, nor implements geared into one another. They are terms, that rest in themselves, termini.[3] Our hand reaches out toward substances, relating them to the finality of needs. But it is not our hand just transporting the nourishment to the hungry mouth, it is our hand depositing something in the home, keeping it in reserve for tomorrow—or marking its position on a path that leads back to the home—that grasps it as a thing, a substance.

Things condense the tranquillity of the home. Contented and at rest in our home, we enjoy their substantiality. We rest within the solidity of the

four walls and sink into the rest of the easy chair. Below our window the
garden gate and the tree-lined road and the bridge over the river are composed and serene. They keep at a distance the threats and provocations, the
sound and the fury of the stock exchanges and the battlefields.

At rest in themselves, these substances do not gear into the things about
them or onto our forces; they emanate a savor, a resonance, an aura. Our
active forces are freed from them, but they softly invade our sensibility,
which comes to rest in them.

Things do, it is true, reveal the consistency and coherence of their forms
in being manipulated and put to use. Looking in the cellar for something to
hammer in a nail to hang a picture on, or looking on the ground for something to hammer back the nails on a shoe whose heel has pulled off, we
attend to the chisel or the stone as something hard enough to drive the nail
into the wall or drive back the nails of our shoe, and of a size and shape that
we can get a grip on. Something that can serve as a hammer takes form in a
system of driving arm, nail, and wall or shoe. The form is not envisioned as
a geometrical shape, nor as contours inasmuch as they are the ways a substance is closed in itself and excludes other things from the space it occupies. The hammer's form is the ways its force of resistance or drive fits in
with other things—with the grip of the hand of the user and with the other
things movable, breakable, or assemblable with its force. The forms of things
grasped as implements are the ways the shapes of things convey and orient
force. The matter, the material composition, appears only as the cohesion
of a form. As we hammer we know the steel of the head and the wood of the
handle only as the consistency of the form that drives in the nails.

But things do not momentarily take form in the unarticulated elements,
in the flow of light and shadow, heat and damp, along the ground, with the
specific function the manipulating hand simultaneously outlines and makes
use of. It is because they are already there, detachable substances, in themselves and at our disposal, that we can envision uses for them. The utility
and the value that a thing can have are separable and come after. A thing
can have several uses, or remain unused and encumbering our home; it can
wear out, become useless. A tool is not a transitory relay of our body that
extends its force in an instrumental field. It is by being in our possession,
available, that a detached substance can function as a tool. Use presupposes possession.[4] Before things become implements (*Zeuge*), annexed to
the body of the user, prostheses, they are furnishings, *meubles*[5]—movable
goods, detachable substances brought into the zone of the home, tranquil-
ized, and kept in reserve. Attending to and dealing with things is not making of our outlying environment a workshop; it is furnishing our home.

A house is equipped with means—with kitchen equipment, with tools for cleaning and for repairing. It becomes a home by filling up with goods, with easy chairs, books and recordings, a fish tank, rocks gathered on walks, and pieces of driftwood. Once we have attended to the mechanisms of home equipment enough to have acquired the proper use of them, they revert to a substantial presence in contact with our sensuality. The living-room furniture, the drapes, the lighting acquire the density of a sensuous harmony. The invigorating smells and air and rigor of the gymnastics court or ski slopes envelop the room of the student athlete. The rocks, driftwood, and debris of urban construction fill the room of the sculptor with a vibrant disorder.

The town that becomes our home town is not just the area where the factory, grocery, laundry, and hardware store are within reach. It is the zone with the tree-lined streets for strolling, the park, the central square and café where we meet friends and acquaintances. Even the shops are not just arrays of equipment and implements offered to our needs; the store windows are tableaux. We do not really do window-shopping on Saturday afternoons: we look at the window displays and at curious or beautiful things we have no desire to buy.

The sensuous properties of things do not only provide data for identifying them practically and conceptually. Our gaze is focused and supported by the dense brown of the wood and sinks into it, our touch is centered and condensed. Our body comes alive and becomes sentient and diagrams of movement form in it. The things support us, sustain us, exalt us. They buoy up our gaze, fill our hearing, nourish our energies, restore our movements. The delight that illuminates our sight, the tact and sensuality that refine our touch, the refinement that makes high-spirited our hearing come from them.

The concept of means misses their reality. The taste for things, the appetite for reality, is not an agitation to compensate for inner lacks. The water we drink is not just a means to lubricate our inner organs; the thirsty mouth drinks too much or too little, savoring the body and the bouquet of the wine, tasting the luminous mirth of the spring pouring out of the rocks. The foodstuffs obtained to refurbish depleted body protein and evaporated body liquids dissolve, for the taste that savors them, into terrestrial and celestial bounty. In the berries we gather as we walk through the meadow we relish the savor of the summer. The substances that nourish us are not means for action that will seek for more means which are each time means for something further. After a good dinner, we turn to squander our energies on flowers planted in the garden in the glowing sunset, in kisses and caresses lost on an affectionate cockatoo, on the somnolent body of a lover. The colors and the shadows that contour the visible and lead the restless gaze in aimless circumnavigations through the environment do not simply serve to locate what we need or want. Sight is not an intentionality made of distress or desire. Vitalized, illuminated, and nourished by the substance of colored and translucent things, sight becomes high-spirited life. It caresses the colors, forms, contours, and shadows, making them glow for themselves with their own lights.

The form does not so much expose and make accessible and graspable the inner nature of things as clothe them and conceal them. Under his or her clothing, someone's nakedness is intact, apart from the environment, and abstract. Under the clothing, someone's nakedness does not belong to a world; it exists elsewhere, and to make contact with the nakedness of another is to make contact with the otherness of the other.

Under their forms which have made things graspable and domesticated, their inner natures are clothed and concealed. Their natures remain decent and abstract. The functional forms of things which make them implements or furnishings cover over their substantial natures. The fiberglass, metal alloy, or plastic substance of the automobile remain abstract and unknown under the molded forms; the form of the stone axe, which detaches it for our eye, leaves the substance which is uncovered by the broken and decayed form in all the abstract generality of "stone" or "fossil substance." Roquentin in the public garden senses how ungraspable is the substance of the bench under the forms and functions it exposes to the light.

The identity a thing acquires by virtue of its detachable form is not the identity of its constituent essence, which it rather covers over. The identity it acquires by virtue of its form makes it susceptible to being compared, exchanged, and quantified. It can enter a system of exchanges as currency, and be exchanged for currency. The anonymity of money for which things are exchanged reflects the anonymity into which their substances recede under their graspable forms.

But in the sensuous density of these things there are directives. The armchair offers repose and calls for composure in the midst of agitation and contention. The worktable calls for devotion to craft. The dining room silently calls for respect for the shared sustenance of the earth. The hi-fi set imposes respect for the lofty aspirations of music. The paintings on the walls, the photographs in the albums lift our eyes from egoist gratifications unto temples, landscapes, and persons loved and admired that trace out the paths of destiny. The plants, the aquarium are not implements that serve us; to live with them is to care for them, to sacrifice for them our time, our projects. The farm woman knows that the aluminum kitchen utensils, which she will not replace with ostentatious and fashionable utensils, have the goodness of frugal dignity in them. The slum dweller finds in the squat-legged bathtub with cracked enamel in which water flows and reposes a lesson in the endurance of modest things and lives too.

To have a home is to actively care for the things appropriated. We have to shelter things from the inclemencies of the weather and from our own and another's careless or reckless collisions with them. We have to be attentive to the needs of things that grow of themselves. We have to be attentive to, and supply for the needs of the land, the plants and the trees, the herds and the flocks.

Exotic Things

The paths leading from our door to the things of our environment also lead on into the outlying regions of the alien. Our departures from our home are not all predatory sallies to acquire implements and possessions. Away from the restaurants and casinos, we walk the arid and sun-flooded mountains of the Côte d'Azur.[6] We are walking, nothing but walking, with no aim or goal, walking in the sun of high noon. The hands are forgotten, they are no longer groping and grasping. The understanding, the agitation of mental activities has been so flooded with light, our mind is so dazzled with the radiant epiphany of the sun that the thin crystal constructions which our mind assembles in an inner darkness are no longer visible. All we are doing is looking. We feel all our life pouring out of our eyes. Our gaze departs, buoyed up by the beams of light, swept down the beams of light, and, like them, absorbed and lost in remote distances where they pick out no patterns or messages for us.

The things we come upon in the outlying regions of the alien are themselves alien forms. The carved rock in the clearing in the forest in the Guatemalan mountains, the bleached twisted log on the sands are not correlates of our hands that impose their uses on them; they are forms made by the growth of a long-dead tree and polished by the sea, made by geological upheavals and carved by a priest of a vanished people and softened by the rain and the moss. The albatross is a form varying itself rhythmically and drawing vanishing arabesques in the Antarctic sky. In the summer meadows the patches of grasses in seed and the thick spiny leaves coiling around the stalk of a thistle form snares for our eyes, into which each time a wave of our life sinks and is lost. In a foreign city the pagoda, the parks, and the colors and designs of the shantytown crystalize into ensembles which present us with unknown shapes and substances dense with imperatives for oblivion-seekers. When people first discover the coral seas, they often buy underwater cameras to take from the ocean depths its enchanted colors and forms, motivated by the desire to share them with the surface-bound. But one quickly learns that the forms and colors fixed on photographic paper stabilized what existed in shimmering movement. In the depths of the ocean one is only a visitor.

In the vicinity of the home, the separateness of things comes from their detachability, graspability, and transportability. But the separateness of things also comes from their taking form in the region of the alien. There, a thing takes form as an attraction or a repellant. In its substantiality it draws our mobility; in its form it refracts our gaze to its surroundings, its own inhuman setting. Alien things are charms and omens; they function as matrices of expropriation.

Indeed, the clothing and the forms of people are not so much how the others are exposed and accessible to our understanding, as how he or she commands our behavior, imposes discretion and tact.

Our look stops on a bleached gnarled log on the sands by the sea. The sands cease to be glitter to become a hollow on the beach where driftwood from the sea come to rest. We come upon a face carved in a rock set upright in the midst of the forest in the Guatemalan mountains. The forest undercover ceases to be shadow flowing under our feet to become a clearing in the forest where an immemorial shrine broods and waits. Such things crystallize as snares in which our look, our touch, our life flowing outward is channelled and sent further into the alien. They are entries into the inhuman. We find ourselves drifting far from our home toward the time of ancient gods of lost peoples, toward the geological epochs of the oceans and the continents.

The zone of the alien is the region where the order of the home enters into decomposition. It is where the things that furnished the home, no longer cared for, pile up, break, blister, decay. It is the outer regions exposed to erosion and to meteorological and geological catastrophes.

It is the zone where the thrusts of our life are excremental, where they eject our forces without return, where our voice seeking no reply issues in laughter and tears. As we wander in the alien our substance is left behind in waste and corruption. It is the zone where our vital energies stain and befoul our way with sweat, secretions, spilt blood, and semen.

SEVEN

➤ *Action with Things*

Implements

Our gaze does not pass through our eyes as through open windows upon a world and is not surprised to find those eyes in the reflection on a wine-glass. The visible disks of our contact lenses, a microscope, and a telescope guide and focus our gaze, as does the cliff and the airplane bearing our gaze over the sequoias. We go to the balcony to see its view upon the city. Our gaze that is drawn to the carved stone come upon in the shadows of the forest in the Guatemalan mountains is refracted off it to the trees about it and the skies above to see the faces it turns to them. To make the other sides actually seen is for us to move to join them, and their anchorage on the earth supports our bodies turned to look at what is visible to them. The back of our desk has a visible reality which is not simply conjectural; the visible wall behind it maintains it visible for us. The sequoia is not an opaque profile projected in front of us by our gaze; the other sequoias, the sea, and the mountains and the skies maintain it visible in its whole reality.

We do not simply perceive the sword-shaped outline of the sequoia; to see its reality is to see its inner lines, its upright posture and upward thrust of force. We perceive it with the stability of our stand supported by the ground and by the other trees and grassy mounds which support our upright posture on the same level as the sequoia, and we know its upward thrust of force as it pulls our gaze upward. Lying on the ground under the sequoia, creeping through the forest undergrowth, circling it in a helicopter, we join the eyes of the other animals and birds who see it at high noon, in the winter, and in the night. As we advance in a tunnel, we follow the

light that outlines the walls and the tracks before us, and they are not terms
but relays for our gaze. Things seen are things with which we see.

When we listen to the flamenco singer, we do not simply reconstruct the
words and their meanings in our minds; the wailings open our throats and
tighten its walls and the hoarse purrings set them trembling. We hear the
song with her voice. We understand the message the panicky child brings
with the breathlessness and the outbursts of his voice, and hear it with the
choked silence of the room and its draped walls and tense floors. We hear
the scream of the eagle with the winds and the rock walls of the canyon.
The animal in Kafka's tale who hears a muffled sound in his burrow rushes
down tunnels where that sound is heard more clearly, and tears through
walls where it would be heard by other smaller burrowing animals and
grubs. When he finds no tunnels, no other burrowing and sentient animals
or grubs that hear it differently, the sound detaches itself from reality and
loses its terrestrial reality to become phantasmal or metaphysical.

When, in the cave, batteries gone dead in our flashlight, we grope at the
rocks, our touch spreads their gritty relief before us as the mass of our
hands press up against the rock and skid across it. The force of our hands
draws on the sustaining force of our sprung stand which draws on the sustaining force of the cave floor and walls. We feel the force and mass of the
rock that struggles with our force. The rock discovered tangible by our
hands is not afloat in an intangible darkness; it refracts our touch to the
other rocks whose forces feel it in our place. They lie about it as sites we
could occupy to feel this rock. Gloves will not be a barrier that insulates
our touch within itself; they will convey our touch upon expanses whose
abrasiveness or stickiness would impede the pressure and scope of the bare
hands. A blind man feels the sidewalk and the wall with the tip of his cane,
and the plumes of our hat are antennae we have incorporated that feel the
height of the ceiling when we are climbing up the staircases of a mansion.
It is not on the surface of our skin inside but with the bulk of our leather
jacket that we feel the narrow passage in the cave. We feel our way across
the unstable rocks of the mountain path with the wheels of our bike.

Every stand we take to view, hear, approach, feel and manipulate things
takes up the supporting force of the ground and supports itself on their
stability and outcropping. The opaqueness of the colors of things, the density of their sounds, the cohesion of their tangible substances does not simply stop the probings of our sensibility. The forces in things do not simply
obstruct us; they relay our forces. It is first by taking up the supporting
force of the ground and the outcroppings of things that provide standpoints
and paths that our energies become forces that move and that perceive.

The things induce us to join our forces to theirs. Their forms are not simply shapes, boundaries, or contours; they are dynamic axes, concretiza-tions of orientation. We perceive how their forms fit in with the shapes of other things movable, breakable, or assemblable with their force, and how they fit the grip of our hands. The understanding that identifies imple-ments is not a contemplating what is here in front of us now; it is a touch-ing what is here as a relay on the way to what this thing is oriented toward, what it leads to, what it conducts us to. Implements are grasped on the move as we reach for them and manipulate them. To go to the cellar and find a hammer is to spot something that can serve to pound in the nail or crack the walnuts. To recognize a vertical plane as a door is to see that we can open it and exit through it; to see a horizontal plane as a corridor is to see it bearing our movement across it.

It is the user, the usage, that apprehends the nature of things found and fashioned to be useful. If you want to understand shoes, ask a dancer, a runner, and a construction worker. The shoemaker himself must ask them. If you want to understand a motorcycle, ask a biker. Who would fly hang gliders designed and manufactured by the earthbound? Fliers buy hang gliders designed and manufactured by Bill Moyes, the first birdman to make and fly one, and first to glide into the Grand Canyon.

To see that we can bicycle to Pittsburgh is to foresee that our tires may blow, the gears break. Nothing useful is useful only for an instant, nor for-ever; all things, in being used, are used up. Every implement may break, misfire, explode; they harbor the possibility of the death of the agent and of the deletion of the field. Every lure may be a snare, every path an ambush, every stone on that path may be a trap beneath which lies the abyss. Sens-ing the recalcitrance of things, our hand senses its own possible impotence.

Relays of force, implements take form in a field of possibilities, an in-strumental field. We opened doors and saw at a glance that this is the kitchen, this the bathroom, this the bedroom. In one setting a bottle of amber oil emerges as possibly cooking oil, in another as possibly soap, in another as possibly genital lubricant.

The Ends of a World

For the user to deal with an implement is to envision a certain practicable field with which the implement connects his powers, in which it maintains and orients his position, sustains and facilitates his advance. When the hiker reaches for her boots, her view does not stop on the shape of a mass of leather; she turns to the mountains, the crisp air and pellucid light, the rocks that rise sovereign over those that scurry back and forth in the plains. Her boots are not for her raw material that sustains the shape the cutter has put on it, but a force sustaining the forms of her advance, a power to forget the mud and the thorns. In the materiality of the boots, she sees the consistency, the reliability that sustains the harsh rigor of mountain paths. The shape of the boots is not for her that geometrical diagram which guided the shears of the shoemaker but a form that corresponds to the contours of the rocks over which mountain goats leap and of the hollows of the brush-covered resting places of deer. In the form of the boots she sees the orientation of her forces toward those paths; in their materiality she sees those paths becoming practicable. The hiking boots exist on the mountain path; their consistency, their durability, their reliability, their flexibility, the affinity of their leather for the warmth and the damp of the earth are felt in the hike; their firm shape, their lines of tension which are lines of support, exist and are known in the rocks and the cliffs. The boots belong to the mountains, and make her belong in mountains.

It is for his neighbor, the spectator, that the motorcycle is so much metal of a certain shape cluttering the view into the backyard or obstructing the driveway; for the biker, his bike is power, speed, roar, phallic thrust that he feels in the confidence and assurance of his body weaving through traffic, plunging by the semis on interstate highways, in a landscape dissolving in hot sunlight and roaring winds and nights when the small lights of rooms in which the sedentary murmur before television screens streak by like meteors. The solidity of the motorcycle is revealed on the dirt trails, its streamlined form revealed in the gale winds bringing the Pacific coast down interstate highways.

The utility of things is not produced by an image of an end, absent from the field of practicable reality, being formed in the mind of the maker who then shapes raw material. Raw material has internal properties and structure which interact with other substances. The serviceability of their natural forms and the reliability of their material natures are discovered in usage. A farmer does not build up the fertility of his land and build up his herds by assembling raw material and imposing a willful form on them, but by protecting the topsoil and caring for the cattle that are born and grow of themselves. The builder in the tropics discovers which woods crack and warp or come to harbor boring insects, and which palm leaves or grasses will serve well and long in thatching. The shaping of a form delimits, focuses, and stabilizes the reliability and serviceability of its nature, which sustains vectors of force with further things.

The mind of the maker discovers the ends for which the things at hand can serve by surveying the outlying field; the things he or she makes will extend the lines of access. The ends which make us perceive our environment as so many routes and pathways and dynamic interconnections are exterior and command us.

It is the fertile fields exposed under benevolent skies that beckon to him who lives in caring for the land, the living things, and the open skies and that make things at hand and things that can be fashioned and assembled useful. It is the open road that insistently summoned Walt Whitman and Maxim Gorky and Jack Kerouac and makes road gear of canvas sacks and dried fruits. It is the India in the Jain temples of Rajasthan and the ancient port of Mahabalipuram under the sea and in the faces and the pain of harijans that looked at Gandhi seated behind the windows of third-class carriages of trains for a year of his returning that delineated salt and spinning wheels into instruments of liberation. In building a home on the flank of the mountain exposed to benevolent skies, in crafting a boat built for the open seas, in lighting fires on the festive night, in forging the bullets of revolution, we come to inhabit the mountain range, we come to dwell in a world of open seas, we enter the immemorial antiquity of feasts, we move on the intercontinental theater of a future advancing upon a world oppressed in the present. Our action brings us to the ends of a world.

In using things found or crafted, we do not simply invent these ends which bring to flush a practicable order in the things about us; we re-present, within our minds, the ends that are outside, on the hillside under the skies, down the open roads, in the remoteness of medieval wonders and immemorial feasts, in the pain of others programmed in chanceries beyond the seas. It is not the maker that makes the final cause; it is the final cause that makes the maker. It is the dance that makes the dancer and the shoemaker.

When I arrived at the old university town of Leuven in Belgium for graduate studies, I found a room with three other students in a house in the fifteenth-century walled quarter on the edge of the town known as the Grand Béguinage. The river Dyle, upon which the old town of Leuven was built, ran through the Béguinage, and the house we occupied was set directly on the river. The béguinages were a kind of nunnery established in the Lowlands during the Hundred Years War, when the men of Europe exterminated themselves in religious fanaticism. In the béguinages pious women grouped together in settlements walled for protection, and devoted themselves to the spiritual and corporeal works of mercy. Unlike conventional nuns, of the three vows of poverty, chastity, and obedience they took only a vow of obedience; they retained their wealth, and if they found a husband, they could leave. Each nun of the Grand Béguinage had her own house, and servants. The nuns had been gone since the French Revolution, and the houses had been rented to the poor.

When we moved in the house, we found piles of waxed milk cartons in the cellar, and we too saved our empty milk cartons. Then, once a year, on the feast of Fière Marguerite, we brought them up. Fière Marguerite had been, centuries back, a maid working in an inn in the town who had a reputation for kindness. One night men to whom she had rented lodging raped her and beheaded her and threw her corpse into the river Dyle. The following morning at daybreak the Duke of Leuven looked out of his window from the castle on the promontory

over the town and saw in the river something floating upstream. He sent his men
to investigate; it was the body of Fière Marguerite. On the eve of the feast of
Fière Marguerite, we, as had the inhabitants of our house before us and those
before them, brought up all our wax milk cartons from the cellar and lit them,
and dropped them one by one from our window into the river Dyle below; their
fires floated gaily through the night of the sleeping town of Leuven. The Middle
Ages, its faith, its legends, its violences and its longings for the transcendent,
settled down around us, and the pious béguines, their daily activities sewing and
cooking for the poor and binding the wounds of men returning from wars, and
their lonely and ardent gazes upon those men, returned to our house.

Was then this year's accumulation of empty wax milk cartons and our matches
the means with which we created the feast? And did we make the feast because
we first made, in our minds, the idea of the feast? Is not feasting something that
has existed from time immemorial, that already existed in the Neanderthal caves
and about its fires, that recurs with the turning of the year, and which in Leuven
had acquired its own form along the river Dyle and in its medieval houses, its
cathedral and its castle, its inns that welcome pilgrims and merchants and trav-
elers and students? We found the feast in the memory of our neighbors in the
Béguinage, in the piles of milk cartons left in our cellar as they had been left
there before by those whose place we took in the Béguinage, in the layout of the
medieval town and of its shrines about its river. The feast did not vanish when
its concept was forgotten in the minds of men; it recurred with the river that
flowed through the town and upon which the cycle of the year brings back the
day of the ancient wonder, and directs once again the hand of the cook, of the
winemaker, of the seamstress, and of the lute-player. The finality that produces
the feast in Leuven, and made our evening once again festive and legendary and
medieval, is the moving waters of the river Dyle, the cathedral where the body of
Fière Marguerite is maintained enshrined in memory, the old stones of the houses
of Leuven, where the Middle Ages, its legends and its marvels, its violences and
its hospitality are retained. And that makes the old milk cartons, their waxy
materiality, their buoyant substance known in the festive fires that dance on the
night waters of the river Dyle.

The ends are not terms, subsisting in themselves, closed terminations,
where some movement comes to an end. The finality that produces the
dance shoes and the dancer is the open vortices of the universe, where
sunlight plays, where birds circle in the open skies, where butterflies draw
staccato rhythms across the meadows, where all things are at play in the
fields of the lord Shiva Nataraj. "'O Zarathustra,' the animals said, 'to those
who think as we do, all things themselves are dancing; they come and offer
their hands and laugh and flee—and come back. Everything goes, everything comes back; eternally rolls the wheel of being. Everything dies, everything blossoms again; eternally runs the year of being. Everything breaks,
everything is joined anew; eternally the same house of being is built. Everything parts, everything greets every other thing again; eternally the ring
of being remains faithful to itself. In every Now, being begins, round every

Here rolls the sphere There. The center is everywhere. Bent is the path of eternity.'"[1] It is this epiphany of a world the other animals know, the horizons where sunlight dances over the forest floor, waves dance across the meadow, spiders dance across their webs, and octopods dance across the reef that summons forth that movement in us that is not going anywhere, that movement driven by melody, rhythm, periodicity which is dance. We do not simply invent these finalities which extend an instrumental order in the things about us; we re-present, within our minds, the ends that are outside, on the hillside under the skies, beyond the open roads, in the dance floors of nature.

The Discontinuity of Practicable Spaces

We can from a lookout point try to see the map of the city or of the valley below and locate the cathedral and our home at the intersection of parallel streets, locate the next town at the bend of the river. We can map out the action centers and the flow of traffic. But our home becomes real in the inhabiting of it, where a geography of primary and secondary paths open from it and return to it. The cathedral becomes a cathedral not for the pedestrian or automobilist who takes it as a landmark to fix the direction of movement across the city, but for the believer and the unbeliever who find in it the precinct of the sacred, the focus of cosmic and sublime dimensions and the oracle where the line of destiny is traced. It is the horse that stands before us with its spirited eyes and charged muscles that opens about it directions and paths in the density of the savannah. The motorcycle that stands before us in the evidence of its compacted power extends open roads across the continent. The cliff looms up before us and draws us along with the wolf, the eagle, the winds, and the sun, and extends below us paths to adjacent cliffs and into the forests and into the town.

A thing first solidifies in its reality and then refracts about itself other things that view the faces of it we do not yet see, and extends about itself the paths to them. Out of the flow of the sand and the sun, it is the bleached log we come upon that delineates about itself the beach as a harbor for things received from the sea. The cave over the sea on the broken lava crust of the island that harbors us and shows us the recesses in which it has harbored other animals and people before us extends about itself the volcanic core of the island, the loneliness of the ocean beyond and the tempestuous skies above, and the habitat this island was for a destroyed civilization.

The practical fields that extend about a thing—the sites that take form when we come upon the reality of a thing—are limited and discontinuous. When, rummaging in the cellar one Saturday morning, we come upon a wire-cutter we had forgotten we had, its thick steel blades connect up with electric cord, clothesline wires, fencing and these in turn to repaired lamps, clotheslines strung across the yard, or flights built in the garden for doves. But these lines of instrumental connection do not extend across the universe; they come to an end in an illuminated corner of the reading room, they give way to a garden bower where doves murmur in the vines and shade. We go to the cellar to fix a broken chair with drill, screws, glue; the phone rings and we plan a trip with a friend, mapping out an itinerary, jotting down things that have to get done—have the car greased and oiled, get a passport, get injections from the doctor; suddenly there is a scream and we drop the phone, hurl out the door and grab a stick to thrash the cat that has caught a blue jay; on the way back to the house we glance at our watch and realize it is almost time for our appointment with the hypnotist to stop smoking . . . He who grasps the hammer does not comprehensively envision the carpentry of the whole world. The practicable fields form so many discontinuous practicable layouts in the density of a sensuous reality made of light, warmth, the murmur of the city, the vastness of the ground, the tranquillity of the home. Between and beyond them, there are innumerable impracticable fields.

Does it not happen that we find the onward drift of our environment disconnected from our actual movements and operations? Does not each life extend across metamorphoses, in which it finds itself reborn with tasks that were nowhere yesterday; does it not find whole fragments of its past drifting behind it, unintegratable like dreams in the daylight reality about it?

The ends, exterior to us with the exteriority of an imperative, are exterior to one another. The consistency and coherence of a world is that of circular paths about resting-places which laterally issue upon other fields of circular paths about resting-places.

The means upon which the movement of an action rests hold that movement as ends that exclude other ends. Around the meal of the Guatemalan campesino the door is closed to the trafficking and urgencies of the roads and the laborious body comes to rest. The motorcycle absorbs all the sensibility and skills and intelligence of the biker developed for other destinations. The pigeons and the canary which started as means to distract the adolescent boy shut up in his slum house end up making that house their home and that slum boy their caretaker, their kin, making him Birdy.[2] The currency of exchange for the capitalist metamorphoses into an end in itself for which the rain forests and the birds-of-paradise and the ozone shield of the planet and his own life are sacrificed. The vistas of the practicable terrain are not stages of one linear itinerary of a single life-enterprise; a world does not extend as a highway into which all roads issue conducting us to our cremation pyres at Varanasi. The unending paths themselves become ends, for the nomads who depart from every oasis in the Sahara, for the hobos of industrial America, and for the motorcyclist.

Implements and Elements

Things do not take form at intersections of an instrumental complex first laid out across the void. A field of paths and obstacles opens in the light. The light is not a network of instrumental references but a sensuous medium. Graspable contours surface in the density of the night. Signals and threats take form in the rumble of the city, in the murmurs of nature. These are not maps extending in the void. A traffic sign solidifies in the flow of the landscape and the radiations of the night. Clouds shift in the blue radiance of the sky. Stars beam in the hard density of the night. Our desk takes form in the pervasive mellow tone of a room which is not a spaceship in uncharted voids but a harbor in the warm and perfumed density of the resounding night. The jug glows not in the intersection of axes it extends but in the tranquillity of the home. Things take form across levels that extend across the fathomless and plenary depths of the elements.

Work draws things from the elements. The hands of themselves grope and grasp in the elements. There is not first a project, a plan elaborated, a finality fixed which activates and controls the body; the hands reach out, grasp, tear up, knead, crush. There is an element of groping in the most skilled manipulations.[3] As we work at our workbench in the cellar, building a cabinet, the layout fades back continually into the indeterminate; we fumble for the hammer, the screwdriver, and the screw we just put down and which has already sunk into the sensuous density of the environment.

The basic comprehensive movement, which understands their identities and their functions, is in the handling of implements; our hand moves as a sense organ, gathering information. But it moves also as a sensuous organ, fondling substances and textures, stroking the grain of the wood and the sheen of the saw blade, captivated by the rhythm of the hammer-blows and the pirouettes of the car on the mountain road, rubbing out the shapes of things to reduce them to buoyant or fluid or vaporous depth or solidity that extends indefinitely into the depths of the earth. Our hand enjoys the random play of its movements, enjoys being surprised.

Our hand that reaches out for things does not make the outside more and more determinate. As we work, as the cabinet takes form under our hands, the working space fills up with wood shavings, tools left here and there in disarray, spilled nails. We make our way down the paths of the garden, to look for the onions for our meal or to gather flowers for a bou-

quet, and we leave, and leave the rest to rest or to drift in the indeterminate. As we make a meal, the kitchen space fills up with knives and mixing
bowls, husks and scrapings, and pots and pans in disorder. Action then
does not lay out the axes and determinations and instrumental connections of a world. It stakes out a zone of the practicable, and, in inhabiting it,
this zone transforms or unforms into an unpracticable density in which we
rest and dream.

It is in the proximity with things that the most remote axes of a world
become present. But the horizons also close in, the beckoning paths fade
out, the gearings and the axes of force thicken and become opaque when
we come to dwell in things. About the few things that are really things with
which we live—an old coffee mug, a carved and padded armchair, a violin,
a pearl-oyster shell on the window sill—the wide world, the common world,
breaks up into so many discontinuous spaces full of dreams and memories.
Even more, these spaces themselves etiolate and get absorbed into the opaque
substance of those things, like the root of the chestnut tree before Roquentin
thickening into something unnameable in any world.

Does not the finality in things also come to an end in them? Water we
know in the savoring and in the drinking, berries we gather and that melt
in our mouth as we walk through the meadow do not catch our eye as
refurbishments for our cells and muscles and means for our projects; they
are substances in which sensuality glows and fades away. The materiality of
things is not just there as the materialization of the dynamic form we grasp;
once grasped and brought under our eyes and in our home, the instrumental forms of things dissolve into the density of their substance. The movement of the carpenter that takes hold of the hammer passes through it to
the nails and the shingles and the house and the stormy skies and the work
done in the home to be sheltered. But once on the job, this relay-course of
finalities dissolves into sunlight and bracing air, and in his hand his hammer becomes a rhythm that prolongs itself. He can be contented with that,
contented with hammering in the sun. The objective intention thickens
into a sensual attention that ends in the hammer, and the carpenter can
enjoy the rhythm and reverberation of the hammering and enjoy this very
activity as a content. We walk down the path to get somewhere, but we
enjoy walking and we can leave our house just to walk. When our look
sweeps over the landscape, surveying resources and envisioning tools, we
also see the fields rippling with the meaningless hum of insects, the rhythmic flow of the green hills, the sky speckled with birds veering and revers-
ing. The carpenter's hammering goes smoothly, by itself, a rhythm that prolongs itself of itself rather than an operation being piloted by an intentionality; his eyes drift over the landscape and the street below and his look

loses itself in patterns and contours of substance. He savors even the fatigue that blurs the outlines and the connections, and the exhaustion that welcomes the night. The expropriated Guatemalan campesino, toiling on the brink of starvation, clings to his native mountains and skies.

The Agent Delegated by the Things

The skyward ascent of the giant sequoias makes us stand tall; the brush makes us crouch to make our way through it; the currents of the wind and the billowing columns of the thermals give the level to which the posture of the hang glider responds; the punch press mandates the position and moves of the punch press operator; the limbs of the trees command the posture of the tree surgeon. The parched and dusty pages of the research books dictate the slouched figures we see, by night, in the carrels of the library. The powdery wings and coiled antennae of the moth command the fingers and hands and posture of the naturalist studying it in the back room of the entomology museum. The motorcycle commands the splayed limbs and racheted wrists of the biker.

Action is effective and is our own in the measure that we respond to the ends we find with our own powers; in responding to them we make our limbs and members and sensitivity into powers and make them into ourselves. Every implement opens upon a field where it can conduct us in different directions and can be used in different ways. The selection of things we will make and use is an individuation of ourselves.

Our body that mobilizes itself emanates a quasi-percept of its own visible configuration as seen by the things it sees, a quasi-percept of its tangible bulk, its sounds and odors as seen, touched, heard, smelled from the outside, of the reliability and serviceability of its substance and forces in view of the ends that command them. It perceives itself in the body image with which the exterior ends see it. This image is not specular but imperative, it is practical; we direct our car through traffic with the image the other cars see of it; we direct ourselves through the glade with the image the trees see of us; we touch a child's bruise and a bird's broken wing and feel the force of our hand that the bruise and the broken wing feel; we modulate our voice not with the tone and force of voice we can hear in the chambers of our skull but with the echo that voice sends back in the voice of another. With our body image we make ourselves a skillful chauffeur, a man of the woods, we make ourselves tactful, we make of our body not a resonance chamber but a communicating medium.

The action to make things into means engages in things that make a means of the one who acts. The motorcycle commands the user to reconstruct his posture, his musculature, his skin, his manual and mechanical skills, his imagination and his reason to serve it; his cycling makes him a biker. The land the Guatemalan Indian inhabits, the milpa he cultivates which demands the utmost of his rationality and leaves no indulgence for caprice and fantasies, are not means for him; he lives not only from them but for them, they are his dignity. The frijoles in baked-clay plates his wife lays out on the table for him and their children are not a means for the refurbishing of depleted body-cells in view of labor for ends beyond; in the repast their cares come to rest and their laborious existence finds an hour of accomplishment.

EIGHT — *The Production of Purposes*

The making of implements has been taken to be distinctive of human action by thinkers who pass over the leaf-mold gardening of ants, the breaking of mollusks with rocks by gulls, the nest-building of birds and dam-building of beavers. Making has been conceived as an imposition of form upon matter by the agency of human force and skill. True production of implements was taken to be distinctively human because it was said to presuppose the conception of a purpose, the end for which the product was the means: the maker who makes an implement first makes an image of the use of that tool in his mind. The image of the end would determine the form to be imposed, and make a product a means. Homo faber, making first his own purposes and remaking his environment into means, would achieve sovereignty, recognizing no directives and no claims put on him by the outlying environment.

In our contemporary industrial market economies, it is not its own nature and its properties linking it with its natural setting that makes a thing useful to us, but the form industry has put on it. It is not willow bark in its nature as willow bark that we find useful for our headaches, but the extracted and purified essence synthesized into aspirin tablets. Timber is first cut into rectangular boards before it can be useful; the trees themselves are first hybridized, thinned out and pruned, before they can become useful as timber. There are whole plantations now where biologically engineered species of plants grow not on the earth but in water, anchored on floats of plastic foam and fed with chemical blends. There are reserves now where genetic engineering is producing new species of patented plants and animals.

The substances of which things are composed are treated as pure raw material, prime matter, without natural forms resistant to the forms manufacture imposes on it. And the raw material is itself manufactured—refined and alloyed metals, plastics, synthetic fabrics, information bytes.[1] The table of elements is no longer an inventory of irreducible physical nature; atomic fission and fusion make the elements all subject to transformation.

The outlying environment does not seem to impel and direct action; instead it lies about us as so much cement or plastic to which any forms can be cast, any purpose assigned. Manufacturers contrive new uses for new raw materials and design forms that can be mass-produced. One makes oneself a laboratory technician, an industrial designer, a manufacturer by imagining in one's mind finalities for resources transformed into consumer goods, goods made to be used up in the usage.

This does not mean that the modern industrial world is engendered by a Copernican revolution which locates the law of production no longer in the external finalities for which implements are useful, but now in the will of the producer himself. The designers, the decision-makers, and the manufacturers who do not select the products to be produced by consulting the purposes of the users do not consult their own values and taste; the decisions are made by marketing research calculations of what cost-effective transformations can be made in the current directions of consumption.

The producers only imagine chairs as the finality of their transformation of raw materials, and equivalent chairs as the finality of the replacement of furniture; industry only requires that materials be transformed into chairs and that furnishings be periodically replaced. Yet the chairs are proposed to the users, and to make consumer goods enter into circulation the manufacturers appeal to the finalities of the users. And these finalities derive not from mental productions in the minds of the users but from the exterior finalities that open the horizons of their existence: home, hospitality, good posture, and good health for a world that awaits.

Advertisers can, to be sure, induce consumers to imagine that a synthesized drug will bring them good health, a cellular phone will break down the walls of their isolation, a vacation resort will restore the land and the ocean to them. The purposes conceived, the representations of ends caught sight of, can be edited, recoded, beautified, transmogrified. But although we use our automobile only to roll to one end of the city and back again, transportation evokes the existence of remote and enchanted destinations or the roar of the sun and wind in the open road. Although we use our PC only to play video games, the Internet evokes the existence of others—people with sensibility and convictions we could not produce in ourselves.

The video games we play evoke the existence of luck and destiny irreducibly alien to the invention of our purposes. The Nestlé baby food the father in Bangladesh buys is more expensive than is local food that would make his wife strong, and does not have the natural immunizing agents mother's milk has. Yet he buys it because the billboard shows babies fed Nestlé as strong and vigorous as Americans.

NINE — *The Pageantry of Things*

*E*verything that is resounds. A voice conveys the warmth or coldness and vigor or timidity of someone speaking. The tolling parades the substance of the cathedral bell, the creaking materializes the dry wood of the stairs in the amorphous night, the crackling delineates the hard grains of the hail. But sounds also dematerialize the substance of the things they resounded and extend their own patterns, their pulse, rumble, melody, or din over the space vacated. They drift off things and link up with one another, and we hear a Morse code or jazz of sounds ricocheting in the free space.

Things do not only show their obstinate occupancy of their own places and their contours to our surveying look and manipulating hands. They project halos over themselves and cast shadows on other things. They scatter reflections in mirrors and in eyes and in water. The water of the garden pool projects shimmering waves on the screen of cypresses behind it. The dome of the Taj Mahal refracts its light upon the faces of the crowds in the dusty streets. From millions of light-years away, stars cast their dancing lights on mountain lakes.

The things that are really stabilized as things in our environment, the things possessed, brought into the realm of the home, lie at rest there, substances kept in reserve. But the furnishings of our home also spread about themselves auras and patinas, shadows and densities. When we sink back into our wicker chair as it whispers again marshland murmurs, the patterns of the room vibrate off the layout and shapes of appliances, cabinets, and lamps.

The colors of a face do not only outline the surfaces and carpentry of that face, but interact with one another in a swarthy, lustrous, ethereal, or ardent complexion. At high noon the colors of the forest below disengage from the contours of the leaves and the trees into a billowing of dense green fog.

The professor is occupied in reading the explanations he has prepared to communicate to the students in the room. But the way he holds his lecture papers, his gestures, his complexion, the shape of his skull and the fall of his hair separate from this professorial presence, and form a foppish, buffoonish, or loutish physiognomy. The instructor disappears, as though he had left the room, leaving there only his trappings and paraphernalia.

A rabbit nibbling its way across the garden doubles up in the image of a child or a dwarf. People who are pursuing their tasks look like fidgety woodchucks scurrying about. The walls of a house double up into a facade whose windows are eyes and whose door is a mouth. The trees extending their bare branches against the wintry sky metamorphose into hands scratching and gesticulating fretfully. The hills rise out of the plain in the voluptuous twilight as breasts of a landscape prone in a swoon or in sleep.

These appearances are not transitional appearances that lead to the real properties of the things and vanish when they appear. They are not true and are not false appearances either. They do not function as signs relaying the gaze to the things themselves. They do not have that transparency; they thicken, materialize for themselves. The rhythm and musicality of their facades, shadows, reflections, and auras obscure our view into the position and composition of things which are uncovered, discovered, and grasped in action.

It is not that things barely show themselves, behind illusory appearances fabricated by our subjectivity; it is that things are exorbitantly exhibitionist. The landscape resounds; facades, caricatures, halos, shadows dance across it. Under the sunlight extends the pageantry of things. The twilight does not put an end to their histrionics. In the heart of the night the pulse of the night summons still their ghosts.

These apparitions are pushed aside when we grasp the appearances of things in concepts. To grasp hold of a hammer is already to comprehend it; it is to close our hand around its essence as an implement that can direct and concentrate force, and it is already to comprehensively hold in view a field encompassing nails, shingles, and boards. It is through action that we comprehend.

When we grasp things and fix their natures in concepts, these concepts offer the succession of things to our powers and connect up with other concepts in a dialectic. Yet when we set out to grasp things in rigorous and lucid concepts, we find those very concepts engendering images that are not images of their referents. Allusions, equivocations, evocations, evasions, insinuations refract off their crystal shapes and bewitch the very mind that cut those shapes.[1]

When we approach a lawn mower, the visible profile we see in the corner of the garage leads us to the handle side, the blade side, and the underside; it unfolds a time of progressive development and exposure. When we see its brown wood handle, we see how the wood was brown and will be brown. The facades, caricatures, projections, and reflections of things double up the linear and progressive time of action with a time of fate. The shadow or reflection of the chair we see in the window endures in a present without possibilities, not pregnant with another, future side or force. When we look at the face speaking and see the professor teaching, we see the expression and form of that face evolving in the elaboration of sentences and paragraphs. But when we see instead the double, the caricatural form, the foppish or buffoonish or loutish physiognomy, it appears immobilized in its fate.

These apparitions exist in a rhythm or a tempo rather than in a time with past, present, and future. A tempo keeps reproducing the Morse code of the dripping faucet. A pulse of the forest links up the splotches of light and shadows. They do not evolve or continue of themselves nor cause one another; their rhythm or their tempo commands them like a predestination.

The rabbit nibbling its way through the garden doubles up into an image of a child or dwarfish human not because our mind actively selects images and links them up, but because our mind is captivated by, caught up in a pulse that collects and reproduces sounds and apparitions. We are not grasping the carpentry of things in their appearances nor subjectively fabricating images of them, but find ourselves caught up in their images, their shadows, their reflections, halos, the harmonics of their colors, the rhythms of their forms. The facades, caricatures, projections and reflections of things are interesting; they do not outline something of practical interest, but involve us in themselves. We find ourselves among them and carried on by them into a time of fate.

This is a distinct state of anonymous consciousness, different from habits, reflexes, and instinct. When we walk or dance to music, the movement is not automatic and unconscious; consciousness is acute, but without intentions or initiatives. We no longer direct our attention. We follow the music anonymously, like and with anyone who listens to it.

Seated in a train, we look out of the window, actively seeking to identify things, landmarks, towns, but soon the color and forms of the mountains disengage from the map of the landscape and distract us and our hearing gets enmeshed in the beat of the train wheels turning on the rails. Our gaze no longer probes and surveys on its own initiative, but follows the rhythm of trees and hills. Walking through the forest, the shadows link up in a fibrillation which lifts our eyes from the substance of the trees and underbrush and from the diagram of our gait and the shape of our body image.

We become the splotches of sunlit flesh among the flakes of sunlit leaves. We become our shadow moving among the moving shadows of the forest. The flight of our gaze takes its place in the promenade of the clouds in a space without limits and without tasks.

The density and tempo of noninstrumental apparitions brings us the irresponsibility that charms as nonchalance and grace. It frees us from initiative. We do not continually push our way through implements and obstacles; we take refuge in the beat and melody of apparitions. We drop out of the progressive time of initiatives, summoned to the time of fate.

TEN — *Phantom Equator*

Multiple Sensory Domains

The colors, the textures, the resonance, the scents and savors condense into things that induce our postures to center our sensory surfaces upon them and conduct our movements toward them. But the colors also disengage from the things to play off one another. The visible ceases then to be distinctively visual and forms a realm of events and epiphanies unto itself. The sounds depart from the things to link up with other sounds and lead our hearing away from things, and the resonant ceases to be something we listen to and for. The blue of the sky and the green of spring, the tones that announce the symphony, the mossy floor of the night are the entries into and summons to these other realms.

For our sensibility to be saturated by the chromatic, the sonorous, or the tangible is not to retreat from the field of real things and adhere to the surfaces of our own organism. To the contrary, the unattached colors, the rebounding tones, the tangible engulfing our touch draw our whole sensibility into impracticable spaces full and complete in themselves.

At the airport in Lima, our eyes scan the paths, identify the counters and the gates, find the charter line, search the runways for the Cessna, try to identify the pilot. Our eyes guide us as we follow him through a maze of paths in the construction site under the muddy drizzle called *garúa* that will hover over the city for the winter months. Our eyes locate the seat belt, study the instrument panel. The plane takes off across the wet runway, rises into the murky gray fog and emerges into the sun above. The flight from Lima to Nazca will take two hours. The sunlight spreads out unlimited depths of azure sky. Below, the fog is a powdery blanket that extends unwrinkled on all sides. To the right, below it, there is the invisible feature-lessness of the Pacific. Far to the left, the peaks of the Andes push irregularly through the mist to accompany us in the flight with a distant rhythm. The blue radiance above and the white softness below are not the visible fea-tures of a landscape but a luminous dream over a world that we have com-pletely lost touch with.

We walk down the paths of the floodplain, the raised mud walls car-peted with the dusty green of the compacted grass. The rice paddies extend on all sides, mirrors of the sky. The ripening rice blur in the breeze into a clear yellow mist suspended over the blue that is not of the water and the drifting white that is no longer that of clouds. The yellow does not materi-alize the substance of the plant stalks; it spreads in an ether where green shadows flow about it.

We enter the concert hall, locate our seat; we look at the musicians pick-ing up their bows and sticks and reverberating the violin strings and the taut skins of the drums. Our eyes move from one instrument to another in the orchestra pit. Then the music begins, and the tones now disengage from the surfaces upon which they were vibrating and weave into the space between us and the instruments. Our hearing begins another movement, from one tone to the next in a lyrical space that dilates and condenses, expands over a vast horizon, approaches from distances nowise limited by this renaissance salon whose ornate mirrors present on each of its walls only the other walls. This space is complete unto itself and the musical forces, more than tones, do not evoke or depict visible and tangible things, but materialize emergences, events, and destinies inexhaustible in them-selves. At the end of the concerto, we look about as though awakening from the caverns of a trance and relocate ourselves in the hall with friends and with refreshments outside.

By day the pavilion in the old Balinese princely residence in which we have taken up lodging offers all its furnishings at once to the glance that surveys its narrow confines; from the covered patio before it, the walled garden exhibits a panorama of flowering trees and meandering brooks with small bamboo-arched bridges offering a path encompassed in one view. Returning by a moonless night, we climb the steps through the gate to make our way through a space reduced to the tangible. The high gate steps have to be measured one by one by the groping foot; they materialize very differently now from when the eyes measured their breadth and height. We have to locate the level of the path below; the indeterminate closes in. For the hand that gropes for the door and bed, these things do not have the simultaneity of all their surfaces and contours they had for vision; their extension and substance form along and adhere to the movement of the touching hand. The tangible does not form into objectives as does the panorama of things at a distance that vision encompasses; it rises in relief in close proximity and across movement. The duration that it takes to delineate their contours loosens the simultaneity through which they were the contours of things, as a melodic pattern of sounds, while it has a more substantial presence, does not have the thinglike unity of the pattern of the written score. We find ourselves in a space made of oppressive presences, petrifications, liquefactions, transubstantiations.

The cooking and sewerage smells of Venice or Chandigarh, in the measure that we get absorbed in them, enclose us in their own swirling and dense space that obscures the spectacle of extending avenues and architectural monuments. The perfumes of a Persian garden introduce us into a drifting and radiating space that dissolves the exiguous garden walls that had confined vision. The damp of the monsoon in the cities of the Ganges, the asphalt heat of the strip cities of the American Southwest in midsummer leave about us the perspectives and distances of the visible and tangible cities as unmoored mirages.

These colors, tones, odors, saturating our sensibility, extending their levels imperatively about us, require not a laborious and task-centered posture but a vitality drifting in a play of phosphorescence, dancing in the moving pathways of melodies, exposing its surfaces to the caresses of the moss, the tropical damp, wholly lungs in the midst of scents rising at high noon or sliding through the sultry night. They command us to reconstitute our bodies as ecstatic, melodic, carnal and no longer competent bodies.

Painters, musicians, haute-cuisiniers, and perfumers will represent the visual, the sonorous, the gustatory, and the olfactory in layouts that do not simply represent, as signs, the things. Aesthetic theory will disengage the laws that govern the effects colors and lines, tones, savors, or odors have on one another. An artist does not admit that his representation was produced by a decomposition of his sensory integrity: artists do not believe that textures or tones are so much raw material upon which they depict simply a form they have a priori programmed in their own reason. The colors on a Tibetan tang'ka, the concertos of Bartok have a consistency and coherence that the artist came upon by following the ordination with which colors and tones are given. If an artist can disengage himself from the practicable fields to devote himself so exclusively to colors and tones, it is because he finds himself receptive to an imperative he finds in the colors, that their own ordinance be seen, or in the tones, that their own ordinance be heard.[1] If she can take her work seriously, it is because she is sure that not only for her but for the others also, to be a sensitive organism is not only to be a prehensile system wired to grasp the carpentry of a practicable field but an organ that follows the summons of colors into another domain, that follows music into a sovereign order.

We might hesitate to call science the theoretical elaborations with which aestheticians, musicologists, acoustics researchers, perfumers, and wine-tasters represent their knowledge. It is true that their observations are not objectifying, the phenomena they observe they do not locate on the coordinates of empty geometric space and linear time, simultaneity is not for them defined by the general relativity theory of physics, the regions they circumscribe and organize by correlations are not translatable into the region of the physics of vibratory events. But their knowledge has its own rigor, its controls, and its concepts, and, by extending the isolating method of scientific observation of entities into an isolation of fields of observation, it advances toward the state of reliable empirical knowledge by fragmenting further the domain of science in our time.

Depths of the Night

Sleep is not coma; our sleeping sensibility retains enough contact with the levels of the ground, the warmth, the damp, the tangible to awaken to them and locate on them the paths strewn with things to which one awakens.[2] Like the shadows which set forth the contours of things, the terrestrial night maintains our tasks for us and lays them out under the light for us again when we will have recovered our competence.

But sleep is not only commanded by the imperative of the day, which requires our restored competence exhausted by its tasks. To go to sleep is to enter through the corridors of the terrestrial night into a night not mapped by the stars and where we see with closed eyes visions that beckon to our sleeping sensibility.

The great black bird which hovers, falls, and becomes a handful of ash in the dream does not hover and fall in physical space; it rises and falls in directions extended, Maurice Merleau-Ponty says, by the tide of our respiratory and vital rhythms, by the aspiration of our sexual desire.[3] Yet this unpracticable space is not an inner psychic space; it is the great black bird which exists in flight, and not the emptiness of our craving, that establishes the levels of the space of dreams.

The space of dreams is described negatively as a space where distance does not separate the identities nor the causality of forms, which can instantly metamorphose, a space where surrounding sites do not maintain a thickness of lateral sides to the bird or the facade of a temple.[4] The hold the dream-image has on the dreamer is described subjectively as fascination rather than obedience. But the oneiric apparition positively extends its own connections and lines of depth and remoteness. It is not simply an afterimage or a fragment of things found in the practicable layout of the day; its shape and its traits are strange. They reveal an alien depth and an enigmatic significance.

The psychoanalytic interpretation of dreams willfully identifying each oneiric man, woman, or monster with ourselves only collapses this alien depth onto the banal map of our daytime affairs. A more sophisticated psychoanalysis projects it onto the space of cosmic or private myths. Those who have instead recorded these nonterrestrial apparitions and metamorphoses without the bullheaded intent to adjust some prosaic practical or social incompetency in themselves have discovered the interpretations all leave behind the essential, the uncanny sense of the apparition, the unexemplary plot of events. They have recorded epics which project only to further epics without resolution. The oneiric apparitions summon our sensibility to the night beyond the protective terrestrial night, a night of unlimited disquietude.

The imperative of the night reveals its force not only when one follows down the corridors of the night not horizontal to the day but in depth, but also in the night that looms in the high noon of the environment. These are moments when we do not see things as having insides which consist of more visible things, destined to take form in the light, such that eventually all the content of things extends as a succession of phenomenal profiles—moments when we sense the beginningless, endless presence of night in them that remains while all the phenomenal profiles our initiatives pull out of things file out and pass as an inconsistent phosphorescence. There are times when the panorama of paths and tasks that summon with their urgencies appears as a screen behind which an immensity without tasks summons us to an assignation to which we will arrive divested of our competence and our I.[5] Examining the fossil of a trilobite in full daylight, there comes a moment when it is this night we pass into. Beneath the well-lit room and garden, we sense the night in the floorboards, in the core of the earth.

The nocturnal passions, the compulsions of antiheroes and underground men, the materialists whose passion is not for the terrestrial or the subatomic, the bhikkus immobilized in a heightened sensibility tuned to nirvana, the Orphic initiations—are they not misunderstood as longings for another world in which civic roles are inverted, in which king is slave and slave is king, man is woman and woman is man, human is goat and goat is human? Are they not passions destined for the night itself, obedience to the force of an imperative that holds us more imperatively than the transitory imperative of the practicable fields? How faithfully Isabelle Eberhardt

wrote of these oblivion-seekers, was herself one of these seekers after the
night that awaits no day to come![6]

Unpracticable Spaces

Phantasms, visions, erotic obsessions, and hallucinations link up in constellations. They open abyssal corridors where distant forces synchronize
and induce transformations in one another, where nearby forms and events
disintegrate or metamorphose on contact.

> A schizophrenic patient, in the mountains, stops before a landscape. After a
> short time he feels a threat hanging over him. There arises within him a special
> interest in everything surrounding him, as if a question were being put to him
> from outside to which he could find no answer. Suddenly the landscape is snatched
> away from him by some alien force. It is as if a second sky, black and boundless,
> were penetrating the blue sky of evening. This new sky is empty, "subtle, invis-
> ible and terrifying." Sometimes it moves in the autumn landscape and at other
> times the landscape too moves. Meanwhile, says the patient, "a question is being
> constantly put to me; it is, as it were, an order either to rest or die, or else to push
> on further."[7]

The caricatures and masks that absorb the sensibility of the dreamer,
like the color that saturates our eyes, inaugurate a level which disengages
from the verticality of a world upright before the upright posture to delineate another direction and directive. The schizophrenic who looks out into
the garden which the others see and sees there a stranger the others do not
see, who hears voices where no one is seen speaking, enters another space
which shows through the practicable space, undermines it, and summons
him to push on further. There are multiple spaces extending their own
latitudes, for which the practicable world of things fixes no equator. There
are journeys from which we do not return enriched, with a booty of spices
and gold, souvenirs and snapshots. There are voyages to which we are summoned from which we do not return.

The One-World Hypothesis

The phantasmal theaters of dreams, hallucinations, erotic and psychedelic
visions do not give themselves out as private and fabricated spaces made of
distortions and errors. This, Merleau-Ponty explains, is because the real
and common world does not give true things in a system we understand.
There is absolute certainty of the world in general, because it is only by
invoking the coherence and consistency of the world that we revoke into
doubt any particular appearance, and do so by replacing it with another

appearance drawn from the reservoir of the world, and because any other realm of entities, whether that of the scientific representation of the universe or any metaphysical or theological representation of ultimate reality, derives the entities it admits from observations and verifies them by soundings in the world of perception,[8] and therefore could not be employed to relativize the belief in the reality of the world we perceive. But there is no absolute certainty of anything in particular, because a thing is the termination of an indefinite exploration, a task, and exists in the interrogative mode. The world "takes in without discrimination real objects on the one hand and individual and momentary phantasms on the other—because it is an individual which embraces everything and not a collection of objects linked by causal relations. To have hallucinations and more generally to imagine is to exploit this tolerance on the part of the antepredicative world, and our bewildering proximity to the whole of being in syncretic experience."[9]

For Merleau-Ponty, the multiplicity of realms each with its own ordinance does not impugn the primacy of praktognostic perception or confound the normative force of the practicable world. "I never wholly live in varieties of human space, but am always ultimately rooted in a natural and non-human space."[10] The images, doubles, masks, caricatures, phantasms that populate multiple unpracticable fields owe their presence to the grain of the sensible made contact with in perceptual prehension. "Even if there is perception of what is desired through desire, loved through love, hated through hate, it always forms round a sensible nucleus, however small, and it is in the sensible that its verification and its fullness are found."[11] "As I walk across the Place de la Concorde, and think of myself as totally caught up in the city of Paris, I can rest my eyes on one stone of the Tuileries wall, the Square disappears and there is then nothing but the stone entirely without history; I can, furthermore, allow my gaze to be absorbed by this yellowish, gritty surface, and then there is no longer even a stone there, but merely the play of light upon an indefinite substance."[12] The perceptible things show through their dream-doubles, hallucinatory caricatures, and erotic mists, as the canvas shows through the painted landscape, the crumbling cement under the building, or the tiring actor under the dramatic character. And "human spaces present themselves as built on the basis of natural space";[13] this is true of spaces explored in dreams or hallucinations or erotic obsessions, as it is true of the all-encompassing metric space in which the scientist elaborates his representation of reality. "The sun 'rises' for the scientist in the same way as it does for the uneducated person, and our scientific representations of the solar system remain matters of hearsay, like lunar landscapes, and we never believe in them in the sense in which we believe in the sunrise."[14]

Not only does our dreaming consciousness have no access to entities save the awakened perception (or the peripheral sensibility that never fully sleeps and continues to be sensitive to the levels and sensorial regions of the world), and has nothing but drifting fragments of perceived things to materialize in the vital and erotic dimensions in whose tides they rise and fall, but, Merleau-Ponty writes, the dream-field itself owes its existence to the waking state that recalls it. "During the dream itself, we do not leave the world behind: the dream-space is segregated from the space of clear thinking, but it uses all the latter's articulations; the world obsesses us even during sleep, and it is about the world that we dream." "Though it is indeed from the dreamer that I was last night that I require an account of the dream, the dreamer himself offers no account, and the person who does so is awake. Bereft of the waking state, dreams would be no more than instantaneous modulations, and so would not even exist for us."[15]

The carnal physiognomy to which the eroticized perception is directed is indeed different from the physical shape of another as envisioned in a practical perception and coded by pragmatic and polite forms of social interaction. The voluptuous tones that give it its sultry density are different from the colors that make its texture and pliancy visible to a perception that synergistically focuses in on it. But it is the perceptible anatomy of the other that anchors the voluptuous phantasm for concupiscent longing.

Dreams, hallucinations, erotic obsessions, and psychedelic intuitions "endeavour to build a private domain out of fragments of the macrocosm, . . . the most advanced states of melancholia, in which the patient settles in the realm of death, and so to speak, takes up his abode there, still make use of the structures of being in the world, and borrow from it an element of being indispensable to its own denial."[16]

The field of real things then admits monocular images, reflections, mirages, noises, and fleeting tactile impressions, which the deviant consciousness elaborates into another space.

The practicable field of perception is for Merleau-Ponty the one world and it contains the corridors that dreams, hallucinations, erotic and psychedelic phantasms open in it, as the dimensions of the canvas contain the dimensions of the scene painted on it, even though there is not one universal set of geometrical dimensions upon which the spaces opened in dreams and in erotic obsessions can be measured. These spaces are absorbed into the geography of the practicable world, "as the double images merge into one thing, when my finger stops pressing upon my eyeball."[17]

I perceive everything that is part of my environment, and my environment includes "everything of which the existence or non-existence, the nature or modification counts in practice for me": the storm which has not yet broken, whose signs I could not even list and which I cannot even forecast, but for which I am "worked up" and prepared—the periphery of the visual field which the hysterical subject does not expressly grasp, but which nevertheless co-determines his movement and orientation—the respect of other men, or that loyal friendship which I take for granted, but which are none the less there for me, since they leave me morally speaking in mid-air when I am deprived of them.[18]

The world remains the same world throughout my life, because it is that permanent being within which I make all corrections to my knowledge, a world which in its unity remains unaffected by these corrections, and the self-evidence of which attracts my activity toward the truth through appearance and error. . . . I may be mistaken, and need to rearrange my certainties, and reject the being to which my illusions give rise, but I do not for a moment doubt that in themselves things have been compatible and compossible, because from the very start I am in communication with one being, and one only, a vast individual from which my own experiences are taken, and which persists on the horizon of my life as the distant roar of a great city provides the background to everything we do in it.[19]

And since the unity of the world is not that of an intelligible system, not grasped in synthetic concepts and principles, but that of a style (as we recognize the style of a city while all the things in it are rearranged and replaced), it is the style in our perception, the postural schema with which we integrate our sensory-motor exposure to it, that prehends it. The world which is one individual that encompasses everything is the practicable world, and if it is not there as a given but as an imperative, it is an imperative that our sensibility be a praktognosis, and that we maintain ourselves integrally as practical organisms.

Multiple Realms

But is it true that the unpracticable spaces are constructed with fragments of real things lifted off them and elaborated into a private space by the deviant consciousness? Is it not true that the things themselves engender, along with their graspable contours, images of their presence in multiple locations and in impracticable spaces? It is the thing that produces the monocular images of itself on our retinas, the pool that makes itself visible on the sun-streaked cypresses. But is it the graspable substance of things that engenders these apparitions?

Does natural perception believe it is getting closer to the shark in discerning the viscous matter of its flesh under its power, its ferocity, its grace, its dominion in the sea as old as and uncontested through three ice ages? What kind of primacy would the practical perception have that sees goals and the paths and means to reach them in the cobblestone lanes and moss-covered houses of the medieval town? Would not the vision that penetrates to the practicable layout of the things itself derive from the revery that lets the tones and the rhythms of the tile roofs and amber street lamps lift off in another wave of duration, that of the immemorial toil and repose, legends and festivity that slumber in its trodden paths and shrines worn smooth by innumerable reverent hands?

The gilt door of the thatched-roofed Balinese princely house presents simultaneously its domesticity, as a wooden door, and its glory. The wood is humble and terrestrial by reason of the gilt it displays; the gilt is glorious because it is the splendor brought to wood. The home is princely because it is clay bricks, exposed bamboo rafters, from the terrestrial sources of the land, that are carved and gilded to enshrine the luster of the civilization that presides over the island of Bali risen out of the sea in volcanic eruptions and sacred favor.

Does the practical focus that envisions someone's anatomy as a prehendable substance really have ontological primacy over the erotogenic surface, the voluptuous mirages that refract our gaze turned to strangers? Is the reality in things that which takes hold of and is taken hold of by the synergistic mobilizations of our practical postures? Are their sensuous density and substance that resist the manipulative hand and invite the caress, their twilight colors that seduce and soften the focus of the gaze and communicate with the sensuality of our organism rather than with its postural axis, in some way derivative? Is not to exist as a sector of the geographical space laid out in perspective simultaneously to exist as a landscape of revery? The nocturnal trees that rub their twiggy hands and gesticulate in monstrous gestures we so readily recognize in old lithographs—have we not always seen the trees with these caricatural versions of themselves?

A thing reduced to its simple location in a here-now instant of presence is not real and is not perceivable, Merleau-Ponty says; a thing is real by presenting itself in a wave of transcendence, sending echoes and simulacra of itself back into the past and into the future, projecting itself in us as a diagram of our own forces. A thing is, we argue, by engendering images of itself, reflections, shadows, masks, caricatures of itself. Things are not reduced to their reality by being reduced to facts; the "pure facts" of empirical observation are abstracts of intersecting scientific theories, logics, and effects of technological engineering. But things are also not reduced to their reality by being perceived in their practicable format. It is because they engender carnal, caricatural images of their characteristics, turn phosphorescent facades on the levels and horizons of reality, that they also engender a practicable format. Reality is in this parturition.

The things exist in a movement which does not only project their integral essences down the tracks of practicable reality; across a wave of duration they refract off masks, veils, simulacra, shadows, and omens. The monocular images, phantasms, lures, and forms made of shadows make the things visible and are the visibility the things engender. The surfaces of things are not more real than their facades; the reality that engenders the phantasm is engendered by it.

Merleau-Ponty puts the inclination to obey the night itself, to let go of the general framework of a practicable nature, on the side of the abnormal and the incompetence of neurotics: "The distress felt by neuropaths in the night is caused by the fact that it brings home to us our contingency, the uncaused and tireless impulses which drive us to seek an anchorage and to surmount ourselves in things, without any guarantee that we shall always find them."[20] But is not the neuropathic distress instead produced by the willful effort to bring back a practicable world when it is the night that summons?

No dream, hallucination, erotic obsession, or psychedelic trip knows itself as the personal construction the philosophical formula "private domain put together out of fragments of the macrocosm" explains it to be. The artist who paints a clustering of colors that has its own consistency and does not disintegrate before our eyes as so many patches of paint on the surface of the canvas, the composer who arranges sounds in a consonance or dissonance that holds together has no consciousness of being a demiurge who imposes form on amorphous material by an a priori decree of the will. The painter, the dreamer, and the libidinous organism find themselves pushed further on by the urgencies by which the dreams, the doubles, the shadows, and resonances materialize an ordinance that commands him or her. Does not everyone who follows his dream, his erotic obsession, his vision, the beat and cadences of his music find that he constructs representations of his dreams, his erotic field, and his artistic visions only by subjecting himself to the fields in which they unfold as to imperatives? No one makes himself a dreamer or a visionary; those we admire—perhaps everyone we admire—are men and women who came upon a field imperative for them, the field of a visionary imperative, a musical imperative, a nocturnal imperative, a passionate imperative.

As our steps advance, the visible domain laid out as a geographic projection in which things are distributed in lines of perspective turns into a landscape made of the voluptuous contours and hollows of things and of the waves and rain that caress, of mossy forests and nocturnal fragrances that fondle our surfaces and penetrate our orifices. The night beyond night summons the insomniac to an abyss that does not lead to the day and its tasks. The unpracticable spaces of visions, of murmurs and melodies in which no one signals another, of the palpable and the impalpable that caress and the night that engulfs, and the practicable field of objects-objectives are disjoint expanses come upon along the zigzag itinerary of our days and nights. The space of the purely chromatic, the range of harmonies and dissonances, the labyrinth of voluptuous contours and seductive hollows, the ether of obsessions and phantasms, and the vistas of the essentially nomadic vital space that shows through the grid of the common coordinates—these are not private constructions built out of fragments of the macrocosm, disconnected mirages that ill-focused eyes send to drift over the equator of the practicable field of substantial and graspable things. The practicable field of things is itself suspended within their latitudes. They are not private constructions, which like the invisible and impalpable space in which the community of scientists elaborates a representation of the field given in perception, exist only by hearsay, spaces we do not believe in and cannot inhabit, spaces contained within us. Each is a realm of exteriority not reducible to our representations, an exteriority that exists with the exteriority of an imperative. The nomad is summoned not by distant things fixed on one equator, but by multiple spaces, multiple ordinances; the equator is itself phantomal.

ELEVEN — *The Reasons of the Heart*

The Weight of the Given

As soon as we open our eyes, the light, the depth of the tangible, the hum of the environment beset us, soliciting, enticing, badgering. The exterior is not an empty and neutral but a resplendent, beguiling, bleak, or stifling expanse. Reality weighs on us; we cannot be indifferent to it.

The light surprises, oppresses, delights, and directs us. Terra firma endorses, uplifts, and orients us. The warmth caresses us, calls us forth. The elements summon our enjoyment and the strength of our endurance. The desolation fills us with anxiety yet draws us. The decomposition horrifies, disgusts, and excites us. The night overwhelms, and haunts us.

The levels sustain us and open before us. They come together in the zone of intimacy, which tranquilizes us and composes us. They come apart in the outlying regions of the alien, which we do not survey from above but feel in disquietude, yearning, and enchantment.

Disquietude and vulnerability, exultation and composure are pervasive states, ways we find ourselves affected by the elements and the levels. They subsist as we turn in one direction or another, take initiatives or abandon them.

Moods are relationships with the outside not in its form, as a practicable layout, but in its force. In mood, the outside affects us, afflicts us, weighs on us.

The arid spread of the roads and barren hills and the gloom of the leaden skies above are not just viewed at a distance; we feel, within ourselves, their oppressive weight. In uneasiness and in dread our eyes scan the environs, sensing dangers and threats that the surfaces of things harbor; the menacing substance of nearby and remote things weighs heavily against us and we feel it in the coldness of our skin and the unsteadiness of our nerves and legs. In enthusiasm the force of the environment surges through us; in confidence the ground sustains us as an inexhaustible reservoir of sustenance.

In and through feeling, the elements and the levels are *given*. For being to be given is not just to be deposited there, in front of us. What is given crowds in on us, imposes itself on us, weighs on us. For us to find ourselves is to find ourselves as subjects—not as spontaneous or creative source-points, but as loci of subjection. It is to find ourselves implanted in what has come to pass.

We stand on the top of the mountain and if it does not seem to us that simply there are so many lines extending across the field of our vision, as when we stand in front of a map or a painting, it is because we feel the distance, the vastness of the space. In the movement of the wind in the fields below and in the clouds above, we feel the force of geological and cosmic time.

When, as on vacation, we are freed from the pressure of tasks, or when the unending recurrence of days beyond the day's work makes the tasks appear pointless, the very emptiness of a practical field where all the resistances and obstacles have been removed weighs on us. Tedium, the sense that nothing matters, that all the things spread out in town for us to occupy ourselves with are tawdry and pointless, is a suffering, a suffocating.[1] In the inconsequentiality of the tasks we feel oppressed by the world that afflicts us with those tasks. We feel weary and exhausted with the weight of the days, having to endure the weight of the emptiness where there is nothing to do.

The light, the sonority, the tangible density that affect our moods can engulf us, obturate our view, weigh down our hands with weariness or hold them in their vibrancy, such that we are embedded in the density that settles down upon us and survey very little.

Mood may be subjection not to the whole space but to an isolated thing, when something focuses our attention and weighs down upon us or engulfs us and obturates our view. Our substance is invaded with a mood when our eyes do not circumscribe the possibilities in the forms of things but settle into the depths of the ardent redness of the ruby or the crystalline frailty of the wings of a dragonfly, when our ears are enchanted by the laughter of a woman or by the five little notes Marcel Proust speaks of in *Swann's Way*, and when our hands are no longer gathering information or manipulating but drumming on the side of the bus or combing the wind.

Things are not only structures with closed contours that lend themselves to manipulation and whose consistency constrains us. They lure and threaten us, support and obstruct us, sustain and debilitate us, direct us and calm us. Things do not only project their appearances across different perspectives, in different media, and on the surfaces of our sensibility. They also enrapture us with their sensuous substances, their luminous surfaces, and their phosphorescent facades, their halos, their radiance, and their resonances.

The smallest things can obsess us with their tones. How the strong gleaming teeth of the child in the slums who laughs can send flashes of light through us! How the lonely circles the condor flies in the wake of the storm touch us, displacing all the diagrams and directions of our willful acts! How the fear in the eyes of the raccoon trapped in the headlights invades us! How the humble endurance of the fossil mollusk absorbs us!

The Outpouring of Emotion

It is not only nutrients we need and hunger for and threats in the environment that attract our attention and release our forces. Euphoria and torment, sensuality and rapture thrust us into the thick of a world. Our movements are not spasmodic reactions to outside forces, nor initiatives programmed in advance; they are moved by emotions.

An object or event lures and concentrates the currents of feeling in us. The thrusts of emotion bring it into focus, frame, crop, view that object or event from a distance or in extreme close-ups, view it from an odd angle or through a slightly open doorway, or as reflected on the surface of a pond or in a mirror, or view it in the mist or in the shadings of twilight. The currents of emotion pick up its glimmer and glower, purr and howl.

An emotion is not just a movement of intentionality generated in the subject that hurls itself against the given and inert reality. We laugh with the sunlight, feel buoyant with the exuberance of springtime, languid with the sultry ardor of the night. The rapture of the deep spreads with the streaks of sunlight zigzagging across the waves; the bliss of the hang glider soars with the thermals and the sea winds. The tenderness that spreads within comes from the contact with the warm and delicate down and skin, throbbing with minuscule torments and pleasures, of the ostrich chick cupped in our hands.

Moods give their scope, and their force, to the outward movements of our feelings, our emotions. In the force of our moods, we feel the forces of the ground, the light, the warmth, the zone of the intimate and that of the alien sustaining us, surging through us.

Emotions then do not only discharge their forces on the outside environment; the outside is also the source of their forces. Rage does not come from the overheating of the organism itself; love does not derive from inner needs and wants only. Outside forces surge into us and drive our rage and our love. Our environment is full of free and nonteleological energies— trade winds and storms, the oceans churned by internal rivers, the continental plates that drift and crackle like ice frazil, the clouds hovering over depths of outer space streaked with cosmic radiations, and the frolicking of robins in the fluttering leaves. When disquietude and gaiety and frenzy form in us, it is their free and anarchic mobility and energies that surge through us.

If emotion hurls more force upon an obstacle or lure caught sight of, it is not simply that it sees the whole world in one of its configurations—that it fears the whole ocean in one of its storms, the whole earth in an unstable path on the cliff, loves the whole universe in the passion it devotes to an oil-sodden seabird or to a woman. It is that the force with which we fear and love is the force of the tempestuous oceans and the forces of avalanches, the strong colloidal forces in nature that maintain separate beings, seabirds and women and not a chaos of atoms in collision and disintegration.

The force we feel ourselves absorbing in moods impels us to move onward into the depths of the elements, into the openness of the levels, or to seek zones of more blessed light, more ardent night, less bitter cold, firmer ground. The desolate moods are not paralyzing; they impel us to endure, to be patient. The rage that flares before an obstacle and, instead of standing back to devise technical procedures to bypass it or overcome it, pits the force of our material substance to destroy it, does not experience itself as unnatural; it finds its form in fires, storms, avalanches, earthquakes, and its force in the wind and the sun that stoke its fires. The awe that surges before the Andes and Machu Picchu has a force that quickens the heart, electrifies the gaze, keeps the body climbing for hours in the thin air, and plunges the sensibility deeper and deeper into pre-Columbian and geological time. Every thinker who has tried to go back from the concept of the phases of his own experience to the time of history and geological time knows how the mental force to forge consistent concepts is weak without the force of this awe.

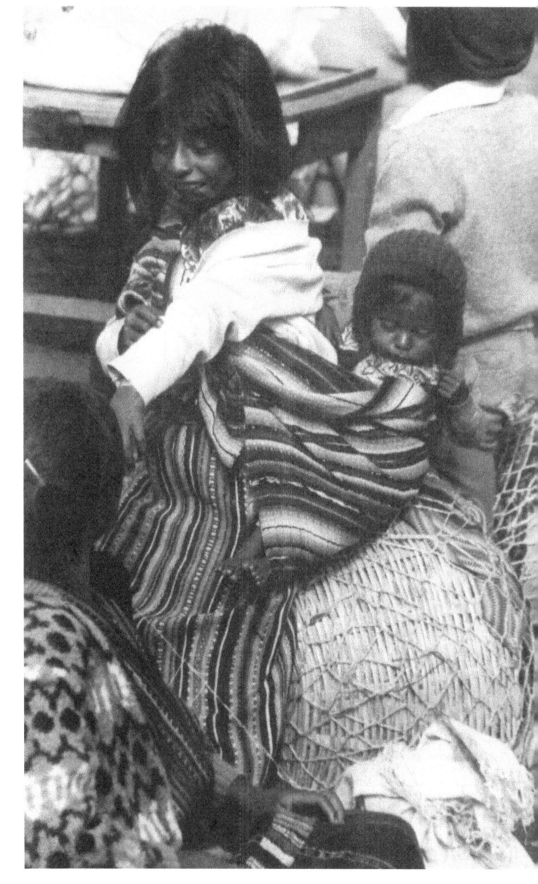

TWELVE ~ *Other Passions*

*I*n awakening to the night, the light, the warmth, and the terrestrial depth, I do not form a discrete being enclosed within boundaries. My enjoyment is not distinctively mine; the night, but also the light, the air, and the earth, are depersonalizing. We see as eyes of flesh see, we see the twilight fall over the forest as innumerable eyes of flesh see it fall, we move and rest supported by the depth of the ground as are other terrestrial animals and plants. We feel kinship with anyone who walks the summer evening. In the forest we sit down in the resting places of the deer. In the sea we dive with dolphins as with our kin. The cat sprawled in the summer grass and the iguana that seeks out the first warmth of the day in the east window are pools of sensuality we feel in a continuity with our own.

The levels along which we move—their confluence at the zone of intimacy and their spread in the outlying regions of the alien—are not levels that support us alone. Others share the repose and tranquillity of our home. The level of the light in the outdoor café that veers toward neutral is the level that the couples and groups about the tables adjust to so as to see, like we do, our complexion and theirs in their gradations of hue and density. We harken to the intruder with the hushed stillness of the birds and insects of the forest; we join the caterpillar stroking the leaf.

The practicable field that opens about us is from the first open to others. The chair we sit on, the hammer we wield, the car we drive require a certain posture and diagram of movement. But there is leeway for a certain range of variations. They are made for someone adult in size and strength like us, but not for us by name—made for anyone within a certain range of size, strength, and age. In sitting in an upright chair in the library, recycling in our head and on paper the theorems of Euclid, we make ourselves a student, another student. The rainbows in the soapsuds in the bath water have to be looked at with a certain focus and movement in order to be visible, but once we have seen them, a certain range of variations becomes evident, and we see what could be seen in another way, and by another. As we are led to the real color and shape of the statue in the park through its transitional appearances, so anyone can be led.

We step on the flat places of the mountain path as another clears them; in the factory we take our place before implements and tasks, a place another has vacated and will occupy when we vacate it. We pick up from others how to eat with chopsticks and swim the breast stroke, and by eating this way and swimming this way we pass them on to others. We pick up from others how to see the bird in the sky and the irritation of the kitten and the malfunctioning part in the engine of the automobile.

The shapes and impulses of life about us are not so many boundaries drawn by our own eyes and interpretations added by our own minds to an environment that is given as so much matter.[1] Our eyes catch on to the inner lines of force and the inner substance of sensuality of the leopard. We feel our substance being invaded by the evident life and the sensuality of the leopard and our posture being directed by him. Before the sequoia our upturned posture, our upward aspiring look, our yearning for the sublime are ordered by the sequoia. It is with the fluid motility of our own bodies that we watch and understand the mountain stream. We do have the power to crush the penguin chick and knock over the sunflower with a blow, as we may block and muddy the river, but our cruelty and our disdain feel the panic of the chick and the vertical aspiration of the sunflower.

When another stumbles in the street, our body knows already what support to give. We put ourselves in the place of another, strengthening his or her diagram of effort with our own. It is by envisioning his or her implements and tasks as though they were arrayed before us that we see someone not as a pattern in the field of vision, but as a beginner on the job, another harassed commuter, another woman. It is with the diagram and direction of movements in our own limbs that we see the coyote not as another piece of flotsam and jetsam in the flooding river but as a fellow-being struggling with the current. It is with our hang glider arms that we watch the condor in the mountain winds. When we free the cormorant from the oil slick, our hands know the effort to add to its efforts and they sense its panic and its pain.

We have learned our hesitancy, felt our assertiveness and our incredulity, learned our obstinacy, felt our irony and our boredom from the surges and tumults in the fields of emotional force in others. They vibrated in our bodies as we captured the tones, rhythms, pacings, emphases and retreats of the gestures and voices of others. Thus we came to feel and express smugness, rebellion, disdain, and gratitude. We pick up from others how surprised or frustrated to feel when the rain falls and how excited to feel when the team hits a goal or when the new samba is pounded out in the street. We also pick up from them how to disguise our feelings and make what is only a show or pretense of feelings. We pick up from a kitten how to share carnal affections and from a puppy how to burst through the tall grass and from the fish in the surge how to navigate the canyons of the coral reef.

When two strangers in a foreign airport laugh at an absent-minded gesture one of them has made, or at the sententious declarations of an official, there passes within them a current of intense communication. Laughter breaks over the room where the things lie closed in their separateness and stupor, a free tumult like that which the waters and the air communicate to one another. As they laugh, they are no more separate than are two waves, though their unity is as undefined, as precarious as that of the agitation of the waters.[2]

The grief that opens to the pain of an accident victim in a foreign land communicates its compassion to any bystander. The fear and the pain of the marchers attacked by the police spread like a wave to the ranks behind and to the people watching from windows.

Acts of courage strengthen the hearts of everyone who witnesses them. Joyous exhilaration demonstrates its evidence like a comet flaring in the sparkling night. Deeds of heroism communicate as no clear and distinct explanations ever could. Sacrifice demonstrates its reality in the powers of the human heart, and communicates sacrifice. It is through the laughter or curses of those staked before a firing squad that the crests of heroism that continue to rise across the distances and generations take form. The care one living being has for another, for an injured animal, for a plant pushing its way to the sun, are understood in the antennae of our vacuous restlessness. We sink into our languor and sensuality to the point of saturation. Thus eroticism communicates its fever to another.

Language is not the primary medium, then, for communication. It is not in speaking to another that we cease to deal with him or her as an instrument or obstacle, and recognize his or her subjectivity. It is in laughter and tears that we have the feeling of being there for the others. We do not laugh alone and for ourselves alone. Laughter breaks out as a current of intense communication among strangers waiting for the plane.

It is first in the communication of laughter and tears that our inner state represents the inner states of others, is a representative of the inner states of others, puts itself in the place of them and substitutes itself for them. It is laughter and tears, euphoria and torment, sensuality and terror that give rise to language, where whatever we say we say for others, where what we say we put in the words and grammar of the one to whom we say it, where what we say seeks to clarify a world and his own feelings for himself.

Every suffering organism incites cruelty; the mother grits her teeth and finishes preparing dinner, leaving the baby to whimper in its cold wet diaper, the nurse takes her time answering the patient's call-button, the tourist drops a small coin in the hand of the beggar child and turns to buy herself a souvenir. But the spectacle of pleasure also excites the sense of and indulgence in power in the spectator. There's a restless toddler in the seat in front of us in the bus; the mother is falling asleep. We make faces at him, provoke smiles and giggles, we pick up his toy, play peek-a-boo with it. We know a sense of power—the power to provoke, and to increase the pleasure in a baby in a bus in Afghanistan.

What imposes respect is the sense of the other as a being affirming itself in its laughter and tears, its blessings and cursing. This respect is first the consideration that catches sight of the space in which the emotions of another extend.

Immanuel Kant has written that respect for another is respect for the demand for law that rules in another. It is when we see that another acts in such a way that anyone anytime would act in equivalent circumstances that we see the other diagramming an action that commands us also. The core of the person would then be the thinking and decision-making functions. Thinking would be the faculty that can disengage the universal and the necessary in a concrete situation, and it would be seen to command the operation observed. The formulation of extensional classes out of data is thought as ratio, reckoning, or computation. It is the function that can be operated by computers, by Artificial Intelligence, which can be programmed to issue decisions on the basis of the logical calculus of data.

But pulling the plug on a computer or AI equipment does no disrespect to them. If what looks like a fellow living being doesn't form personal attachments, grieve, feel remorse, experience fear, pride, anger, embarrassment, frustration, humiliation, depression, fall in love, empathize, feel warmth, or grow resentful, then it is difficult to imagine feeling any sympathy or concern about it.[3]

The insulted honor of the peasant, the grief of a widow, the affection of a child for a puppy command our respect. The misery of the trapped jaguar, the exultation of the young eagle taking to flight, the playfulness of the wolf cubs command our respect.

THIRTEEN ⟶ *Face to Face*

*P*ushing our way through the crowd we feel something, look down: a beggar child touches us. Coming off the bus in the dust of a town we have never been to before, a stranger extends his hand to us. In a hole on the trunk of the tree felled by the storm, we catch sight of half-feathered young owls peering at us in expectation and apprehension.

To face another is to touch with the eyes, if not the hands, not the capillaries coursing with living blood nor the nerve fibers but the layer of dead cells, the moles and scars, the bruises and calluses of the one who has presented himself or herself. It is to soil our eyes if not our hands with the sweat and the grime, the toxins and microbes. It is to feel the skin loosened and yellowed with aging, to feel the bones of the hand we grasp and of the walk we support becoming dry and brittle. It is to hear the coded and informative words on intakes of air, broken with panting, hoarseness, coughs, laughter, outcries, sobs.

The bare skin our hand touches and the naked eyes our look makes contact with do not, like the surface and contours of wood or clay, from the first reveal the inner grain and substance of a thing. They extend before us a surface of sensitivity and susceptibility.

On the surfaces of another, on his skin, we sense his maneuvers not simply being activated by the instrumental complex about him, but striving to reorient the directions of force in the practicable field and wearied and exhausted by the forces of things that resist him. We sense the limbs of another not simply adjusting to the fixed things and the shifts in her physical environment, but pushing against the hard edges of reality, buffeted and wounded by them. We see the wrinkles with which aging inscribes the pressure of imminent death. We sense her gestures not simply formulating signals and shaping intentions but faltering, hesitating, and offended by what is said or not said. We see the lassitude and torpor into which the expressions he addresses to us sink.

Our look and hand touch a surface where another sentient being is exposed to the harsh reality of things and to the force and the grasping in us. When we make contact with the surface of another with a look that grazes it or a hand that caresses it, our gaze and touch sense the tremblings of pleasure that die away and the anxieties of pain that agitate those surfaces.

We do not perceive—in the sense of observe, look at, inspect—this suffering. When we look at something, sight circumscribes the contours which are enclosing an exterior substance; sight positions the color and situates it at a distance. When we look at skin, at a distance, the sense of susceptibility vanishes; we see only a colored surface firm in its own place, subject to being pushed back or cut.

The alien suffering does not extend at a viewing distance, but afflicts our sensibility immediately. It is felt in our hand that extends to clasp the hand of another as a manipulatable limb, but whose grip loosens under the sense of a sensitivity that touches us. It is not at a distance that we feel it, but in the substance of our own hand, which cringes before the leper, the accident victim on the highway, and the bruised animal. The suffering of another is felt in our eyes whose direction is confounded, whose focus softens, whose glance turns down in respect. It is not at the end of our look that we see the surface of susceptibility, but in our own feeling, in the eye that winces, feeling the pain invade it when it turns over there. When another hails us and gestures to us, our hands halt in mid-air, detached from our working posture and our projects; we feel their grip invaded by tact and tenderness. The susceptibility of another is felt in our voice which is in command of its own order and speaks to command, but which falters, hesitates, and loses its coherence before the nonresponse and the silence of the other.

We can turn away from faces as we can turn away from the surfaces of things; we can push them aside, strike them with words and with blows. We have the power to render a body incompetent and defenseless, we can corner an animal. We can tear away at it, spill its blood, reducing it to carrion and filth. To recognize the sensitivity and susceptibility of another is to catch sight of these possibilities and to feel tempted by them.

Then the one exposed to my eyes and purposes turns and faces me. In the contact the torment of another afflicts me as an appeal, the pleasure of the other presses upon me with the urgency of a demand. She approaches me and exposes the naked surfaces of her eyes to me, the plumes of light in her irises, the night in them that absorbs my day, the liquidity of her gaze that dissolves the directions of the environment about me. He extends the bared surfaces of his hand to me, requiring me to let go of my implements and concerns. Empty-handed, he advances upon me only with the vanishing breath of his voice, disarmed and disarming. Ceasing to extend her order and force into her environment and before me, she laughs, or weeps. Already to turn and greet me is to call for my attention and require it.

The sensitivity, the susceptibility of the hands of another interdict my manipulations, solicit support and tact. The liquidity, the nakedness, the vulnerability of his or her eyes do not expose themselves to me without foreseeing and contesting the violent and violating impulses in my forces.

My eyes glance about to measure the space of his concerns, and to pull back from that space. They are moved to look to her to see what support I can offer, what resources I can put at her disposal. My hand, moved in response to the want and demand that faces me, is affected with tact and tenderness.

A slum dweller in Brazil, after a mudslide or the polluting of his water supply, who reaches out to me reaches out for the skills and resources of my hands. He does not ask that I take over his tasks for him; he asks of my hands the diagram of the operations his are trying to perform and requires the assistance of my forces lest his be wanting. The fatigue, the vertigo, the homelessness in his body appeal first for terrestrial support from my body which stands steady on the earth. If, while extending my skills to his tasks, I do not offer this support, he will prefer to work out the ways and the operations on his own by trial and error.

The homeless woman in looking to me appeals for the image of what my eyes have seen, the directions and operations my understanding has clarified, so that her eyes can find her way and her understanding find her tasks. But her eyes look first for the vivacity and delight of the light in my eyes and the shadows and darkness my eyes harbor with care. Should I turn severe eyes to her, she will look on her own for the path the light shows or trust the darkness.

The unschooled adolescent who has taken refuge in my country from the war ravaging his own speaks to me. His words, which I understand because they are the words of my own tongue, ask for information and indications. They ask for a response that will be responsible, will give reasons for its reasons, that will be a commitment to answer for what it answers. But they first greet me, appealing for responsiveness. His words seek out a voice voluble and spiritual, a voice whose orders and coherence and direction are interrupted, of itself, by hesitations, redundancies, silences, questioning him by questioning itself. In the very explanation and instruction that he seeks, he seeks his own voice in my silences and my questions. If my voice answers without being responsive, he will listen to the murmur of things or confide in their silence.

When we seal our agreement with a handshake, we put into our understanding of and our commitment to our task the trust and that certain indifference to compensations which are already set forth in the clasped hands with which we greet one another, and where the sensibility of the bare hands, the susceptibility of empty hands are made the guise of our presence to one another.

The approach of the vicuña and the oryx, the quetzal and the albatross, the lionfish and the damselfish, the dragonfly and the moth interrupt our engineering of the environment, pull our look up from its paths and its tracking of means and ends, and make an ecstatic movement in our sensibility break out. A jaguar glimpsed in the jungle, an eagle soaring in the clouds, a flight of transcontinental-migrating hummingbirds seen in moonlight captivate our sensibility, trouble our mind, and lift us from the humanized sphere of implements and expectations, sweeping us to the realm of violence and freedom. Our environment ceases to be the prey of our own interests, to show the alien worlds of unfeigned feelings and nobility in which they live.[1]

Like a leopard looking at us in the shadows of the jungle, an eagle soaring over mountain peaks and over us, a dolphin visiting us in Antarctic waters, for someone of our own species to face us is to extend beneficence and blessing upon us. A face speaks blessings by the fire in its eyes and the vivacity of its organs, the spiritedness of its substance, the exceptional expressiveness of the movements that form and fade across it, the harmony or vigor of its contours and tones. His or her hands leave blessings in brief embraces and light touches that were not made to steady our hand. The campesino who tenderly herds his llamas on the parched mountain grass, the untouchable woman in threadbare sari who cleans our bedpan filthy with dysentery give us the courage and the demand to live. The refugee woman who shows her child the colors of the sunset gives us the demand to break the husks of our security and be reborn. The slum dweller who takes the machete of his fallen brother and goes to join the guerrillas in the mountains gives us the passion and the demand for justice. The gleaming eyes of the prince of inner-city streets flash their vivacity to us as he passes. The homeless man extends to us the force of his endurance as we, giving money for his meal and a drink, give him much less. The kisses of a child give us the demand that the powers and the thrones be disobeyed. The one whose laughter is heard in the summer night gives us the demand for ardor and revelry. To walk down the way with someone whose sensitivity illuminates secret splendors and desolations requires that we open our heart to him.

The speech, gestures and facial expressions, eye movements and kinesics of another do not only formulate and offer access to things to us, offer us more pathways in the practicable world; they also set up more resistances in those pathways. They deform and transform and conceal things. They formulate for us her phantasms, dreams, visions, erotic obsessions, nightmares, and give access to the darkness of the nights that within the common night darken about her. The signs he makes not only stake out the paths he has broken for everyone, but lead us into unpracticable vistas where if, following his signs, we do not lose our way, we do lose our own hold on things and on ourselves. A conversation with a stranger is a departure from the commonplaces of our world into phantom cities and jungles we could never have found by ourselves, in which we find we have lost our selves. A conversation with a nomad from Yemen or a boatman in Agatz is a departure toward the desert of his own walkabout, and a descent into a past that was never our present, a future that does not come to us. We read the texts of philosophers with the conviction that they are as revealing for us as when they were composed in cities and landscapes vanished thousands of years ago, with the reassuring notion that the abstraction of the words transports us to an ether from which our gaze encompasses the universal, surveys the universe no longer hidden beyond the narrow perspectives and horizons of our or his particular sensory-motor organism. But in following down the itinerary of the thinker's words, finding ourselves thinking in the track left by an alien thought a thought we make our own, we in fact lose the moorings of our own space in a panorama for which his words were the sole access. We listen, and we read, not to annex an all-encompassing universal space to the order of our own vital space but to lose our own path in the alien deserts of another's walkabout. The face of another is not only a sincerity that guides us to the real things of the practicable world accessible to anyone, but is a seducer's countenance leading us into the hidden places of an alien voluptuousness, an idol dazzling our eyes and transporting them to places where we figure in an intrigue unknown to us, a tragic or comic mask that refracts our gaze into the stage of a historical or farcical drama, and the daylight surface of a night that conducts us toward a night that will not return us to our own day.

To speak is to respond to someone who has presented himself or herself. We catch up the tone of his address, her question, his voice resounds in our own, we answer in the words and forms of speech which are hers. We catch on to the urgent, the frantic, the panicky, the exultant, the astonished tone. We catch on to the level of the purring kitten, the frantic cries of the bird, the snorting of the distrustful horse, the complaint of the caged puma. We catch on to the tone of the blackbird marsh, the hamlet meditating in the Himalayan mountainscape, the shifting dunes under twilight skies.

When we speak, we speak to others. Whatever we say, we say in response to what another asks or has asked. Whatever we say we put forth for her assent, her sanction, her interpretation, her judgment. To agree to speak, already to answer his greeting, is to have already accepted the other as our judge.

When we speak, we speak for others. We answer another in her words. Our thoughts are shaped in the vocabulary, grammar, and rhetoric of our interlocutor. We shape our thoughts and feelings in the raw metaphors, elliptical grammatical paradigms, and staccato pacing of a street kid, in the allusive formulas of nurses, with the facial expressions and body kinesics of Brazilians. We apply ourselves to formulating our thoughts and feelings for them. We catch up the tone of his greeting, her question: his or her voice resounds in our own.

When we speak, we speak in the place of others. We present insights, appraisals, and feelings another will make her own. In answering his questions, we formulate for him thoughts and feelings he had begun and could not finish. We extend the light she had turned to the environment for her. We formulate, concentrate, and intensify his feelings for him.

We speak for the silent and for the silenced. We say what others would say if they were not absent, elsewhere, or dead. We say to the kid working on his motorcycle what the mechanic would say. We say to the music student, depressed and full of self-doubts, what Joan Baez or Arnold Schoenberg would say. We say to the lonely widow guilty over responding to the attentions of a suitor what her dead husband would say. We say to a black youth what Malcolm X would say. We say to an Aymara peasant in Bolivia what subcomandante Marcos would say.

We speak in order to give the other her own voice. We speak in order that the other can speak for himself. Our speech breaks, stops, opens silences, and awaits the moment when it shall withdraw into silence.

Speech becomes grave and imperative when we speak for infants, for foreigners who do not speak the language. When we speak for those in a coma, for the imprisoned, the tortured, the massacred, those buried in mass graves.

FOURTEEN — *Association*

We drop whatever we were engaged in and attend to someone who approached us. What we say picks up what she said. We pick up the tone, the vocabulary, the grammar, the rhetoric she uses, which answered to what others who have long passed by said and did. What we say awaits her confirmation or repudiation, or her question which our answer made possible.

We find ourselves contested in the midst of an endeavor; we answer for what we did and said. In answering now for what we said, we answer for what had been said to us and to which what we said was a response. We speak for those who are no longer here to speak for themselves, who have passed by and who have passed away.

To respond is to commit ourselves to answer for what we answer. We address what we say to him or her who faces us, to what he or she will say and what he or she will be. We answer now for when we will no longer be there.

Responsibility is not limited by what we have deliberately initiated and by the duration during which we pilot our enterprise with our own forces; responsibility is not authorship. To be responsible for our child is to answer with our forces for the defects we did not implant by conceiving that child, that were engineered by the drug companies that others set up or by genetic mutations in ancestors long dead. To be responsible for our child is to have to answer now for that child's welfare when we will no longer be there.

We have enlisted the Sherpa youth on our expedition. To recognize him is to have taken on responsibility for him, to find ourselves commanded by his physical breakdown and his very irresponsibility. We do not measure our responsibility by locating the causes that lie in our own consciousness and will, by recognizing that this youth is stricken with cholera now because no one has taught him the necessities of killing bacteria by boiling the water, by recognizing that if he is loyal in some ways and disloyal in others that is because of the laws of his gods formulated in remote antiquity and of the laws of those who combated those gods with the alien gods of venality, that he is blind now because those who have conquered Nepalese and world economy have ruled it in such a way that he was not able to acquire high-altitude goggles and no teacher was sent to his village to tell him of the perils far above its altitudes. We have to answer for what the British did on their own in the Indian subcontinent two centuries ago. One does not find oneself in a world of one's own making; one finds oneself a Briton in some Indian subcontinent. One is always with a Sherpa youth on some expedition.

Responsibility involves answering for what will come to pass after we are no longer there; it involves answering for and to those yet to be born. It also involves answering for what had come to pass before we came on the scene; it involves answering for and to those who are departed and the dead.

To those who face us, we respond with fluids of our life. We respond with the tears of our happiness and the tears of our compassion. We respond with the breath of our voice, and with the energies and the fervors of our blood. We offer the sweat of our brow and of our chest. We respond to the hunger of an infant, and of the starving adult, with our milk. We give our vaginal flows and our semen. We respond with our blood shed for another.

We respond with our body parts. We give a hand. We support the other who has fallen with the strength of our legs. We respond to the grief of another with the warmth of our arms. We lend our eyes to the blind; we lend our ears to listen for remote cries. We offer our lips, breast, testicles, vagina, penis.

As resources the goods we have at our disposal supply our needs; as property that produces more property they materialize our station, independence, and freedom of initiative. We respond to others with such representatives of ourselves. We send a rose to represent us when we are not there. We put our heart into a poem addressed to someone. When we come we bring a whimsical gift only you are touched by, to leave with you when we go.

(It also comes about that the representative of ourselves with which we respond responds to a representative of the other. We cover ourselves with raiment and coiffure that represent success when we go to meet the corporate executive, the dean, the celebrity. The career, the business, the home we show others represent us not as body fluids or body parts but as a name that means something in the real world. The Hollywood surgeon has dinner with the Japanese film director, the Vassar graduate goes on a date with the Formula One racer. The self that advances from the body is not its representative, but a representative of a trend, a caste, the action, an empire.)

When faced by a stranger, or by a neighbor, we answer to and for our language, our sciences, our society, our history. The boatman on the Amazon answers not only with what he has seen but with what his father and brothers and the people in villages down the river have seen. The physicist, the veterinarian, or the engineer answers with the information and predictive system of her science and of her technology and art. The patient speaks to the doctor about his illness describing it with what little or much he knows of medical language. When we describe a problem with an electrician, we try to supply the kind and amount of data he needs to frame it in the terms of his science and technology.

To the child in the village and to the man retiring from his job in our town, we answer not only with the knowledge that comes from experience but also with the dreams of our youth.

What sadness can there be worse than to have killed the dreamer of our childhood! Nothing the environment and the others can do can afflict us with so terrible an inner desolation. And to answer the youth who faces us only with the knowledge that comes from experience is to speak in order to put to death the dreamer in him.

We answer today for and with the dreams and dances of our parents and our people. If we do not abandon our people and assimilate our lives into the industry and culture of the conquerors, it is not only that our speech takes up the claims of our people to this land and this city, but it does so in the memory of the laughter of our fiestas and our carnivals and in the memory of the enchanted tales told to us in our childhood.

In taking our place at a post others have vacated, we see in the arrangement left on things not only the diagram of their skills that can be reinscribed on our forces but also the outline of singular enterprises that they did not have the power to realize: possibilities they left behind, for others, for us. We discover in ourselves the intelligence and the tact no one else has to love the child the polar explorer has left in our care. Following attentively the path the researcher was able to blaze into the enigmas of viral diseases, we come upon byways she left behind and find there the questions which our cerebral circuitry was alone wired to capture and find a response for. In the vision of justice of the fallen hero and of the resources he found in the oppressed themselves, we find what our lives are for and find our own courage.

FIFTEEN ⟶ *Erotic Demands*

Erotic Allure

Hummingbirds and birds-of-paradise array their extravagantly elabo-rated plumage, mountain sheep and elk raise their crowned heads, coral fish ripple their fins of blazing colors. Living beings that can move evolve seductive display and ritual, artifice, masquerade, and finery. Humans first, and still, make their bodies provocative with plumes and furs, fangs and shells. Until Versailles and its gardens, perfumes were made of the musks of other animals.

Dresses made from the unraveled cocoons of moths brandish colors and designs as astonishing as those of butterflies. Diaphanous, sheer, or sequined fabrics swirl about arms and silk-clad legs or encase them in outbursts of metallic light. The legs are arched on spike heels, the head enshrined in a coiffure and shimmering plumes. Beauty organizes the garb, the jewels, the coiffure into a snare for the eye. Sometimes only a detail flares out—a ruby on the nostril of a woman with freckled cheeks, a gold serpent in the punctured nipple on the hard chest of a laborer, a chain of white shells rolling over the young breasts of a girl in Haiti, a red hibiscus flower in the long black hair of a lanky adolescent fisherman in Sumatra.

Eroticism demands beauty. But neither in humans nor in the other animals is beauty solely produced by lust.[1] The beauty lust demands is a distinctive beauty.

Erotic beauty adds to the body the excesses of feline, avian, and coral-reef ornamentation. The extravagances of renaissance courtesans and geishas are outdone by haute-couturists and jewelers. Erotic beauty cuts into natural human body, changing its skin with tattooings, scarifications, cosmetics, restyling its movements with the artifices of elegance, coquetry, and glamour, elongating its ears and its neck with brass rings, remodeling its inner shape with gymnastics, skull molds, and plastic surgery.

There is the functional beauty of the bared limbs and integrated movements of a draft or race horse, of a skilled laborer, young farmer, or deep sea diver. There is the expressive beauty of a semaphorist or an orator. There is the grace and melodic expressiveness of a dancer. But erotic beauty is idle beauty.

A dress of sheer, almost insubstantial fabric separates her, white linen trousers separate him from the rough and grating tools of workplaces. Powder and cologne separate her and his hands from the dust and spills of work. Jewels of precious stones and glittering metals station her and him ostentatiously apart. Perfume designates an impalpable zone in the midst of the hard edges of reality. Clothing as improbable as the plumage of birds, hair in lacquered or beaded ringlets, jewels of rare stones in intricately crafted settings, and perfumes of rare flowers vaunt the profligate deviation of resources and time from useful or profitable intentions. Upon the worker returning from his or her toil and meticulous, sustained attentiveness to causes and effects, they exert a dangerous fascination.

The erotic body is liberated of the roughness of work and the scars and hardening it effects. It shows neither the coarseness of the laborious body nor the crispness of the managerial body. It is liberated of weight and fatigue. It is a body liberated too of hungers, problemed digestions, excretions, the reproductive processes. It exhibits, at whatever age, the youth of sleepless nights and inexhaustible effusion of energy heedless of sound nourishment. It is liberated of the evidence of the tendons and thongs that flex the skeletal mechanism. It is a body that floats, is spirited and ethereal.

At the same time this delicate and ethereal body is shielded and armored in its finery. The frailty of its diaphanous garb, the white linen trousers and mirror-polished shoes, the thin gold chains dangling in the way of its movements constitute a barrier that the forces of implements cannot cross. It is a body set apart, ostentatiously exhibited outside the paths and directions of industry, feral, divine and demonic.

The mechanic who rolls up her sleeves and the pearl diver who strips to a minimum of protective lining for her abdomen are clothed by the machinery or by the ocean into which their bodies are fitted. The springboard diver emerges clad in the least swimsuit whose bright colors cling to and reveal the contours of what they cover, but her hard musculature, like so many thongs, flexors and tensors, clothes her inwardly with their sober and laborious functions. Whoever goes about her business in the office or city, even though minimally clad in the heat of the tropics, is clothed with the forms, manners, and etiquette of discretion and decency. But the very excess of erotic clothing denudes the body. The furs and plumage, the shimmer and glitter of silk and sequins, the sheen and style of leather and steel cage an animal nakedness exhibitionist and obscene.[2]

The profile is outlined with splashes of the candlelight. The hand lies open, grasping nothing, stirred, when it moves, by the rhythms of laughter or an ambient song. The bare thighs of the lanky adolescent rock against the sweaty flanks of a horse. The throat and belly, unoccupied, are exposed. The tight or filmy dress contours the supple, lithe, and languorous flesh.

The arresting garb exposes the throat and cleavage, the arms, the shaven skull. From the tortoiseshell combs and under the silk strap of a blouse, or the suggestive knot of a necktie, our eyes are refracted to the hair, to the mustache and hairy hands, to the armpits, and to the hairy orifices of entry into that body.

The starched white uniforms of naval officers, with their gold epaulets and the hats, capes, and the mirror-polished boots of cavalry officers with never the least trace of the muck of the barracks and the gore of the battlefield, make them astral men who appear from the outer spaces beyond society. The erotic charge of their uniforms is bound up with the impeccable whiteness and geometry of starched creases that efface limbs made of muscle put to laborious use. Nineteenth-century bandidos and twentieth-century outlaws and high-society con men stud their black uniforms with silver and their bloody hands with precious jewels.

The impeccable dress uniform of soldiers and the black and silver costume of bandidos set forth their hirsute faces or skulls shaven, their hairy hands, and designate the probing penis in the hairy animal hollows with their disorder of blood, secretions, and discharges. The nudity of the naval or cavalry officer, of the bandido or con man, unlike the nudity of athletes in the locker room, is lewd. In the hard rigor of their limbs unsullied by labor and the exposed vulnerability of their abdomens, offered to being touched and seized, the lustful eyes see in anguish and repugnance animal bodies of savage predators destined to be torn apart on wastelands by night. Idle beauty demands lust.

The Imperative Violation

Catching sight, under the glamour, of the wanton and brazen nakedness of the carnal body, the impassioned witness goes to join it, with a movement that does not try to protect or lend a hand to this body no longer functional in its workspace, with a compassion that does not aim to heal or cure, that goes to join it with the movements of kisses and caresses.

He is leaning against the railing of the bridge, his hands holding the railing. The hand that touches one of his hands and begins to stroke it loosens his grip, relaxes the hold. She is laid back on the bed, and one's strokings and caresses loosen the tensions in her posture, dissolve the diagrams for action from her limbs, filling her view with one's face, disconnecting her gaze from the things of the room, disconnecting the agent that was there, the one who surveys and acts and judges.

The body caressed is denuded of the uniform with which it had been clothed—for all clothing is uniforms and informative; when one dresses one dresses in the garb of an outdoorsperson, urban woman, professional, preppy, punk. The caressing hands are not exploring or gathering information from the forms of the body they uncover. They pass repetitiously, obsessively, over flesh they do not manipulate, not knowing what they are doing or what they are seeking. The caressing hand is not outlining the shape of the skeleton nor measuring the width and bulk of the limbs of the body denuded of its physical form. The caress is not a manipulation advancing toward an objective; it is aimless. The hands lose their power to grasp and dominate what they take hold of and their power to move themselves. The caressing hand is not governed by a will that moves it; it is moved—solicited, agitated by the nudity of the other. It is moved—affected, afflicted, tormented.

The erotic nudity does not fit in, is unjustified and intrusive, is inexpressive and exhibitionistic. The caress is not speaking to the other; one describes it badly when one speaks of the body-language of eroticism. There is no conversation, no dialogue, nothing being indicated, no information being exchanged in two lovers embracing and caressing one another. There is no appeal and no demand and no response that is responsible. The caresses violate and profane a concealed, clandestine zone, without discovering a secret or forcing someone out of secrecy. They pass everywhere over the body of the beloved, without leaving traces or inscribing forms, passing again and again over the same surfaces as over virgin territory.

The caresses especially stroke the nonfunctional parts of the body of another, the belly, the thighs, the back, the chest or breast, stirring up spasms of pleasure and sinking the awareness of the other into those opaque, nonmuscular zones of flesh. The caresses excite everywhere in the flesh spasms and torments of pleasure which the consciousness of the other turns to, sinks into, swooning back into her own carnal reality. All his awareness, sensibility, consciousness are there, all brought back from the objects of the outlying environment, all condensed into the substance of her or his body which we hold in our arms and touch.

But there the sensibility, sensitivity, and susceptibility of the other held in one's arms manifest all its alienness, its irremediable separateness from oneself. The caresses are not an initiative or a struggle with something alien, with an alien will; the erotic body denuded itself wantonly from the start and is will-less, neither holding back nor consenting, playful, infantile, a young animal. What inflames passion is the child and the child in the old man, is the man in the woman and the woman in the man, is the leopard, serpent, mollusk in the man or woman, and the man and woman in the bull, swan, crocodile, and octopus.

The imperious demand for kisses and caresses supersedes the demands of industry and science, supersedes the exigency of maintaining our reason, our good sense, our dignity.

The embrace of lovers nowise constitutes an elementary unit of society. It decomposes initiatives into play, language into moans and laughter. Nothing is to be learned from listening in to lovers' talk—lovers' laughter and babble.

The denuded body founders on the rug or hillside, its moans, sighs, sobs, shrieks, decomposing all beginnings of ordered and reasoned discourse, its dismembered limbs shaken with spasms, its orifices open like wounds, its substance turning into steel, gland, gum, secretion, vapor. The one who finds himself or herself caught up in the momentum of this progression is overcome with anguish, horrified by the decomposition and the obscenity where corpse and fetus are there, an anguish which of itself drives one to push on further, into the danger zones, the tabooed precincts, in drunken elation. For if good luck favors us, what we desire most ardently is what is most likely to drag us into wild extravagance and to ruin us.[3]

Voluptuous pleasure is not the enjoyment that sinks into the element and turns upon itself, is not any kind of satisfaction of a hunger, is not any kind of contentment simmering over a content appropriated and assimilated. Voluptuous pleasure is catalyzed by contact with the dismembering, dissolute body of another and by contact with other bodies in transubstantiation, with the excoriated skins of animals hardened and ironed into leather, with feathers and fur detached from the motor and protective intentions of birds and animals, with silk and vinyl exposing themselves as skins, with the flanks of horses pushing up against thighs, with the steel rods of motorcycles pumping like erections, with blades of grass stroking like fingers, with the humus dank with rising wet and microorganisms. Voluptuousness is an outpouring that goes on and on without an end in view where the lover would recover himself or herself and stand back in himself or herself. Voluptuous pleasure is pleasure in its aimless cravings, in its torments.

Violence is the abrupt wrenching out of discontinuous existence. Violence violates what we call our person—our separate and discontinuous existence, source of its own acts, responsible for what we ourselves say and do. Violence is not simply a strong outside force that hurls itself against us.

A force hurled at us becomes violence only when it violates our inner space, when it violates our integrity and what we call our person. It breaks up our individuality. We are not simply left wounded, but shattered.

Eroticism is the inner experience of being violated in sexual contact, and of violating another. The erotic craving is a craving to be violated. When we grasp another's hand for support, that hand stiffens into a rail of bones and tendons and hardens the bony support in our hand. But now the tingling of a caress on our spine turns our bones into gum, and our sheath of motor muscles shivers with chaotic impulses like so much nervous fiber. The posture held erect for tasks collapses, becomes dissolute. One staggers about possessed, no longer in control of one's own thoughts and values, no longer master of one's feelings, invaded by alien feelings. The aimless stroking of a hand on one's abdomen turns it into a gland, a heart palpating with blood and frenzy. The mouth loosens the chain of its sentences, babbles, giggles, the tongue spreads its foam over the lips, the lips cease to shape words in ordered sequences to turn into a wet and open orifice. The toes turned in the empty air no longer strain to support the posture and probe along flesh and orifices like tongues. Glands stiffen and harden, becoming bones and rods. The eyes cloud and become wet and spongy, hair is turning into webs and gleam. Then everything collapses, melts, gelatinizes, runs. Every voluptuous embrace is necrophilic, sinking into a body decomposing and cadaverous, already soaking the sheets and oneself with released inner fluids teeming with nameless and chaotic tinglings, spasms, fluids, microorganisms. The flames of voluptuous pleasure ignite them as they careen and flare apart, in clothing and the wood of the furniture collecting swampy stains, in the air whose minute spheres of water vapor teem with microorganisms, in the soil decomposing into unnameable organisms.

For this zone of decomposition of the world of work and reason, this zone of blood and semen and vaginal secretions, of excremental discharges and corpses, this zone too of proliferating, uncontrollable, nameless fetal life, which disgusts and horrifies us but also summons us, is the zone of the sacred.

SIXTEEN

— *The Summons of Death*

*E*very animal which can move moves to elude or push off forces that threaten him or her; every animal feels fear, knows he or she is vulnerable. In fear—fear of being insulted, mortified, of being abused, offended, of being trapped, of being wounded, of pain—we sense our mortality.

In our strengths we feel the weight of death in things. In our efforts we feel a reluctance of life to undertake, to bear the burden of its own existence. In weariness and fatigue, we sense our life become passive, prostrate, materialized, mineralized.

As we work, our limbs are oiled in our secretions and sweat. Our hands rub them off under the flow of the shower before they irrigate and fertilize funguses. We smell later in our soiled work clothes the stench already of souring body fluids and dead skin cells.

We leave behind the weariness and aching of our eyes when our sight is absorbed in some radiant and alluring object. Suffering struggles to depart, to attend to objects and landscapes of the outlying environment. In the measure that we feel the weariness and aching of our eyes, our vision is held back in itself. The pain of suffering is being mired in oneself. Suffering struggles to retreat behind oneself, to view our painful eyes or hands as does the doctor. In the measure that we cannot retreat behind that pain, our vision is invaded by it and adheres to it. The pain in suffering is being backed up against oneself. Suffering is also the struggle to bear the pain; it is endurance and patience.

An injury incurred first fills the injured flesh with pain, and then with the inexpressivity and insensitivity of stiff-swollen pulp. In our youth, and now at work or in the gym, the swelling power of our muscled body pushes back and also risks injury that requires surgery—pulled tendons, torn muscles.

When the knife slipped and cut into us we felt a bolt of pain, but we feel nothing of the surgeon's scalpel. The anesthesia leaves us groggy for a few days as does the loss of blood, but we also discover blanked out masses of flesh on our body where nerve fibers had been cut. Waking up in a hospital bed after we have broken a leg, we feel a spasm of disgust and horror before the limp swollen limb we bump into under the bedcovers. Utterly disconnected from our inner feeling, we feel it outside like still warm dead meat. Long before we feel what physical contact with the dead body of another feels like, we have felt this surge of revulsion on contact with one of our limbs become alien and dead to us.

Surgery on our hands and especially our face disconnects us from the space we occupied more strangely. Our hand or the side of our face has lost mobility, and when we touch it, it feels like the padding in stuffed furniture. Our hand rubbing and probing our face does not awaken any inner feeling. The expressive muscles of our hands and face with which we face other people have been replaced with that inert tissue. Before, our wanting to attend to another and draw their attention to us, our curiosity, our amusement, our tact and courtesy were not just mental movements; they were diagrams in our face and hands, diagrams forming in flesh and blood. Now our glad greeting, our interest, and our surge of affection feel gagged and muffled behind the substance of our face turned into rubbery pulp.

Sickness and infection enter our body silently, through unnoticed breaches in the invisible masses of macrophages and T-cells that lurk behind the pores open on all its surfaces. We have become aware of them with the electrolyte drinks, protein and carbohydrate supplements, vitamins and minerals we measure out to turn back the states of exhaustion in which the viruses and infections proliferate.

Sickness, a bacterial or viral infection, a glandular malfunction, or a neurological disorder, may well be localized, but the feeling they bring on is not localized. Weariness clogs our body axis and diagrams of movement and a cloying staleness pervades the substance of our body. Our sense organs are no longer transparent windows upon a vibrant outside landscape. We try to read or watch television but our eyes are opaque, and then when we shut them to try to sleep we feel hot and gritty or slimy lumps under our eyelids. There is a sour and nauseous taste and smell to our mouth, our armpits, our breasts, our clammy skin.

Aging does not only make our muscles look and feel like ragged shreds of their former selves, animated by enfeebled pulses of vitality, our skin feels dry and looks marred and stained. Aging makes us feel our movements lagging behind our decision and wish to move, and, more and more, we sense our desires and impulses dying away in the inertia of our trunk and limbs. Our skin feels like hide; when we stroke it, it no longer flushes with the thick pleasure we once knew. And aging feels like sickness—that heaviness, that dullness more and more difficult to shake in the morning.

The pores and orifices of our body continually exude secretions and excrement, but surface or internal wounds turn our flesh into filth. We cough out phlegm, a wound secretes pus. Once a dog bit us. The animal proved not to be rabid; the doctor dressed the wound. The wound scabbed over, and was forgotten. Then one morning, six weeks later, we felt ourselves struggling to awaken, out of a deep torpor. As we woke, we became aware that the room was filled with a greasy foul stench, that of a piece of rotten meat in the room. When we shifted up out of the bed, we realized that the rotten meat was our leg; the wound had abruptly infected. We have seen a dead person laid out in a coffin, or anyhow a dead cat or bird on the grass, and felt there is something serene, composed, in the stillness of the corpse, and an unearthly tranquillity. Now we begin to feel horror and repugnance before a corpse, of the rotting of flesh that pollutes the bed and the ground with its biles and the air with its stench. It recalls the horror and disgust we felt before the fetid infection in our own body, where we first smelt and saw the decomposing, putrid cadaver it was turning into.

After that we feel a new revulsion in catching sight of the malnourished street kids of São Paulo or the homeless aged of New York. Until now we had thought, in aversion, that their suffering was feeling weakness, exhaustion, the numb throbbing of hunger, the misery of unwashed grime and only cardboard boxes laid over the cement to lie down on at night. Now when we notice bruises on their legs and cuts in their arms, all the fetid blood sickness of an infection and the revolting stench we felt steeped in comes back to us. Seeing them in dark alleys, sprawled against the filthy walls, we feel and smell the filth their bodies are turning into.

Suffering is a premonition of dying, and prolongs itself into dying. It takes time to die. Suffering and dying extend a duration in which there is nothing to do, but suffer. The suffering one is reduced to himself or herself, disconnected from any future he or she could project or take hold of. The suffering one is disconnected too from the force and momentum of his or her past. Nothing one has experienced and assimilated prepares one for this. Death comes, of itself. Until it strikes, it remains absolutely out of reach, uncomprehendable, unnegatable, unconfrontable, unpostponable. What is impending is the unknown, not even apprehendable as impossibility or nothingness.

We die in the world, into the world. Dying is being reduced to passivity and prostration, being stripped of the impulses with which we spring out of our own state and substance to play with possibilities and impossibilities. Pain mires us in ourselves, in the thing, the corpse, that will leave us definitively in the midst of the world. Dying is corruption and putrefaction. It is the sinking of our life into the muck and mire of the world, into the outer regions where the order of things and of the world enters into decomposition. These outer regions are also the regions of the separated, the sacred, which possess us and take possession of us, which we reach only by abandoning the world and ourselves.

We die from the world. The harsh edges of reality shut us out. To die is to depart from the world, to go we know not where, to go no where. We see others die, and feel in anxiety and grief their disappearance from our world. What we see in the hateful eyes of another is a will to annihilate us. The naked eyes, the open hands empty-handed, the frail breath of words can become lethal when they grasp on to the forces of things. In the eyes of another black with hatred turned to us, our own death takes on the guise of utter nothingness.

The ancient Stoics banished the fear of death, saying that while we are, it is not; when it is, we are not. What fears death is indeed not our life, but our sense of not having lived. And it is the approach of the shadow of death that quickens the sense of not having yet lived.

The anxiety we feel nowise concerns what we are—the mathematician, hotel manager, mother, or virile male we are. As we took the place of another to become a punch press operator or computer programmer, another will take our place the day we will no longer be there. But in feeling the approach of death, anxiety senses powers in us which have not been actualized.

Under the lurking shadow of death, we sense that there are out there harbors full of possibilities singularly destined for us. We sense that there are forest clearings illuminated just for our eyes, there are enigmas in the environment about us or in outer space for which our brain alone is wired. We sense we could capture, in the singular circuitry of our brain, patterns in the galaxies of outer space or in the movement of viruses, or in the interactions of our brother primates or migratory birds which no one else could understand. We sense that there is someone who waits for our kisses and caresses, and glades and deserts that wait for our laughter and tears. We sense that we could dance like no one can dance, that we could swim lakes like a fish no one has seen. We sense we have in our heart and in the sensuality of our hands a love to pour upon someone like no love ever poured forth.

The approach of death, which darkens the field of time and cuts from us the array of possibilities that are for others, summons us to our own powers. It summons us to discharge our forces into the possibilities laid out singularly before us.[1]

The approach of death quickens our forces and summons them upon the pleasures the environment offers us, the tasks it urges upon us, and the gifts of our forces for which it presents occasions. But death also summons us to itself.

Do we not feel the summons of the death that is in the world, the dying into the world? In vertigo, for example?

> Halfway up the cliff, at a place where a narrow ledge made it possible, he compelled himself to pause and turn to face the emptiness. A cold sweat started on his forehead, and his hands grew dangerously slippery. He shut his eyes to avoid seeing the boulders over which he had sprung a few minutes before, which now seemed to be reeling through the air. But then he opened them again, resolved to conquer his weakness, and it occurred to him as he did so to look up at the evening sky, flooded with the last rays of the sunset. A sense of comfort instantly restored some part of his faculties. He realized that vertigo is nothing but terrestrial magnetism acting upon the spirit of man, who is the creature of earth. The soul yearns for that foot-hold of clay or granite, slate or silica, whose distance at once terrifies and attracts it, since it harbours the peace of death. It is not the emptiness of space that induces vertigo, but the enticing fullness of the earthly depths.[2]

And do we not feel the summons of death in the attraction come to us from all corruption, all defilement, all decomposition? Do we not feel it in the swooning in voluptuous abandon? The sacred, that separated force which intoxicates us, is felt in all the outer regions where the things and the order of the world enter into decomposition.

And do we not also feel a vertiginous peace beckoning to us in all evacuations, all disappearances?

Death then is not simply a fatal accident that befalls us, that arbitrarily cuts short a life which always spreads before itself a future still. It summons us, in so many different moments of life, as a destination.

A fear that marshals all our forces may confront the death that insinuates itself into us in wounds and sickness. Pain and aging may finally reduce us to bitterness and despair. The summons of death may evoke in us defiance or obedience.

Courage is the strength of the heart that hears the advance of death as a summons to engulfment in the elements, to the horror and decomposition of a corpse, to extinction. Courage is made of lucidity and ignorance, strength and patience.

Courage may be the steadfast strength to hold oneself together to act in the interval before death strikes, and to hold oneself together to perform a supreme and final act. This act which endures in defeat by an enemy or by the hostile onslaught of forces of nature may thereby be victorious against the death that does take us. It may be that this momentary victory is the only victory possible before death prevails. The tyrant has a premonition of his defeat upon hearing the one who laughs in the face of a firing squad, for he knows he will hear this laughter again from heroes who even now are going underground or to the mountains.

But courage can exist without victory. Such is the courage of heroes who take up arms without assurance that the cause will prevail, even with the probability that indeed it will fail. Such is the courage of him or her who is shot in the night and fog and still laughs in the face of a firing squad.

Courage does enter into and transform every other trait of the psyche. The respect, the humor, the comradeship of men of courage is different from that of men who do not see courage in one another. Omar Cabezas entitled his account of his ten years as a guerrilla in Nicaragua, *Canción de Amor para los Hombres.*[3] One could sing a love song only for men of courage. Nothing can give dignity to men and women who lack courage. (And every time we feel miserable about ourselves, it is because of some cowardice.) Everywhere in Omar Cabezas's account he tells of men and women harboring the guerrillas in their rude mountain shacks, men and women able to believe in the dignity of their lives in a terrain and society that dooms them to malnourished subsistence, as courageous as the guerrillas. And he, and they, have only their courage to stand and struggle, now that their victory has been destroyed.

No less sublime is the courage to deal with death from disease or drowning or industrial accidents, death without glory, death without the admiration of disciples, death that does not leave the will intact and resolute, death whose sting the intellect that thinks of eternity cannot remove. When dying from disease or drowning or industrial accidents, courage supplies strength so that we shall not shrink back in dread from the pain and shall not be afraid of not being able to endure the time of suffering.

Anyone who has spent some time in a small town hospital, visiting people who have never extended their horizons beyond that town, is struck with the bravery he finds among these people when the time comes for them to die. He would perhaps not have noticed this woman, who was born in this town and limited herself to being a housewife; now she is dying of leukemia, dying without panic, without despair, with animal courage. All of us are braver than we realize. It is imagination and thought that make cowards of us.[4] When the inconceivable has happened, when the terrifying image of terminal disease is replaced by the disease itself, we find the depths of animal courage we had no idea we had.

SEVENTEEN ～ *The Death of Strangers*

To have a friend is to be brought into the sweep of the laughter and weeping, blessings and cursings of that friend. It is to be led by the strength of her hands down paths lit up by the light of her eyes and the torments and courage of her heart. It is to answer for her wants and failings, to bring to her ventures and adventures our insights, our resources, our blessing. It is to shoulder her burdens and support her initiatives when she is stumbling and to heal her suffering with the resources of our health. What greater misery can we know than not to have been there when that friend, having been hit on her motorcycle, lay dying on the highway, when that friend lay dying of a stroke in his home unable to reach the telephone?

We would have been there to help, to get help. We would have been there when there was nothing to be done. We would have had to be there.

The one who suffered the blow that had left his powers helpless suffers the inner violence of pain that pursues its course and extends its time of passivity and prostration. Dying takes time; it extends a strange time without possibilities, without a future. Our friend has fallen into a time outside the time of initiatives, of others, of history, and of understanding. Whether struggling or not, the dying one is not advancing with his own forces into the distance where the last moment awaits; he finds himself constrained to go on without going any where. The skills and understanding with which he took hold of possibilities and a future are disconnected in this time when there is only death coming to take him. The death imminent in any moment disconnects from him the past which supplied resources and momentum for possibilities. He finds there is nothing from what was learned and endured in the past that he can use now; he has nothing to say that others can use in the future ahead of them. The others can find nothing to say to him, from the things they have endured and learned in the past and foreseen in their undertakings.

There is nothing to do but suffer. The intensity of pain holds him back from the course of the environment, backs him up against himself. To suffer is to find himself mired in the pain, mired in himself. Suffering is a struggle to retreat behind the pain, to hold on to the environment, source of sustenance and support, to break out of oneself unto a world. Suffering is also the struggle to bear the pain—the passive struggle there is in patience. He suffers the fear of not having the strength of the patience demanded. Unable to flee and unable to retreat from himself, unable to ride the surge of the environment and reach out for its possibilities, he exists in a time that stretches on, without a future or a past. He waits in prostration and patience.

Enduring the time of dying, our friend is divested of all the hopes and expectations, all the skills and experience with which we were with him laughing and weeping, striving and sharing, embracing and reposing in the itinerary we followed in our environment. He has become a stranger. He dies in a dying that is not his own. He is but a force that endures the time it takes to die and the pain, until this force is broken in gasps and sobs.

The skilled hands of the surgeon extract the bullet, suture the torn tissues. The component hands of the nurse anaesthetize the pain, wash, feed, and support the mutilated body. But the fallen one still has to suffer and to die. And we, who have come to help, can do nothing but suffer. But we stay. We have to stay. We find ourselves compelled to stay so that our friend will not be alone in her dying. To be a friend, who has accompanied her in the take-off of exultations, down the path of initiatives where obstacles drawn up against her were also drawn up against us, and who has accompanied her in idleness, is to accompany her in this going on that is not going anywhere.

In the compassion that can do nothing to heal the violence that shatters the fallen one or relieve her pain, there is fear that we shall not be able to endure the suffering of the other and fear that she, mired in pain, may not be able to obey the summons addressed to her. But we do find that in suffering with her, in enduring the time of dying, our embrace extends to the dying one strengths that we did not know we had—the strength to suffer and to die.

The grief maintains our compassion, our will to accompany our friend in her suffering, our will to suffer with her when it was not possible to suffer in her stead. When no medication or comfort was possible, grief may understand that our friend had to obey the summons of death, and in suffering and patience found the strength to do so. The grief, when our friend dies, understands that one has to grieve.

How alone we are in our compassion, separated from everything we have in common with the fit and from everything we build with the strong! And our compassion for our friend is a compassion for a stranger. In suffering and in the time of dying our friend is bereft of all the possibilities that were possible for him, and for him with us in our friendship, as he is disconnected from all the resources, skills, experiences, and momentum he had made his in the time past. He suffers as anyone suffers, and dies a stranger to his death and to us.

The misery we know when we hear someone we did not know died alone in his room without being able to reach a telephone, and when we learn that someone was thrown into the ditch along the highway by a hit-and-run driver, is the misery we know when a friend died when we were not there.

We understand that a society that would abandon those who are dying —of irreparable damage in collisions, of incurable diseases—to die alone would disintegrate as a society. Our association with one another is not only an association in health and enterprises. In associating with one another in health and for undertakings, we find ourselves exposed to the susceptibility, fatigue, and suffering of others. We sense that while we together extend the time of possibilities and undertakings, another time is being extended in the body of another, the time of suffering and patience in which we are together. Our society is also an association in our mortality.

On the surfaces of others, on the skin of their faces, we see being formed and expressed indications and knowledge, we see their convictions, their will, their determination, but we also sense sensibility, sensitivity, and susceptibility. We sense the tremblings of pleasure that die away and the anxieties of pain that compress someone in his own skin. We see the wrinkles with which aging crumples a life upon itself. We sense the lassitude and debility into which what she declares or proposes sinks. We see the flares of insight and determination in his eyes and we also see them engulfed in the hopeless darkness of those eyes. Along the expanses of their skin, their weariness, their aging, we sense that people who take their places in the posts of society and industry and whose forces take up the resources of the past and reach for the possibilities of the future also exist in another time, the time of endurance and suffering.[1]

While their diagrams of force reach out for our forces and our resources, the surfaces of others expose themselves to us. From a distance the pleasures and torments we sense on them turn down our eyes. We do not join hands with the skills and resolve of others without sensing their susceptibility. Our hands extended and manipulating are halted before coming to grips with them. We cannot count on them without sensing their vulner-ability, their suffering. From a distance the force and skills of our hands are detained in tact and tenderness.

The dexterous hand that has learned tact, the eye gauging the information and intentions on the faces and stances of others whose focus has softened before the susceptibility that shows through, and the voice that hesitates before the silence and the suffering of another—extend to all be-ings. The perception that perceives things finds in the things its tasks and in the levels its ordinance. But there is another understanding in percep-tion. It does not only find in the patterns, shadows, perspectival deforma-tions, and mirages the givens of sense that give the direction and the direc-tive which understanding obeys to locate and determine the things. It is also afflicted with the passing of the substance and the shadows of things.

We cannot touch the eyes of another, or the leaves of the trees, without touching their fragility. We cannot make contact with the skin of another, or the pebbles of the river, without sensing their porousness. We cannot lie with another, or under the clouds, without suffering the impermanence. Our touch understands the transience of the silver-filigreed wings of the flies and the opaque leaves of the moribund giant sequoias, of the polyps in the muck of the deep oceans, and the celestial constellations burning them-selves out as fast as they can.

This understanding is in our caressing hand that accompanies the pass-ing away of what it touches with the sense of its own susceptibility and mortality. This understanding is in our gaze that is no longer on the look-out for objectives, but goes where these things go. It is in our voice which becomes reticent before the silence of their endurance and their transience.

There is a consolation in our hand moved by tenderness over the tran-sient surfaces of things; it is not a consolation for our mortality but an accompaniment of things in their transience. This accompaniment is in our hand that touches with tenderness the fallen tree, in our voice that finds the unjustified calm to keen the moans and wails of the beasts that die, in our insomniac eyes that watch the stars flickering in the immensity of cosmic voids.

Memory is not only a depository at the service of the understanding that fixes the objects and the laws beneath the surface patterns that pass. There is also a memory of the surfaces, of the shadows, the reflections, the pat-terns, the masks, the vortices and the rapids in the river of the time of endurance and vulnerability. This memory is the form of consolation, not of one who retains their forms for himself, but of one who accompanies them in their impermanence. One has to remember.

Grief then is not only the harbor that retains by memory all that was the life, the forces, the exultations of the one who is dead. There is in grief a deeply troubling attraction for blood, putrefaction, and corpses. Grief continues to suffer, to be rent; it prolongs one's own decomposition. The Papuan woman who cuts off her finger upon the death of her child or lover throws her own body outside of the sphere of work and reason and consigns her body to decomposition. The ravages of our grief are perhaps less public because we sense that the zone where our world of work and reason enters into decomposition, the zone of spilt blood and corpses, is more invisible, more excremental, and more sacred.

In the time of dying, disconnected from the possibilities and the future one's own skills take hold of and disconnected from the resources and momentum of one's past, one dies as anyone dies. There is not only the extinction of the I in the time of dying in advance of the blow of death; one rejoins the mortality and susceptibility and thus the life of all that lives and suffers. There are times when we hear the dying one speak then of the extraordinary lightness of this time of dying, the sort of beatitude without happiness, the sovereign elation with which one dies as one—anyone, everyone—dies. This lightness is invincible, an ecstasy and a sentiment of compassion for suffering humanity which involves the happiness of not being immortal. We, who are not yet dying but find ourselves, in the midst of the time of initiatives, discourse, and history, already in the time of compassion and dying, understand such words.[2]

It is in this compassion that the dying one understands a summons to revolt and cry out the injustice of it no more, to demand help in driving it off no more, a summons to die. In the assent then to die there is not only the resignation of hopelessness and the longing for nothingness as deliverance from the suffering; there is also a surreptitious friendship with the death that comes which is a friendship with all that lives and dies.

EIGHTEEN ~ *Walkabout*

There extends about each of us our vital space, with its auspicious and inauspicious latitudes, its individual geography of passageways and horizons, its directions of ascent and descent. Its levels and paths delineate, in the midst of the avenues and highways where the others circulate, the mountains and valleys in which nature distributes its species, and the cosmic vastness in which the ultra-things, the moon and stars, navigate, an itinerary for our own life.[1] In our vital space tasks to the measure of our forces, voluptuous fields and rhythms others do not see or hear, theaters of historical or cosmic dramas to which others are but spectators, make our body, trained, disciplined, and coded by others, a substance with sensibility and compulsions of its own. It is a space in which the Main Street of our town is but vaguely marked alongside of the thoroughfare of our concerns and pleasures, in which the concert hall figures but not the adjacent power plant, in which the factory figures but not the university, in which Salvador fixes the horizon but not Brasilia, in which the rain clouds hover maternally or the sacred mountains summon. It is the space in which continents extend to our view raw materials and markets or stage great historical dramas of empire and revolution. It is a landscape sultry with voluptuous contours and dark places of intrigue and adventure, danger and security.

It is illuminated from refulgent centers where our eyes one day recognize that they were made to see this: the streets of *a cidade maravilhosa*, the walled medieval town covered with vines and silence between glaciers in the maritime Alps illuminated from the storm clouds, the cliffs where the condors nest. It is recognized when, beneath the map of air-traffic routes and highways, we recognize the landscapes of intimacy and the enchanted lands of the remote.

In aboriginal Australia the girls are progressively given the skills of women; the boys are not educated or trained but initiated. The decisive stage is the "walkabout"; the youth leaves the camp alone for a year of wandering. He will learn by himself the terrain and the directions, the places and the ways to find water, the properties of the plants and the ways to catch and use the other animals, the dangers and the exultations. He will find companions in the other animals, the stars, and the spirits of the desert. When he returns it will be as an equal; he will know the equivalent of what the community has learned and shares.

Among us, in our sedentary empires, there is no initiation; at different stages of our lives we are transferred from post to post in the grids of the modern disciplinary archipelago—hospital, schools, barracks, factory or office, prison or asylum, hospital, nursing home. We do not leave the common paths and workshops, stadiums and market-places; the outer deserts, and outer space, are mapped in advance. Yet we too sense the second space of our walkabout lying between the channels and the tracks and the assigned posts. The space of our own desert summons us out of our infancy cradled in the arms and placed in the space of others.

There are those who never locate their vital space, who leave their birthplace only to march in squadrons or to sit in cubicles, their life a dexterity programmed by computers. The land of their collaborators, kin, and intimates is for them a land of exile from a homeland they have never known; they may circulate the planet without ever finding the space of their own walkabout.

To locate our vital space is to locate in the common world whose latitudes are fixed, where outer space itself is cartographed, an exit, a departure that opens in a wave of time. Somewhere in the midst of the terrestrial that extends beneath our feet as the provenance of our first birth and our births to come, a path on the other side of the horizons breaks free. The fallen bird nestled in our childish hands will lead us to a post as guard of a nature reserve in Sumatra. The black hand that touches our child face leads us one day to marry a woman in Agatz. A street kid lying in filth in São Paulo looked at the child we were, brought along on our father's business trip, and twenty years later, now trained as a nurse, we find our way back to him.

Our vital space is not plotted from the bird's-eye view, or from the view of a sedentary animal which fixes its dwelling and measures the environs in widening circles that keep the lair in view. It is a landscape where the rivers and the harbors, the deserts and the cliffs and the passes are events not displayed in an array of dimensions and equivalent paths, but located only by the path we break as we go. The distances are not seen in a surveying gaze that encompasses, in simultaneity, the remote things present and exhibited; they are measured in a clairvoyance for what summons us. They are distances illuminated, on the glowing horizon, by the lights of Paris; the Toltec city of Teotihuacán slumbering in the mists of our America; the great stupa of Borobudur rising against the wall of smoking volcanos to the impermanence, the compassion, and the no-self.

The space of the desert is measured by the year of the walkabout. The space of our destiny is a space whose axes are trajectories of time. It is the space of our life, but it extends back, for the musician, to the spaces charted by Vivaldi, Beethoven, and Bartók; extends back, for the Sandinista militant, to the cloud forests of Nueva Segovia whose paths were open to the mystic Sandino. It extends ahead beyond the frontiers of our death, where our life forces, without us, will be borne on by enterprises, revolutions, and by the anonymous discourse of culture.

The summonses arrive as contingencies, in portentous omens—the photograph of a man of the Nuba come upon by chance by Leni Riefenstahl, disgraced Nazi actress and filmmaker, and which led her, at the age of 70, to be the photographer of the facial paintings of Ethiopia; the seat in the Selma bus that made Rosa Parks pass into the space of nonviolent revolution extended from India. The nomad on the solitary walkabout must know what chance encounters are portentous, which hills gleaming on the desert horizons have to be crossed.

We have, in modern Western culture, for the conduct of our lives only a science of determinism and chance and an ethics of freedom and decision.[2] The archaic discourse on luck or destiny survives only in the disqualified columns on astrological charts in our newspapers. But it was because determinism and decision did not come together that we found the lover for which we now can live; it is because the course section we had decided fitted for our career program was, because some chance encounter on the way delayed us, closed five minutes before we arrived to enroll, that we found ourselves in a section we did not want, seated at a desk opposite someone we would not otherwise have met, and who is now the sun under whose caresses we live a life for which passion is imperative. The imperatives that extend a space of our own are vitalizing forces that do not have the form of law but of portentous events.

He or she who has a hold on his or her own vital space can then recognize the laws of the practicable world and the deviant axes of the visionary, melodic, phantasmal, oneiric, and erotic spaces and the abyssal depths of night and night beyond night. And he or she can formulate programs which are commitments.

On Our Own

The vital space is made into a private space whose directions are projected simply out of our own will or longing when it is understood as the space in which we find our powers come into their own, the space in which we find our vitality sustained and harbored, find our sensibility over its extension and depth awakened, the space in which our body finds its integral mobilization. It is true that when we find ourselves in our own vital space, we move in the conviction that our eyes now see that for which these eyes were made to see, our hands have found the Stradivarius they were made to play. But our flesh is but malleable clay taking on the forms of the common world until it comes to hold itself together through the force of obedience to what summons it. It is because the summons to the space of our destiny weighs on us that we find the force to vitalize a sensibility for things others do not see or hear or feel, that we find the force to produce artist fingers, distant vision, the militant vehemence that churns the wells of our emotions, and the reverence that is a reverence of the body and not only of words. It is because we expose ourselves, in our walkabout, to the portents and necessities that press upon us with the dawn of the day, to the visions that obsess the nights of our own desert, that we become someone on his or her own, with something of our own to tell in the community of those who have each his or her vital space, the community whose camp is not the homeland after the exile but the meeting-place of nomads, itself displaced from day to day or from season to season according to the omens.

The nomadic directions of our own itinerary are extended in the time of endurance, where nothing is ensured and nothing promised, not even nothingness. And in which we encounter the others that face with their vulnerability and the things that surface with their transience. The vital space is also the space of suffering and compassion.

NINETEEN

— *Importance, Urgency, Immediacy*

Hypothetical and Categorical Imperatives

Our actions, initiatives where we maintain a sense of ourselves, are projects; they posit objectives. But they also reveal imperatives. Discussion of action is more often dominated by the theme of freedom than that of practical necessities. It is true that there is no action unless we can act, unless we have the strength, skill, and practical understanding required. Further, action requires us to be able to see some future result or product to be obtained by the action—that is, to represent to ourselves finalities we have caught sight of outside of us. What can be done is determined by the layout of things, by the good that beckons, and by the forces and resources available.

Within the course of doing what we want to do, the material structures of the paths, the implements, and the obstacles appear as directives which regulate our action. We have to go buy firewood and clean the ashes from the fireplace if we are to have a live fire for our lovemaking. We have to put in insulation if we mean to live in this house in winter. We have to work out these mathematical data if we are to know how much insulating material we will have to buy. In working out this mathematics, we have to follow the rules for calculation. These imperatives Immanuel Kant termed "hypothetical"; it is the fixing of the objective we want that makes the material structures of things imperatives. But we need not posit this objective; we do so with a desire we are free not to set out to realize.

Need, hunger and thirst, obtrude with an urgency that determines action. If hunger and thirst determine a sequence of actions, the material structure of the paths, instruments, and obstacles acquire an imperative force directing action from the urgency of the hunger and thirst. Hunger and thirst have a direct and unequivocal relationship with what the action they launch leads us to, and which is both a means to satisfy hunger or thirst, and a good, an end, that terminates them. The objective aimed at by need is not a means, or a symbol, of anything further. The action ends in savoring the food and drink, and in the contentment that simmers over a content assimilated where there had been lack and need. If, sometimes, we eat and drink in order to have the energy for a project or game we have decided on, it is not the force and urgency of hunger or need that now drive that further action.

What has to be done, overriding our wants, is determined by the intrinsic importance of what is in danger and the intrinsic importance of what needs us in order to exist. The good in question may be our own survival or welfare. Nourishment, shelter, unpolluted water and air have to be secured. Our homes have to be protected against electrical fires; the city has to be protected against floods. But realities outside us also present themselves as having to be spared, protected, or promoted. This becomes the more clear in the measure that we come to know them. Although we can dismantle ancient temples and sell the parts for our own enrichment, the more we know those temples the more evident it is that to subordinate their existence to our private wealth is to denature them. Every artist knows that a great symphonic composition or a grand painting will not exist unless he subordinates himself to their creation, and they will not show themselves and exist unless we listeners and viewers make of our eyes, ears, and sensibilities recipients and stages for their epiphany. Although someone with enough capital and equipment can cut down the sequoia forests for his own profit, the more we perceive and know those forests the more evident it is that the living stands of sequoias have intrinsic importance as an awesome living spectacle of beauty and grandeur, belittling but also inspiring us, but even more that to subjugate their rare great life and great age to the puny pleasures a human will derive from cutting them down for private profit is a perversion.

The layout of things of intrinsic importance shows what has to be rescued, protected, repaired, restored, or nourished. The action required becomes clear when we appraise the forces and resources available. Urgency imposes what has to be done. What I have to do may conflict with what my desires and even my needs impel me to do; it may well be that it postpones or interferes with what I want to do and with the urgency of my hunger and thirst. What has to be done is, in Immanuel Kant's terminology, not hypothetically but categorically imperative.[1] Immediacy to where and when I am makes what has to be done what I have to do.

Are there not innumerable such cases among our actions? Strolling in the sequoia forest, I come upon a discarded, still smoldering, cigarette butt in the dry leaves. I am here, and what has to be done has to be done right away. I am the one in the car who sees the calf breaking through the fence on the side of the road. But also *I* must do it—because I can. My neighbor, drunk and enraged, is threatening his wife with a gun, and I am the only one who can talk to him. This child in Amazonia has a severely infected cut, and I the tourist am the only one in the region with the money to fly him to the hospital.

A clear sense of *what I have to do* is constant with artists. A dancer heads for the studio for the day's work, ignoring all the tasks and pleasures she could share with others and that solicit her on the way. In the studio *what I have to do today* is clear to her and unquestionable. It is also clear that she has to be a dancer—not because she aims to get rich and famous, but because dance must exist and her body is made for dancing.

Is not the clear sense of *what I have to do* constant with everyone who is engaged in a work that is important—an ambulance driver and a cleaning woman in a hospital, an engineer designing a bridge and an electrician installing a heating plant in a home, a retired person patrolling crossings for schoolchildren and a retired person living by the sea where the seabirds are engulfed in an oil spill?

What I have to do is not determined only by what results can come from my skills and resources. My leg in a cast, I have to wait with the mother while all the neighbors are out searching the woods for her missing child. I have to stay with a dying friend, though the doctors and nurses have done everything that can be done. I have to stand for a minute of silence during the burial of children killed by a gunman in another country. I have to grieve for the species of birds exterminated in the war.

When I decide to do what I want, I discover what I have to do, but in fact what we want is not determined by a fiat of our free will. How often we feel that what we want is determined by training, habit, or obscure and unconscious fears! How often when we feel we can do whatever we want, we find that in the course of doing it the desire for it has faded away! How much of what we do we do only to make the time pass!

Is it not that I discover *what I want to do* only when I discover what I have to do? It is in gradually mastering the necessary skills and expanding his imagination over what can be made or built and what not or not that way, that the high school dropout finds that being a carpenter is what he really wants to do. It is when she had to leave her job in a lawyer's office to care for his invalid mother that this woman finds that nursing is what she really wants to do.

Throughout our lives, something in us understands that certain ways of action, certain ways of speaking, certain ways of feeling are just not ours. It may well not come from a sense of the end of our lives impending; it may instead come from the sense of the youth, the newness of our lives. To sense one's youth is to sense all that one has to do that is not found in the role models of adult society or of youth culture, not found in what can be learned by lesson and paradigm. The runaway youth, dropped out of school, hitchhiking, refusing to anaesthetize the poet in himself and become a notary, understands the imperative urgency of *What I have to do*. For the chained lion cub the open savannah, as for the high school dropout the open road, is categorically imperative.

There are dangers I have to foresee. There are people I have to avoid, lest they poison my life with their authority or their cynicism. There are people I have to strike down. There are times when I have to speak up, with my own voice.

Before the sequoias I know that my eyes had to see them. In Istanbul what I have to do is stay in the Hagia Sophia. In the Colca Canyon what I have to do is wait, for hours, for days, eyes open to the skies, until the condor appears in the sun. The transcendent things determine what I have to do, and relegate the rest to unimportance.

The Conflict of Imperatives

In expending my funds on medical treatment on my son who requires repeated and immensely complicated surgery, and in giving him all the attention and support he needs, I neglect the wants and needs of my other son and my spouse. In famine times the bread I give from my stores to the stranger is taken from my own family. It is not only the stranger who knocks on my door who faces me, but the strangers in remote lands, in Rwanda and Bosnia, who today face us in the appeals and demands brought by satellite-relayed television in our living rooms. In turning to the one who faces me with his or her joy, I turn away from those who have no one but me to look to in their pain.

Because an imperative is a practical necessity, it prevails over what is undoable. Because opening my stores to the famished refugees would give both them and myself and my children but one meal before we all starve, it cannot be imperative to do so. I cannot be obliged to leave the farm I am cultivating to go to the deserts of Ethiopia to assist engineers trying to dig wells. I cannot be obliged to turn from my neighbor whose house is on fire to study how to make all building materials nonflammable.

Still, it is true that contemporary media, which present us with the faces of famished and debilitated peoples in other regions and other continents which our prosperity exploits, and which give us access to the economic, political, and technological information which make progress toward solutions possible, constantly change what we thought was doable and what doable by us.

No doubt the very notion of justice always goes beyond what is doable. Every sacrifice of my attention, my time, my resources to another already opens the horizon of justice for still another, and for all. Each time I answer the greeting of one who passes in the street, I sense the demand to respect all the others, and the other animals too. Without the passion for justice and truth, whatever I do with my neighbor—or with my comrades exploited with me—becomes a reciprocal egoism and whatever we agree upon becomes our ideology.

PART TWO — *The Imperative*

TWENTY

— *Images of the Imperative*

The ancient Stoics had located the imperative in the world order; for them the organization or the arrangement of the universe functioned as an order, a command laid on humans. The Christians had located it in the creative origin of humans and of external nature; for them the dictum with which, according to the first chapter of Genesis, the divine will creates functioned as a command laid on human thought and human intervention in creation. Immanuel Kant comes upon the imperative when he thinks, and reflects on the activity of thinking. He finds the imperative in the faculty of thought.

The Force of the Imperative

The imperative is met with at once. Whenever we form a concept of something, we find ourselves obliged to conceive content correctly. As soon as we set out to relate our concepts with one another, to reason, we find we are subject to the principles of right reason.

The imperative itself is not a concept, with which we represent some content. It is a command that we conceptualize correctly. It is not a principle or a law or an order. It is a command that there be principles and that our thought represent order—or that we represent the unprincipled and the chaotic correctly.

The imperative is a given, a fact. It is the first fact, for empirical facts can be recognized as facts only by a thought that conceives them correctly and that represents them as the givens retained and related in the order thought presents. Every cognitive act with which empirical facts are recognized is an act that receives the full force of the imperative before it receives the impressions the environment gives.

As soon as thought begins and maintains itself, it does so in subjection to the imperative. Thought is obedience; subjectivity is constituted in subjection.

The thinking subject which arises and makes itself present forms representations. It forms concepts that hold together, retain, and re-present the phases of the surface effects of the world which pass even as they present themselves. It establishes cohesion and comprehensibility in the passing flux in which content is given. The imperative commands understanding to be consistent and coherent. Thought formulates relationships that comprehensively retain the concept that represents what is passing here and now with the concepts that represent what is passing elsewhere and what has come to pass and shall come to pass. With its concepts and relationships, thought establishes order. The imperative commands thought to order.

The imperative itself is ungroundable and unrepresentable. Every principle from which one might try to derive it and every argument with which one might try to demonstrate it already presupposes a thought subjected to the imperative to formulate principles with correct concepts and to reason rightly. The force of the imperative is the command one obeys before one formulates the law.

A thought that conceives the impressions received on one's sensibility with coherent and consistent concepts and that organizes its representations according to universal and necessary principles, alone thinks something. It represents the impressions presented to it in a representation of objects arrayed in a space and time in which they are exterior to one another and to itself.

The imperative weighing on thought commands that thought think and that it think content—open itself to the exterior. It commands that thought relate the content it conceives in the right order and open itself to the whole field of the exterior.

In order to think truly, one must conceive content, which is given. This constraint is not a determinism, an adjustment of the sensibility of an organism that responds to the physical pressures on it. The mind can formulate empty concepts, can reason with content it knows to be fictitious. It can elaborate transcendental illusions. But thought must be empirical. The mind can attend only to the phosphorescence in one's own eyes, the tinglings and pleasures and pains in one's own organism. But perception must be intentional: it must represent the causes and occasions of one's sensations as empirical objects. The mind must formulate a perception of, and a conceptual representation of, the environment as exterior. The world presented before the mind as a layout of exteriority, where intentionality turns to exterior objects, is extended under the force of the absolute exteriority of the imperative.

Thought is not a reaction provoked by external things, but an action with which the thinker moves spontaneously over external things. But, for Kant, thought is not a natural inclination of our psychic constitution. We do not think spontaneously as we imagine or daydream or whistle while we walk. We find ourselves commanded to think, ordered to order.

The Form That Is Imperative

The thought that reflects on its own activity represents the consistency and coherence of its concepts with the concepts of the universality and necessity of their forms, and represents the consistency and coherence of the order of its concepts by formulating the principles of reason. The universality and necessity of concepts is not a natural product of our psychic propensities. The principles, the laws of thought, are not psychological laws, regularities de facto observable in the associations of mental representations. Thought which can conceive as incoherently as one can imagine and relate its concepts as inconsistently as one can daydream, recognizes that when it does so it does not conceive correctly and reason rightly. To conceive correctly and to reason rightly, thought must will to do so. The imperative weighing on it commands thought to be in command of its will.

Our thought represents for itself what the imperative commands by formulating it in the form of laws of thought. It formulates as imperative the maxims of the will that are universal and necessary. The formulated principles are indeed products of the representational power of thought. By formulating the imperative forms, thought puts itself at the origin of the formula and makes of its will activated by the principles it formulates its own project. The rational agent acts, Kant says, *as though* its will is subject only to the law the faculty of reason itself legislates.

But the laws of thought are not simply a program which thought sets up for its own operations. The principles have to be formulated with consistent and coherent concepts in a consistent and coherent order. They are so formulated by an exercise of thought that is already subject to the imperative. The imperative is obeyed before being formulated. The principles can be formulated because they are obeyed.

The formulation, which sets before the mind the form that is imperative, does not set before it the force of the imperative, which makes the law binding. The force of the imperative remains exterior to the form with which the representational power of thought has presented the imperative before itself. Each time thought sets out to effectively think something, that is, to represent something coherently before itself in the relative exteriority of this represented presence, it acknowledges the absolute exteriority of the imperative that weighs on it.

The mind has already found itself, felt itself, subject to the weight of the imperative when it sets out to formulate the law with an act of thought. The entry of the force of the imperative is an event in an immemorial, unrepresentable past, an event that has already come to pass in the locus at which thought arises before the act of thought presented itself. This event is the a priori fact which precedes and makes possible the a priori forms with which understanding understands empirical facts and which it represents as its own laws. The imperative is an absolute fact, a *factum*, an event with regard to which thought is passive, which thought suffers.

Thought Become Practical

There is a sensitivity for the imperative for law in thought's spontaneous activity of formulating coherent and consistent concepts and representations of the relationships between them. This receptivity, this intellectual feeling, Kant identifies as the sentiment of respect. Thought arises and is constituted in respect.

Kant narrows down the meaning of the term "respect" to distinguish it from regard—where circumspection circumscribes one's own space and consideration lets the other have his or her own space—and from admiration —where awe is receptive to the force of what is superior. Respect is respect for law or, more exactly, for the imperative for law; respect for persons, Kant says, is respect for the imperative for law they diagram in their positions and moves.

Kant describes respect phenomenologically as "something like fear, something like inclination."[1] The imperative is known positively not when the representational faculty would posit before itself, as its own program, a formulation of the law it enjoins, but when respect produces representations of exterior objects and of the system of those objects, whose consistency testifies to the mind's obedience. Thought arises and moves spontaneously, bent in the direction of law. Negatively, the imperative is known through "something like fear"—something like the pain in fear.

The imperative that weighs on our thought requires that thought command our sensory powers to expose themselves to particular data which it can grasp with universal and necessary concepts, and command our practical faculties to move through and manipulate the flux of data in ways it can organize coherently and consistently. The imperative that commands that thought will to think requires that our sensuous and practical faculties be ordered according to intentions issuing from our understanding and reason. The imperative commands our rational faculty to be in command.

Sensible data are not only effects collected by moves that expose our sensory surfaces, but affects. Sensory affects collected on our sensory surfaces irradiate as pleasures and are felt within as energizations of our powers, or sting and throb in pains. Our sensory-motor nature is vitalized by pleasure and debilitated by pain. Our sensory faculties, and the motor faculties that move them, are not only receptive to the phenomenal data, but responsive to them. They represent what is presented on them as lures of pleasure and threats of pain. Our practical powers do not only move to expose our sensory surfaces to sensory data, but are moved by them.

Our sensory and motor faculties are moved not in isolated circuits, but as a whole. The "core vital force"[2] is confirmed by a gratification offered to any of its organs and receptor surfaces; our whole motor vitality shifts in response to what lures our eyes. The core vital force of our sensory-motor nature moves with a sensory will, an appetite for pleasure and an aversion to pain. A will that is activated by sensuous representations is activated by the particular lures of pleasure or threats of pain with which the each-time-contingent contours of sensuous patterns are presented. It is a will ordered from without. The core vital force of our sensory-motor nature is a will attached to the particular and the contingent.

The core vitality of our sensory-motor nature, activated by the particular and the contingent, is itself particular and contingent. The core vital force in us that wills pleasure which confirms it, wills to maintain itself, but does not will to will unconditionally. The anarchic intermittence of impulses and appetites, activated by external contingencies, makes it a particular whose will to live is contingent. If the contingent lures of pleasure the empirical field offers the core vital force are not as great as the pains they inflict on it, it can will to suppress itself; it can will suicide.

Understanding is particularized as *my* understanding in requiring content from my sensory surfaces, which collect each time particular data, and from my powers for movement and manipulation, which expose my receptor surfaces to data and adjust to a layout of the phenomenal field that is each time particular. The imperative is put singularly on *me*. The *I* arises in the measure that the sensory-motor vitality is no longer diversely and contingently activated from without by the lures and threats of external sensuous nature and by the appetites and fears of its internal unconscious nature, but commanded by a will activated by a representation produced inwardly by thought.[3] The command put on me by the absolute exteriority of the imperative is a command that the I arise and be in command. The *I* that understands is constituted in this obedience; the subject is constituted in subjection. Respect is "something like inclination"; the I arises and posits itself bent in the direction of law.

The thought commanded by the force of the imperative requires a sensory-motor vitality commanded by a will for the universal and the necessary. Thought is the power to disengage, in every particular and contingent

pattern, the universal and necessary concepts and structures. A will activated by the representations thought puts to it will be motivated to will and
to act in all circumstances and always. It maintains itself in force unconditionally. The rational agency constitutes itself as a will that wills itself, an
identity that maintains itself in presence—an ideal presence.

The immediate effect of the rational activation of the will is the reduction
of sensuous impulses and appetites to impotence. Their activation by the
contingent lures of pleasure with which the sensuous faculty represents its
objects is intercepted and held in suspense. The sensuous appetites are not
desensitized but deactivated and they engender a negative feeling of distress. The feeling of the sensuous impulses of my composite nature being
reduced to passivity and suffering, not deadened but mortified, is the underside of the feeling with which the psychic apparatus knows its receptivity for the imperative for the universal and the necessary. This suffering is
something like fear in respect which, positively, is something like inclination. I sense respect for law in effect in the mortification the core sensory-
motor vitality blocked from its objects knows. This mortification, this dying that does not die which the law commands is the inward knowledge the
I that arises has of its obedience. The suffering I feel within my sensuous
vitality is the weight of evidence I have of the force of law weighing on me.

The Imperative Models

In order to make my force in my particular empirical situation an exemplar
of law, I need an advance representation of the figure I must compose of my
powers. I need a representation that is concrete, sensible—an image—but
also general, such that it can be transferred to other concrete material and
can present my presence in advance. The free imagination finds itself from
the first commanded to produce a generalized image. Such images are needed
for the practical judgment that must guide the rational will. These *imperative images* are generated from intelligible general representations which
Kant names "types."

There are three possible "types." Thought which must think content
forms coherent and consistent representations of the data its sensory-motor powers can collect in moving among sensible things, in manipulating
the field about it, and in interacting with others. Nature, the instrumental
field, and civil society are the three possible representations of systems ordered by law which the understanding and reason subject to the imperative
must produce. They are the three possible representations of the exterior
with which imagination can produce a representation of myself outside of
my actual situation, as an entity governed by the imperative for law. My

practical imagination must produce an advance representation of myself by transferring these models upon myself. The conception of law is not the same in the three images; all three "types" are required.

1. Nature as a Model for Action

Act as though the maxim of your action were by your will to become a universal law of nature.

What has a nature of its own in the empirical world is a multiplicity of elements governed by an intrinsic dynamic order. The whole of the phenomenal field is represented by the theoretical use of reason as nature inasmuch as it is depicted as governed by universal and necessary laws.

The human psychophysical constitution comprises a multiplicity of impulses and appetites which are reactive, excited by the surface effects which its sensibility represents as appearances of particular sensuous objects and as lures of pleasure and threats of pain. This sensuous sensibility attaches the practical will each time to the particular and the contingent, and produces an anarchic intermittence of impulses and appetites and a core vitality whose will to live is itself contingent. When this sensuous sensibility is intercepted by a representation of the universal and necessary formulated by reason and put to the practical will, when the core vitality is commanded by the faculty of thought, then the disparate powers given by nature in the human constitution are made into a nature.

Kant takes the species' trait of thought, which distinguishes humans from other natural species but which constitutes itself into a separate agency in conflict with the human sensory-motor vitality, not as a sign that the human psychophysical organism is destined, by an imperative external to the inner workings of nature, to an extranatural or supernatural status, but as an index that a human must, of his own thoughtful initiative, make himself natural, make himself into the integrated nature he is not naturally.

The imperative depicted as an imperative to become natural is not the Stoic idea that man, whose sensory passions make him a disturbance in the cosmic order, must use his reason to discover and to fit himself into the order of universal nature. The representation of man as a nature is not a cognitive representation of man as a part of nature. It is not derived from the existing scientific representation of external nature. It is not produced by the advance of the theoretical knowledge of universal nature which depicts man as a diversity of substances and functions regulated by physico-chemical, physiological, and psychological laws.

The entirety of the observable represented as a totality, governed throughout by the laws formulated in empirical science, was in Kant's time as it is in ours an idealized representation produced by imagination. For the theo-

retical use of thought this idealized representation is, however, an imperative image. Practical reason is obligated to draw upon this representation as
a model for the reconstitution or composition of the sensory-motor faculties which supply thought with content. The model imaginatively represents one's composition as a nature. This imperative image is the necessary
means for its practical realization. Human nature is not natural but composed in and by its own action.

2. The Instrumental Field

*Act so that you treat humanity, whether in your own person or in that of
another, always as an end and never as a means only.*

The second "type" is an instrumental field. An instrument is a value; its
properties and its place and time are represented as exchangeable for other
properties functioning in other times and places and for other entities in
those times and places. An end is a good for which values are exchanged.
Goods do not terminate the instrumental layout; they can be exchanged for
further goods. An end that is not exchangeable in turn Kant terms a *dignity*.
In the economy of production raw materials are exchanged for manufactured goods, base metals for noble metals, commodities are exchanged for
the production of a monument in which the idol is enshrined; henceforth
the economic community will expend its resources to defend the dignity of
its monuments and its idols. The unexchangeable end, the dignity, is not
outside the instrumental order; it is what organizes the instrumental field
unilaterally and makes the intermediaries means. In fact, however, when
one looks at existing instrumental fields, one sees every good remaining a
good only until it is attained, then it becomes a means in turn. In every
society the most sacred idols have their price; the more irreplaceable and
priceless are the monuments of a society the more useful they are to the
economy. (One raises the taxes needed for the restoration of ancient monuments after statistical projections of the tourism revenues.) The unexchangeable end, then, is not given in perception but in imagination. But this image
is imperative; it fixes a direction in the economy of an instrumental field.
Without it the instrumental field would disintegrate in the multilaterality
and reversibility of all its lines of exchange.

The sensory faculties, which represent the surface effects presented on
them as lures of pleasure and threats of pain which activate impulses and
appetites, transform a radius of the phenomenal flux into an instrumental
field. In the field of action sensuous objects figure as means for the core
vitality.

The imperative which commands thought to be in command requires an
advance representation of the powers which deal with the content given in

the practical field. The imperative which makes the rational will maintain itself in force in all circumstances and always, sets it up as an unexchangeable good and requires the subject to imagine his own sensuous and motor faculties as means. The representation of an instrumental field—not the perception of existing instrumental fields, but the image of an instrumental field whose lines of force are unilaterally fixed by the existence of an unexchangeable good—is transferred from the outside upon the agent himself. One must imagine one's sense organs and appetites, one's practical faculties, and one's core vitality itself to be means, and depict the maintenance of the power of thought as an end that is not a means for anything further, a dignity.

This in turn requires that the content collected on the sensory surfaces, which are represented by the sensibility affected with them as sensuous objects, means for the maintenance of the core vitality, are to be taken as values to be exchanged for other ends. The sensory content is no longer to be represented as possible pleasure-objects serving to confirm the core vital forces whose appetites terminate in them and as painful obstacles that threaten to debilitate vitality. Instead, the sensory content is to be represented as a layout of means for the use of a rational will that is interested only in the universal and the necessary—a multiplicity of objects arrayed in a consistent and coherent order. The affective impact of sensuous objects is to be taken as a means to conceive their objective properties; the particular properties of sensuous objects are to be evaluated as interchangeable instantiations of what are grasped in stable concepts. Objectivity is not produced by supplementing the data collected on one's own sensuous surfaces with that collected on the sensibility of others. There is no necessary connection between the objective properties of an object and the pleasure it gives. Objectivity forms as the surface effects, which function as affects in which one's appetites terminate, are taken as means for another good.

Objective objects—the objectives of a sensibility commanded by thought —are in turn means for the use of a rational will which is not a means for anything further, is a dignity. When thought exists, it exists imperatively, and maintains itself by conceiving objects and ordering them. Thought arises as the locus of impact of the force of an imperative which has come to pass without being representable in a formulation thought would put before itself. Thought arises because it is commanded to arise and to command, and not because some remote and problematic good in the instrumental field of our sensory vitality requires it as the means. The rational will arises as an existent end in itself, commanded to be in command.

When the rational will becomes practical, it does not act to order the outlying objects into a layout that would conduct the appetites of the sensory-motor organism toward their most unobstructed satisfaction. Nor does it act in order to reorient the directions in which means are exchanged for goods which are in turn exchanged for further goods, such that all the lines of exchange terminate in the rational will itself and establish it as the unexchangeable good. Thought arises as an existent end in itself, and the practical will it commands acts only to order the field about it in such a way that nothing violates its dignity.

The use of the instrumental field, in which our sensory-motor vitality is stationed inasmuch as its sensory affects move it, as a "type" for our practical imagination involves, then, a double extension of the instrumental order. The order the agent finds or institutes across the field of his practical initiatives is transferred upon himself; he is to organize his own disparate faculties into unilateral means for his rational faculty; he is to make his core sensory-motor vitality a means for the *I*. At the same time the type of organization of what a sensory-motor organism represents as a layout of objectives within reach, is extended over the universe. The phenomenal exteriority beyond the scope of operations of any organism—an expanse in which a radius of possible sensible appearances, pleasure- and pain-surfaces, light up about one's organism—is converted into a vast instrumental field. All natures are represented as potential means for a rational organization pursued by a practical agent. Thought represents the universe in advance as a dominion awaiting its orders.

It is this imperative image that makes possible respect for the other. In the imperative image of all nature extending as a field of objective objects, always and everywhere means for one's own unexchangeable dignity, the other arises as another locus of the same imperative. Respect for the other, as an entity on his own, a nature that is not simply to be ordered as a means for one's own ends, is respect for the imperative for law that rules in his heterogeneous faculties. To respect the other is to respect the law that commands in him and commands me also.

One does not know, in any given case, that the positions and movements one sees in the psychophysical functioning of another are in fact caused by a representation of principle he himself puts to his will—just as one does not know, in any given case, that the operation one perceives one's own faculties performing was not instead programmed in unconscious drives and regulated by the confluence of external forces.[4] Causal efficacy, Kant conceded to Hume, is not given in the perception of the concomitance of events; still less is the causal efficacy of a representation of principle to activate the will and the nervous circuitry of one's body perceived. But one believes—one must believe—that it is possible that the representation of principle can alone activate the will. One believes—one is commanded by the imperative laid on one's understanding to believe—that one can command one's psychophysical composition to execute actions that will be instances of the universal and the necessary. And one believes, one must believe, that the particular diagrams of action one perceives in the other's phenomenal figure can be understood as instantiations of the universal and the necessary—and that the other has in fact so represented them in advance. Respect is the clairvoyance that senses from the first that the other is an exterior locus of the exteriority of the imperative which I find in my faculty of thought but cannot represent in a formulation that has its source in me.

The belief that an imperative commands the moves of the other one sees, is immediate. This belief does not, like a rational hypothesis, arise in the measure that reliable observation of the stands and moves of the other in the empirical field makes it plausible that other laws than those of the physical universe and those of psychophysiological natures are needed to understand them. As in the case of understanding my own nervous circuitry and energized musculature, as in the case of the irregular orbit of a comet, I am obliged to suppose that any phenomenal datum that is not an illusion holds together with the laws that make it an integral moment of nature. If the other can present the phenomenal form of an operation in the field of means whose moves are programmed by principles represented in his thought, this figure of the other is engendered, not at some advanced stage of understanding the multifarious functioning of his psychophysical organs in physical nature, but out of an immediate sense of the imperative for law in him—a force of law sensed as binding his understanding as I sense it weighing immediately on my own.

As the sense of the imperative, felt weighing immediately on my thought which commands the I to arise and to command, requires me to form an imperative image of myself in the field of action as an existent unexchangeable good for which my sensory-motor powers are means, so the sense of the imperative in the other weighs on me and commands me to produce an imperative image of the other as a configuration of psychophysical functions in the service of the dignity of his rational faculty. This representation does not result from my understanding of the psychophysiological laws that make his perceived figure rationally comprehensible to me and locate it in nature. The imperative image displaces the perceived figure.

In the respect for another I recognize that the exteriority of the force of the imperative—inassimilable to a principle that has its source in my spontaneous formulating power—is the exteriority that constitutes alterity. For the other is other not by occupying another place in the exteriority of nature; he is another nature unto himself, as I am. He is other than me not by virtue of the sum-total of phenomenal differences his psychophysical organism shows from my own; he is other as an authority to which I find myself subjected. I find my understanding sensitive to the imperative for law as what rules in the positions and moves of the other. It is this sense of another locus of the imperative that weighs on my understanding that makes me understand the succession of his positions and moves as determined by representations of the universal and the necessary which his understanding puts to his will. It is this sense of another locus of the imperative that makes the other appear to me as a being on his own, a nature unto himself, a being that activates itself, a dignity in the field of means—and thus genuinely *other*. The otherness of the other is constituted by the exteriority of the imperative. The imperative image of him I form as a figure in command of his own operations dislocates and displaces the objective perception of him I form in the field open to my cognitive initiatives.

This is why it is that the feeling of being contested, being summoned, is immediate, coming with the first intuition of being approached by another, and why it is that one is relieved, acquitted, when one begins to see the color and shape of what is there. In the measure that one sees what it was that moved him—the discomfort of the chair, the raw wind—in the measure that one understands why he spoke as he did—the surprise of finding me here, his immigrant's faulty command of the idiom the situation calls for—in the measure that one understands why he felt as he did—how my shape fits into his archetypes of authority-figures, father-figures, rebel-figures—one dissipates the sense that his law binds me; one's perception and synthetic understanding of what one perceives justifies oneself.

The feeling of the force of the imperative in oneself, which is the origin of the rational faculty, is a rational feeling; it motivates itself. It is confirmed, not by perceptual evidence of the causality with which one believes the force of the imperative activates the practical will and the nervous circuitry and musculature of one's body, but by the feeling of suffering in one's intercepted and blocked impulses and sensuous appetites. The suffering I feel within my composite nature is the weight of evidence I have of the force of law weighing on me. Thought is not something apart from or prior to this suffering. The representation of the universal and the necessary which thought formulates displaces the sensuous representation of the particular and the contingent, and the representation of the pleasure-object is exchanged for the representation of the objective object; the sensuous powers are not deactivated but subjected to the I and affect it with their distress. The thoughtful subject arises and maintains itself in this affliction.

It is also the sense of suffering that makes rational the a priori belief that the other is other with the alterity of an imperative. This exteriority of the imperative is located in the phenomenal field in which the other figures inasmuch as one does not simply perceive a psychophysical organism responding to the pressures and lures of its empirical environment, but senses a nature jarred and buffeted by the forces about him, suffering the dictates of an imperative for law that does not reign immemorially in physical nature. One does not see the efficacy of an inner program regulating his organs and his limbs; one winces, one senses the pain. One does not perceive the pain where it is, in the psychic depth in which his nervous circuitry knows itself; one senses it at the surface of contact. The imperative image of the other as a set of sensory-motor powers at the service of his dignity, which displaces the representation of him as a part of objective nature, is located in the practical field in the perceived figure of a surface of exposure, of vulnerability, that suffers. The figure of the other as a rational agent on his own is this surface phenomenon of a susceptibility. The sense of his suffering justifies my sentiment of an imperative in him that commands me also.

The discordance between the other as a psychophysical organism, which the imperative laid on my understanding demands I understand as wholly subject to the laws of nature, and the other as a rational agent whose imperatives bind me, is not a diplopia of the other perceived and understood and the other as the term of belief synthetically represented by my own imagination. There is a displacement of the other from the depth of nature to a surface phenomenon in which the force of his alterity acts. What we can call a depth perception of the other is the perception of his phenomenal figure, which extends into an understanding of the physiological processes that expose his surfaces before me as a phenomenal surface, an understanding of the psychophysiological laws that move his appetites and impulses toward the sensuous objects which leave surface effects on him and lure him, and an understanding that extends beneath the surfaces of his body I perceive and the sensuous surfaces of objects he perceives toward the physicochemical and electromagnetic processes of the depth of the universe behind them. The imperative image that displaces this depth perception is the figure of the other as a surface of susceptibility. It yields a surface impression, not simply of the de facto vulnerability of a physical substance whose space has to exclude and resist the force of inertia of other physical substances, but of a suffering produced by his own action in obedience to law. His thought, which exchanges representations of sensuous objects with representations of objective objects, arises in this suffering; his action, which orders sensuous substances as means such that his impulses and appetites no longer end in them, moves in this suffering; and his dignity maintains itself in this suffering.

The representation of the positions and moves of the other as commanded by his own representation of principle is not reached at some advanced point of understanding the psychophysiological processes behind them and the physicochemical events in the depth of nature behind him. It is not a cognitive representation. It is an imperative image produced for my practical judgment in dealing with him. It is produced immediately out of my sense of the imperative in him that weighs on me, a sense of an imperative whose location in him is motivated by an immediate affective sense of the suffering on the surfaces which the axes of his active body expose to the things and to me.

This surface does not cleave to his depths, but cleaves to me. The sense of his suffering justifies my feeling of an imperative in him that commands me also. I sense it as an imperative suffering. To feel this suffering is at the same time to respect the imperative for law, the universal and the necessary, that binds me also. The hedonism of my sensuous appetites is arrested by this suffering, afflicted by it, interdicted by it; I sense the sensuous objects of the field not as immediate lures of pleasure but as independent entities that beset the rational agent. To begin to think is to begin to reorganize synthetically the sensuous substances, affecting my sensibility as lures of pleasure, into objects, objective objects understood in function of the necessary and universal order represented by thought and entities exposed to the other, entities to which the other is painfully exposed. The suffering of the other is the origin of my own reason.

3. Civil Society

Act as if you were through your maxims a law-making member of a realm of ends.

The third "type" is civil society. An individual interacting with others represents the multiplicity of individuals as a totality formed by association. Their association maintains itself in the form of a civil society. A multiplicity of individuals forms a civil society when they set up a legislative instance for themselves. The individuals will be associated with one another in their parallel assent to this legislation. Then those individuals are regulated neither by the forces of another civil society nor by the contingencies of the natural environment and the drives of their own psychophysical natures. Their society disengages itself from nature in sovereignty.

Have not, however, the civil societies we can perceive in empirical history instead been shaped by men driven by the passions for power, for wealth, and for prestige? Are not their legislations expressions of the drives of their psychophysical natures in the confines determined by the contingencies of nature and the limits of its resources? Indeed, Kant's observations of the French revolution and its aftermath convinced him that the civil societies set up in the wake of the Enlightenment were not rational societies whose constitutions embody the overriding domination of universal and necessary laws over private passion and whose representational parliaments worked out the rational subordination of particular interests to the general reason. Kant understood that bourgeois representative democracy is a theater where lobbies representing the most powerful passions for wealth, for power, and for prestige work out provisional alliances, pacts, compromises, and armistices which function to allow these passions to flourish.

Kant defines passion as a drive that takes a partial satisfaction of the drives in the human composition for the totality, that is, for happiness. The warm passions such as hedonism, lust, or vengefulness imagine that total fulfillment will be in the gratification the blood craves; the cold or rational passions take their objects to be the means that will make all gratifications attainable. The one who pursues wealth imagines that with wealth he can satisfy all his desires, be independent, autarkic; the one who pursues power or prestige imagines that with them he will be able to obtain everything else he wants. A passion, that is, the investment of all one's forces in the satisfaction of one drive, can count for the pursuit of happiness because, Kant believes, there is no representation of happiness.[5] To eudaimonism in ethics Kant objects that from Aristotle to this day no thinker has been able to form a representation of the good eudaimonism takes to be the integral goal of the integral rational animal. One agrees that happiness would be the total and enduring satisfaction of the longings and cravings amalgamated in us; no one, however, has been able to come up with the formula. Happiness is unimaginable, unrepresentable; it is forever but a regulative idea, an idea-limit, an idealizing idea without content, a transcendental ideal of the imagination. The empty character of the idea of happiness explains both the force of passions to give it the content of visible goods and the unsubstantiatability of their claim to represent happiness.

In fact passion obtains its image of happiness from the passions of others. To give content to one's idea of happiness one looks to men whose passionate investment in particular drives yields them exceptional resources. Passionate men do not only associate in armistices, compromises, pacts, provisional alliances, dictated by the rational appraisal of their own interests in a field of limited resources and in view of their own limited resources; they are first associated by their very passions, which derive the content of their empty idea of happiness from the pursuits in which others invest all their energies.

But the wealth, power, and prestige the cold passions appropriate are appropriated from others; the one who contracts his image of happiness from passionate men contracts the image of his own dispossession. A society forged by passionate men dissociates in the measure that its members see in one another agents whose rational passions attach them to particular gratifications whose capacity to represent the totality can only be fortuitous and which are acquired by expropriating others. The existing civil societies, whose legislation seems to represent the form in which those societies maintain themselves, are in fact in a state of constant dissociation by reason of the passions which that legislation represents.

Thought, obliged to imagine in advance the figure of an exemplar of law it must make of its own powers in the particularities of an empirical situation, uses civil society as a third "type" of system governed by law. But the model we use cannot be any real existing civil society we perceive. We must instead imagine another civil society such that the order in it is that of what is intrinsically universal and necessary. Such would be a multiplicity of individuals regulated by principles valid for each and in all circumstances. Each one makes himself a member of such an imaginary civil society when he represents its laws as his own. The most integrated form of civil society is a republic, where each envisages every other individual as a fellow-citizen, that is, as an exemplar of laws that bind him also. Then the individuals are not only associated as parallel agents subject to the same legislative instance; they are associated in lateral bonds that subject each to the others. In his alterity the other appears in the practicable world, not as an instrumental function situated in another place from oneself, but as a surface of vulnerability exposed by an imperative in him that commands me also. In the image of an integral republic, each one would be for the others *other*. It is in this image that thought fixes society as a distinctive form of order.

The image of such a civil society makes possible the image of each citizen and of oneself as a society unto himself. The individual will imagine his rational faculty as an autonomous legislative instance which imposes an intrinsic order upon the anarchic multiplicity of his impulses and sensuous appetites, and constitutes him as a microrepublic emancipated from the orders put on it by the forces of external nature and freed from the anarchic compulsions of its own constitution. With this "type" the sense of the force of the imperative disengages decisively from the notions of physical force and instrumental force and acquires the sense of command. Thought requires the sociological-juridical image of society which gives it a model of what it means to be commanded to be in command. This legislative image of its practical judgment is imperative.

The Coherence of the Ethical Imagination

In Kant's typology, the third type, citizenship in a republic of ends, is not independently elaborated alongside of the other types; in it the imperative's images of practical reason are integrated and become specifically ethical.

According to the first type, one is to imagine oneself as a nature in the midst of nature, that is, as a set of sensory and motor powers regulated internally by universal and necessary laws. By itself, this rule would induce our thought to constrain our sensibility to represent sensible objects not as objectives of sensual appetite but as surface effects determined by the physiological properties of our sensory surfaces and the physicochemical properties of the forces that impinge on them. It would induce us to view our complex of impulses, appetites, and practical volitions as regulated by psychophysiological laws of the same form as the empirical regularities that govern the physicochemical and electromagnetic events of external nature. The first type would exclude the second, the environment envisioned practically as a field of means for ends that could be introduced into it, and oneself envisioned as an instrumental system. It would leave us with the Stoic or technological ethics that uses thought to effect a cold intervention in one's own representational faculty.

The second type induces us to view our sensory and motor powers as means for our rational practical faculty, instead of as functions regulated by psychophysical laws of the same form as the empirical regularities of physicochemical nature. The second type extends throughout the universe and upon oneself the practical representation of the environment as a field of means, and fixes this representation as ontologically ultimate: the outlying universe is represented as creation, created to serve rational man. This representation extends the universe about us as a field of action, but it does so by excluding action contrived to ensure the happiness of our core vitality. The good for which it makes created natures—and our own sensory-motor powers and core vitality themselves—means is the rational faculty. But since the rational faculty arises by the force of the imperative, exists unconditionally, and maintains itself in existence, the universe of external natures and our own psychophysiological nature which we envision practically as means cannot be envisioned as means for the existence of this good. Then the action the rational will can have on its sensory and motor means transforms neither them nor their mundane objects. Action reduces to an intervention in one's own sensory nature such that one's spontaneous impulses not violate the dignity of one's rational faculty.

According to the third type, one is to imagine oneself as a microrepublic whose order is legislated by one's own faculty of reason, and where one's sensory-motor agencies function in relations of command and obedience. The third type does not simply supplement the others but inscribes the first upon the second, such that the objective representation of nature becomes a practical objective of one's own sensory-motor nature. The other appears in the practical field of our interaction as another figure of the imperative which binds me also and whose form exposes him in a surface of suffering which cleaves to me and arrests my sensuous impulses and appetites. I am commanded to view with him the sensible objects as regulated by the determinations of nature, as objective objects, but I see that they are not thereby divested of their sensuous impact; the pleasure-objects viewed objectively now show their harsh edges and lacerating momentum. This is what induces me to perceive them as structures of a practical field, a field of resistances and obstacles and the means to overcome them. Positive action becomes possible as an intervention that uses the objective structure of the universe to reduce the resistant layout of things so that they become for the other the means in the service of one's rational dignity they are in themselves by creation. Such action is to be effected by extending within oneself the relations of command and obedience that constitute our coexistence as rational agents in society. The instrumental field extended across the furthest expanses of the environment by the second type is inscribed on the vision of the world and of oneself induced by the first type, nature and one's own nature as a system arrayed about one according to universal and necessary laws. The image of the other and of oneself as an instrumental system is inscribed upon the image of the other and of oneself as a nature; the image of the other and of oneself as an unexchangeable good is inscribed upon the image of the other and of oneself as a totality integrated by laws; the image of command is inscribed upon the image of order and of force in the imperative at work in the other and in oneself. The image of oneself as responsible citizen of the universe is inscribed upon the image of oneself as a nature surrounded by nature and the image of oneself as an end in a universal field of means.

The Primacy of the Moral Imperative

The moral sense, the sense of the imperative for law, is for Kant a complex experience, where the subject is simultaneously obedient, imaginative, and rigorously cognitive, and where the law is simultaneously an immediate affliction on the faculty of understanding and reason, a form imaged in the spectacle of the world, and a project one imposes on oneself. The imperative for law, laid on the faculty of thought, commands thought to be in command of the whole human psychophysical complex.

Our thought is obligated to understand and to reason, obligated to be thought. The understanding that understands the necessity of coherence and consistency in its concepts and the reasoning that understands the obligatory force of principle understand that they are themselves commanded. Thought understands that it must will to think, must make the imperative for law the energizing principle of its representational faculty that conceives concepts and relates them and of the set of sensory and motor powers of the psychophysiological organism which collect content for its concepts. It understands that law must become practical, understands that our rational faculty must command our sensibility to perceive competently, with coherent and consistent concepts, and must command our practical powers to act validly, according to principles. The sensory-motor vitality in which the faculty of thought is obligated to maintain itself is obligated to become nothing but a rational agency.

Just as our thought, when it is coherent and consistent, understands nature in terms of universal concepts and laws, so our thought must understand our multifarious makeup as having to be governed in its operations by universal laws. When it is so governed, it determines itself by virtue of its own representation of itself, and becomes intelligible to itself. The demand for consistency and for concordance with all instances of like acts will make it possible for the man who acts out of principles to maintain himself comprehensively; the phases of his acts pass but the principles from which they issue do not. The rational apprehension of law will also be an ontological appropriation of one's effective existence. But for Kant the imperative a human practical organism finds within itself is not an imperative that its acts become intelligible to itself. It is not an imperative that a man comprehend himself, that by subsuming all his acts under intelligible principles he have a comprehensive hold on the meaning of all his successive and dispersed states. The imperative is the demand that there first be law. The imperative cannot be deduced from prior principles nor derived from an end, from the telos it does bring about—an explanation that would itself have to be already subject to law in order to be valid. Reason grasps the subordination of means to an end, including any end it would represent for itself, because it already grasps its subjection to the imperative to represent order. The imperative for law is a pure and transcendental fact, prior to every explanation and every purpose.

Subjection to the imperative for law is the condition for there to be possible a world of experience that would be a genuine world, a cosmos and not a chaos, a world of recognizable objects and not inconsistent phantasms. But it is not that thought determines that our functional nature ought to be conformed to law in order to not lose hold of its environment held together by laws and relapse into a sensuous absorption in phantasms. Thought does not obey the imperative for law in order to maintain a hold on the world; it maintains a hold on the world because it is bound to obey law. Thought does not posit in itself an imperative for law in order to understand why the environment makes sense to it as a law-governed totality;

instead thought understands empirical facts of nature in the universal and necessary laws that govern them because it understands the fact of the imperative that requires that our own nature be totally rational. The whole theoretical employment of reason, as mapped out and bounded in the *Critique of Pure Reason,* turns out to be an activity morally incumbent on us. It is the moral imperative that makes sense to thought and makes sense of the world, or makes thought make sense of the world.

A rational project is not motivated in the field; it does not come into existence by being proposed as some good for which reason would be required as the means for its acquisition. Thought is activated by the weight of the imperative, which commands unconditionally. Its effective operation is not an end to be achieved; it is an unexchangeable end that exists from the start. A rational project functions in forming representations for an executive will, but neither the force that commands it nor the causality it exercises can be represented before itself or intuited in itself. The imperative images of itself are given, not the original. Of the existence of this unexchangeable good which the rational faculty is, it itself has no representation; this existing end, which one is, is only something that affects sensibility. It is given not in a representation of oneself but in a feeling of respect for oneself. One feels one's absolute worth as a rational entity, as something against which one must never act.

Portrait of the Rational Agent

The image of rational activity one will give of what it is that one respects when one transfers upon oneself the form of an instrumental field unilaterally fixed by an unexchangeable good, is the image of lord over nature.[6] The Promethean, Western, image of humankind as lord over nature is not, in Kant, an image from which one derives the concept of being an end in oneself inasmuch as one is rational; the reverse is the case. The concept of existing by imperative command and unexchangeable is a priori; it is the meaning of what is given in the sentiment of respect prior to all empirical experience. The productive imagination is imperatively constrained to produce an image of this understanding of oneself that will be operative in a practical field. What one has to imagine is a situation in which one is an end in oneself, and all the rest are ends relative to this one. The image must not be a specular diagram for theoretical purposes only, but must guide action on things where and as they are found. The image then depicts a situation in which all of nature about me really consists of entities that in their being exist relative to me, such that if a thing were bereft of its property of being my property and my implement it would be "reduced to nought."[7] I imagine that the outside world consists of sensuous objects whose value lies in how they serve my rational purposes—and I have to take that image to have metaphysical validity. I depict all nature as really created to serve me, and I who make use of them really created as an end in myself. Thus the Kantian image is not dependent on the experience of the technological efficacy of rational science; it instead involves a theological postulate, a postulate that is imperative if this image is to be efficacious. The image of humankind existing as lord over nature takes the world specifically as creation. In Kant man's sovereignty, his de jure nobility, is a suzerainty under a postulated divine investiture.

It is then not that because man finds himself more and more, by determination of his own will, master over nature that he comes to think of himself as absolute end. It is that the image of man as master over nature is produced by the productive imagination—and produced on categorical command—as a guide in judging in whatever practical field he shall find himself. It is not produced in order that man make himself more and more master over nature. It is produced so that he will judge in practice in such a way as to never violate the absolute worth of himself as a rational entity.

This image of lordship over nature is not only the image of all external nature laid out to serve one, but the image of an action which is sovereign. I am to imagine acting in every practical field as its existent end. I am to imagine making myself in action a dynamic system of powers made functional by intrinsic laws, like a nature. I shall imagine myself, like a state, constituting myself and maintaining myself as a law-regulated body and existing on my own right, as sovereign, because I set up a legislative organ for that body, whose will in its executive acts will henceforth recognize neither the forces that drive men in the state of nature nor the laws of other bodies. The legislative organ I have set up for myself, my rational faculty, makes me universal legislator, for the law, the universal and the necessary, is law by being law for everyone.

The image produced is one of autonomy. I shall imagine my will as not simply subject to the law, but "subject in such a way that it must be regarded also as self-legislative and only for this reason as being subject to the law (of which it can regard itself as the author)."[8] Autonomy is perceived, not in an outer or inner observation of psychophysiological causality, but in the imperative image of one's faculties not just juxtaposed but related by relations of command and obedience, an image derived by analogy from the perception of the juridic representation of civil society.

This autonomy is not, as in Heidegger's interpretation of Kant, the program of a project which the agent has conceived and affected himself with, nor the program of the project to act on his own which he has freely determined or which is the very determination to be free. It is true that self-determination means being subject only to laws one oneself formulates, but this subjection is itself commanded. By the imperative one finds oneself commanded to be master. The legislative bodies of the civil societies we can observe regard themselves—imagine themselves—as the authors of the order they formulate, but we understand that what gives their dictum the imperative force of a decree is the monopolization of armed force in their service. Rational agents who are the authors of the forms of the maxims they give their will regard themselves[9]—imagine themselves—autonomous legislators, authors too of the force that makes of a formulation a law.

The Kantian image of autonomy is not a development of the apperception of the inner spontaneity of the psychic apparatus, by which, it is true, the mind compensates for its finiteness by producing the objects of its own cognition, and in which therefore Kant saw the image and likeness of God in the human soul. The power to formulate laws binding on one's will is not perceived in the power to form objects of cognition. There is not some irreducible inward experience of it, an intuition into one's sovereign nature. Autonomy is an image, which we must produce. Not in order to explain the incidence of the moral imperative on us, which is given as a fact, and as the first fact—in order to obey it. Autonomy is the imperative image of our imperative obedience. A man finds he can act freely because he must.

The image of autonomy, or moral autarky, is not that of authenticity, such as Heidegger has elaborated it.

In Heidegger, authenticity, being on one's own, is a free determination of the existence in the world one conceives. One exists—ex-ists—by conceiving a potential figure of oneself and casting oneself into that figure. This potential figure arises in the horizon of the future, of which the world, expanse of implements, paths, and obstacles, that is, of possibilities, is the articulation. There is an immediate intuition of this projective movement by which one ex-ists; the intuition is not representational but affective, it is anxiety. In moments when the world ahead sinks into insignificance and insubstantiality, anxiety shrinks back from the figure of oneself in the world and cleaves to the potential to exist that wills to be, which one is. Anxiety reveals that the potential figure of oneself one conceives and casts oneself into in everyday life is an anonymous figure already sketched out in the world by others. The effacement of that figure in anxiety functions as an injunction to conceive on one's own the figure into which one will invest one's present forces, a figure of oneself on one's own. This injunction comes from exteriority; it is produced by the shadow of death, the nothingness absolutely exterior to my being, which falls upon the world and, anxiety understands, knows with certainty, is coming for me. In responding to this imperative, in resolutely advancing toward the death that is coming for me, in recognizing that I have to die, not only one day but now—by discharging all my forces into the figure I project on the world—I recognize in the nothingness of death not a fatality but a summons, and the imperative that directs me into the figure of being that is mine alone to be.

The Kantian image of autonomous sovereignty is not an image of a freedom which is conceived positively as power, self-engendering potential, being that ex-ists by conceiving a potential state of itself and projecting itself wholly into that position. It is not the image of an authentifying project, an *Eigentlichkeit*, which, in being faithful to itself according to a law, in conceiving now the universal and necessary structure of the figure in the world it will be, appropriates itself, comes into and retains possession of itself. It is true that subjection to law makes this comprehensive self-appropriation possible, overcoming not the dispersion of one's powers in the anonymous figures inscribed on the world by the powers of others, but the anarchy of one's sensory-motor faculties moved by outside lures and threats and the expropriation of one's vitality by passionate images of happiness. But the intrinsic lucidity of a project of self-appropriation, which converts the recognition of death as a fatality into the recognition of a destiny and an imperative, is not what, in Kant, founds the imposition of law on oneself. For the sense of the imperative weighs from the start on every lucidity and is what bends it toward the sensuous flux as toward the order of nature, bends it away from every nothingness that could disintegrate the world back into a sensuous flux adrift, and bends it into the dying that does not die, the mortification to which it is destined in the world. The exteriority of the imperative is not sensed in the anxiety which is an anxiety lest one not exist on one's own; it is felt in the weight of suffering in one's sensuous faculties that contains something like fear, the fear that with them one may not be able to obey. This affectivity does not contain the intuition of the trembling of a freedom that casts its powers only into the figure of itself it itself selects or engenders in the anonymity of the world, a freedom to not be or to be on one's own. Freedom is an idea one elaborates on the image one needs in order to act as a necessary figure of the universal.

A will subject to no laws but those it itself puts to itself is a will that has liberated itself utterly from all the allurements by which sensuous things attract or repel with their promises of pleasure and pain. It is imagined free at the same time from the laws of the causal efficacy of sensuous nature and from its own natural inclinations. And it is imagined freed from the natural fixation of all its inclinations on the unimaginable idea of happiness, which could only become intuitive in the passionate investments of wealth, power, and status by which passionate men pursue independence—a fixation that subjects me to images proposed by their pursuits, while those pursuits in fact have expropriative designs on me.

The idea of freedom is postulated to make the image of autonomy intelligible. Freedom is not found in an inward experience of unbound, creative potential; it is found in the image of a will that is unconditionally constrained within a form, but the form is only that formulated by one's own representation of law. Freedom is a political idea; its negative meaning signifying a will not heteronomously determined depends on its positive meaning signifying that the relations between one's powers are effective relations of command and obedience. The idea of freedom is not postulated to make responsible civil existence intelligible; instead the constitution of a state functions as a means to construct a psychological model for operations of a will constrained by the form of law. Freedom is postulated to justify that model. For freedom is not an immediate datum of consciousness. The causality of the will on external nature integrally governed by universal and necessary laws, the causality of the will on the nervous circuitry and musculature of the psychophysiological organism, and the determination of that causality by the representational faculty forever elude all experience.

The idea of freedom is produced by thought in order to make intelligible the image of autonomy, which is produced in order to make practical judgment effective. The idea of freedom is not a production of theoretical reason, setting forth an intuition of my essential nature with a claim to cognitive validity. With the idea of freedom, in this idea, what is understood is the fact of the imperative. The idea of freedom is an element of the practical project to produce acts of obedience. The image of oneself as autonomous sovereign is an image one must produce in order to function as rigorous judge of one's performances.

The Executive Force of the Imperative

But is the I that arises commanded to command sovereign beyond the confines of my own body? Can the nature I form by ordering my psychophysiological powers with relations of command and obedience displace the physical order that determines the course of events in external nature and keeps things in their places, and which I am obliged to represent theoretically as a universal and necessary determinism? I have no perception of the force relations of command and obedience could have on the forces that determine the events of the external world and their impact on my powers; might not instead my powers be determined by them?

Indeed, is this I efficacious in my body? Will it be able to act upon the psychophysical processes in which it arises? I, after all, have no perception of the causality my psychophysical powers exert on one another, and indeed am obligated to represent them theoretically as determined by the universal and necessary laws of empirical chemistry, physics, physiology, and psychology. I could have no rational comprehension of the force with which these empirical regularities are displaced by relations of command and obedience. Might not these empirical regularities have a force that commands me? In civil society, the force of physical means is used to impose commands and induce obedience. A prison warden constrains my psychophysical powers by removing the means for their exercise; a torturer undertakes to constrain *me* by means that debilitate my core vital force under the assumption that the universal end of human inclinations, happiness, binds my will. In order to obey law I have to imagine that the representation of ends that lie beyond a field of means can be displaced by an end produced within me which is not the end of my core vitality, and that this end determines my will immediately. Does this immediate constraint have the force to displace the constraint external means can impose on my psychophysiological powers and the force they can have on my vital will? Will my psychophysiological powers and my vital will ordered in relations of command and obedience be able to displace the force of hard reality which, when I act, shows through the image of a nature created to serve me with which I represent it practically, and shows through the universal and necessary laws with which I am obliged to represent it theoretically?

To act in the suffering one knows from the harsh edges of hard reality is to recognize that while one is the author of the formulation of their universal and necessary order, one is not the cause of the layout in which real things are found. We have to believe that action is possible; we know that action is not prestidigitation. In order to believe that acts conceived in obedience to the a priori imperative could be efficacious in nature where phenomenal changes are represented causally, we shall have to imagine that, in their essential being, rational initiatives and the natural events we have to understand as causal processes are destined for one another. We shall have to imagine that the universal and necessary order in which the events of nature are theoretically represented as determined makes them destined for our service.

The image will be drawn by analogy from the teleological order we find objectified in aesthetic contemplation,[10] and generalized by the imagination to extend across the natural order and the moral order. In an artwork come from the hands of a creator, we contemplate a form produced by free initiative planted in the properties of matter and requiring the universal assent of taste. To be able to act on our imperative belief that our morally determined action is a priori destined to be practically efficacious in the hard reality of nature, we have to postulate a common creator of both the imperative laid on the will of a rational being and the empirical regularities which we have to represent as the laws of nature. This elaboration, this theodicy, does not result from external experience and does not serve to ground a sense of our own intrinsic dignity and sovereignty that we would have through an inward intuition of our own person. It issues from an imagination bent on obedience.

The citizen in a republic of ends acts not to satisfy his sensuous appetites but to make himself an exemplar of law. In each of his positions, words, moves, and deeds he acts only in order to diagram the universal and the necessary. He acts as though he is responsible for legislating for himself and for each the universal and necessary laws of the republic. The responsible citizen of the universe does not think and act in order to attain the integral satisfaction of all impulses and appetites of his psychophysiological constitution, his own happiness. While he acts *as though* he obeys only the laws he formulates for himself, he is not the force that lays on himself and on all things that take their places in nature the obligation to conform to universal and necessary law; he is but the one in whom that force gets formulated in the form of law. In his reason and in his words he speaks as the promulgator and in his deeds he acts as the executor of the legislation that rules universal nature. In his action as a responsible citizen of the universe, he intervenes to open the impasses with which harsh edges of hard reality block the advance of the vulnerable body of other citizens who have made the universal law their own law.

The word of the sovereign is law, each word and each move makes the law; sovereign existence is an existence entirely exemplary. Acting autonomously consists in not taking oneself as an exception. The speech of the sovereign one formulates and his deeds diagram the universal and the necessary, put forth the essential for everyone. No word, no gesture, no move admits any divergence between its public meaning and its private intention.[11] Nothing in his existence is contrived to dissimulate. To use one's manifest or public figure as a means for something particular is the general formula for acting against oneself as an existent end. Sovereign existence is an existence always promulgating, public, not only without private interests but without privacy.

Feelings are not simply inert states of being passive with regard to something impressed; they are responses in the direction of inclination. Thought becomes practical by displacing the sensuous representations with the representation of law. In the sensibility the anticipation of feelings of pleasure and pain from sensible particulars is converted into a susceptibility to pain from the hard edges of reality perceived objectively. The force of the sentiment of respect for the imperative—something like inclination, something like fear—is felt, negatively, in the suffering with which it reduces to impotence the sensuous inclinations of one's core vitality, making "life and its enjoyment have absolutely no worth."[12] Its sway is felt with a feeling essentially different from the feeling of satisfaction of inclinations, which is pleasure; it is purely rational contentment. This rational contentment is essentially different from and at variance with the satisfaction of one's core vitality; "moral self-satisfaction is not happiness or even the smallest part of happiness."[13] This contentment is not the feeling of a content; it is not a reward. "Satisfaction in the comforting encouragement of one's conscience is not positive (as enjoyment), but only negative as relief following previous anxiety" (over being in "the danger of being found culpable").[14] And yet it is blissful. A state of will which finds itself in act always, independently of what the contingencies of the world promise or threaten, is the bliss of godlike existence.

TWENTY-ONE

— *The Theoretical and Practical Uses of Reason*

The Forms of Order

*I*mmanuel Kant identifies three domains whose constitution is regulated by law: nature, the practicable field, and society. But it is because the mind first knows what law is, and knows that law is imperative for understanding and reason, that, Kant argues, thought sets out to formulate the medley reflected on human sense organs into a representation of law-regulated nature, to formulate the directions of the instrumental layout as directives, and to represent human multiplicities as civil societies. The force of the imperative for law is not revealed in nature, the instrumental field, or civil society, but illustrated in them. Thought does not simply feel the force and the fact of the imperative in the sentiment of respect; it knows its properties: the imperative is an imperative for law, for the universal and the necessary.

But in fact Kant's text has drawn the properties of the law it identifies as imperative from logic; universality and necessity are the logical definition of a principle. From what logic? From the logic governing the theoretical use of reason. This logic is a formalization of the procedures used by reason at work forming a synthetic representation of the empirical field as nature. It was originally elaborated out of the procedures used in the substantive physics and metaphysics of Aristotle. Kant finds this logic valid for the advanced Newtonian physics of his day. He would not consider the ancient concepts of order in nature represented as Dikè and as Moira, the forms of organization Claude Lévi-Strauss has formalized as common to the native civilizations of the Americas, or statistical concepts of law in use in recent micro- and macro-physics to have achieved the intelligibility reason requires.

Are we not then forced to conclude that the formal properties of the imperative, universality and necessity, are not known a priori but are derived from the "type"? Kantism does not know how to find the form that is imperative from the feeling of respect upon which weighs incontestably the unformulatable force of the imperative; Kantism finds it in an inspection of the cognitive forms of the speculative use of reason which represents the data of perception as nature. Then is not nature, which for Kant is an illustration of the force of the imperative known originally within in the sentiment of respect, indeed the original locus of the form that is imperative? And if we have to discover the form that is imperative for us from the logic of the empirical representation which theoretical reason has already constituted, then we must examine on that representation what makes it cognitive.

In the natural sciences of today we see not only a prodigious augmentation in the accumulation of observations and a multiplication of theories but a multiplication of the forms of theories and a fragmentation of the theoretical order. Scientific thought today employs rigorous and refined versions of the full array of categories elaborated in natural languages. Along with the set theory model for a universe of objects, scientific thought uses a panoply of idealized conceptual models which include cluster-concepts and radial concepts, image-schemas, postural and kinesthetic diagrams, and metaphoric and metonymic mappings.

The most useful function of a new hypothesis and a new theory is not to account for hitherto unexplained and unpredictable facts. The function of empirical theories is empirical; useful empirical theories generate new facts.

Empirical laws have no true necessity. Today statistical laws are instruments for the deduction of probabilities which may even in principle escape precise where-when determination. And the concept of universality as the ruling value for a theory has become problematical. It is true that any new conceptual scheme, model, or method for elaborating theories introduced is transferred to heterogeneous domains and produces theoretical renewal and advance. But in these transfers, concepts introduced into other systems become metaphorical, laws acquire different powers of extension and different meanings, paradigms reorganize but also restrict the phenomenal field accessible to investigation. We do not have the theories of translatability that would integrate microbiology into genetics, neurology into biology, biology into physics, quantum physics into relativity theory. The theories that make the connections between the laws of one discipline and those of another themselves fragment into new disciplines. These theories do not even have the same mathematical form; mathematics itself has lost its unity and fragments into region-specific mathematical disciplines. The universe is the specific topic of a cosmology that does not have the totality of the empirical data of all the other scientific disciplines as the basis of its laws and theories, and indeed elaborates its laws and theories with the least data available or possible.

Kant assumed that the notion of order or organization in the theoretical representation of the field to which perception is attracted and repelled, of the field of action moved by interest, and of the social field constituted by passion to be in principle the same: that just as empirical nature is represented theoretically by univocal and valid concepts and empirical laws, so also hard reality, wherever and however encountered by practical intentions, is organized in universal and necessary directions, and every civil society is organized by rules of a rational form. Technical and political action are not possible in violation of the laws of nature.

Technology does draw on physics, and returns back into it inasmuch as the substances that serve as the data for empirical observation are not natural but technologically produced substances. But the rules for the technological production of those substances are not of the same form as the physical laws governing those substances in nature. Technology is not simply applied physics. The practical properties of a substance are not simply revealed by its physicochemical analysis; they are revealed only when related to the practical end, which in turn is not determined by its physical properties and physical dynamics but by its position within a technically arrayed order.[1]

Kant had taken the representation elaborated in jurisprudence to be the representation of the specific kind of order, in relations of command and obedience, which constitutes the multiplicity of individuals in interaction into a society. He had assimilated the universality and necessity of the laws with which the rational jurisprudence of the Enlightenment represented the order that constitutes civil society with the formal properties of the empirical laws of the scientific representation of nature. But in reality the jurisprudence that formulates juridical practice employs a distinctive form of reason, which does not elaborate the universal and necessary rules of social intercourse and deduce juridical judgments from them, but argues from cases and precedents, with a normative reason which is not simply that of empirical generalization.

Contemporary social science has constituted as separate regional domains multiplicities of cultural observations that had not even been included in the empirical domain of classical social science. New segments of the social and economic sciences have organized into intelligible domains the specific regularities of the monetary order, human genetics, the kinship relations of gender-based societies, the management of human resources, the structure of games, linguistic pragmatics and kinesics, the long-range field of the operation and structural transformation of myths and the short-range field of media-generated representations. Psychoanalysis has made its real advances when it abandoned the neurological and behaviorist concepts that would have integrated the data of the psychic sphere into the domain of general psychophysiology. Cognitive science has made its advances by abandoning interpretative concepts and schemata from general psychology and contriving regional concepts and hypotheses. Linguistics achieved scientific status because the concepts of phonetics, syntactics, semantics, and pragmatics are specifically regional, and the paradigmatic rules it has been able to formulate for the structures and evolution of these strata of language do not have the form of formulas with variables and rules of combination and transposition.

The Models for Action

For Kant, the representations of nature, of the practicable field, and of society function as models of the law-governed system we must make of ourselves by acting. But our practical judgment must not be regulated by the existing representations of nature in the science of our day, the representations of the uses of things in the technology of any existing economy, and the representation of the order of society in any present or past jurisprudence. The practical imagination must not be fascinated by the concrete; it must be abstract and idealizing. We must form an ideal image of the forms of nature, of practicable reality, and the social field with which to project an image of the nature we will make of ourselves in nature, the end we will take ourselves to be in the instrumental layout of creation, and the responsible citizens we will make of ourselves in human society.

In Kant's program, using every representation of a law-regulated totality as a model to imagine what we must make of ourselves, the concept of model is crude and misleading. And the Kantian concept of imagination is willful.

Nature which presents itself to be known requires that we stand attentive, make ourselves sensitive, and move observantly. The practicable field which extends about us to be inhabited and used requires that we make ourselves competent and skillful. The society in which we find ourselves requires that we be responsive to the appeals and demands of others. The development of the natural sciences requires not only a cognitive psychology that depicts the kind of psychophysiological organism that can elaborate natural science but also a conception of how to make ourselves researchers and theorists. The development of technology requires not only an understanding of how the telescope works but how the eye works and how the eye must be used in order to see the stars and not simply light reflections in the glass of the lens, requires not only an understanding of propulsion outside of the earth's gravitational field but an understanding of how to work the instruments in a spaceship and walk in outer space. The development of economics, political institutions, and festive events requires an understanding of how to perceive economic trends, how to respond to the different kinds of authority and to the decomposition of authority in carnival and revolution. What is required is not a representation of our nature, of our faculties as an instrumental system, and of ourselves as microsocieties, but a representation of the powers and forms of response in our sensuality, our sensitivity, our perception, our thought, and our motility.

Today, our evolving implantation in our natural and constructed environments, in the practicable and unpracticable fields in which we act and wait in patience, and in the forms of our associations with fellows of our species and of other species supplies for our thought new projections for what we are required to become. The representation of nature as an electromagnetic field, the representations elaborated in quantum physics and in relativity theory, those elaborated by evolutionary biology and organic chemistry, those elaborated of the codings in one-celled organisms, in organisms which are colonies of sedentary and nomadic cells, and in the earth as a single cell must today shape our images of our psychophysiological natures and monitor our action which must respect the natures we are.

The fragmented, ever partial, format of the cognitive representation of nature, where certain sectors lie fallow or regress as a result of advances in other sectors, functions as a "type" with which the theorist must constitute his or her own mental life. It requires him or her to become an agent, a researcher and an experimenter and also a witness and an advocate. He and she must make his and her thought a field in which disconnected concepts from various scientific domains, from non-Western and ancient cultures, even from myths are taken seriously as ways to observe, in which diverse kinds of laws, paradigms, and schemata are used to relate observations, in which different mathematics and different logics are used to formulate observations and laws, in which diverse models are used to construct theories. He and she must make his and her theories empirically productive; he and she must make his and her thought obey an imperative of productive observation rather than of consolidation.

It is interest and passion that open and develop new sectors of empirical knowledge; sensuous, indeed libidinal, attraction invests the features of real things that scientific observation identifies. The progress of empirical knowledge requires not our human psychophysiological constitution reduced to an instrument of a purely rational agency, but the core vitality of theorists, their sensuality and their instincts, and their multiple practical skills including those moved by sensuality and interest, even their obsessions and superstitions. It also requires their base as well as their noble instincts,[2] their partialities, hubris, disabused skepticism, pugnaciousness, and vindictiveness. The exercise of our theoretical faculty induces us to envision our own psychophysiological and social constitution as a segmented field without ideal simplicity and unity, without an internal pyramid of command and obedience, without comprehensive self-possession, where what counts is the production of new observations and experiences within ourselves and the production of new relationships within our senses and our powers, and new organizing skills.

The scientific representation of nature is always a collective product; what new sectors are opened up are opened to other researchers, what sectors are left fallow or closed is determined by economic and political institutions and interests; when certain sectors enter into regression a certain range of reality is occluded from human passions and practices. Scientific work requires not the social order of modern mass-democratic societies, where social interaction is officially regulated by universally binding legislation and unofficially by the technologies of the disciplinary archipelago, but societies that contain the maximum possible of internationalism and revolution without disintegrating.

Today the representation of the social field segments into nonisomorphic representations elaborated out of the practice of political theorists, economists, sociologists, and linguists. But we are also constructing theoretical representations of the ways we associate that are not relationships for production and for power. For our associations are also exultant, dionysian, festive, carnivalesque. They are also associations of oblivion-seekers. They are also communities of those who have nothing in common. Thoughtfulness not only respects the economic, sociopolitical, and semiotic orders that regulate the circulation of goods, persons, and messages in association with others, but also the elemental ordinance that makes us a telluric, uranian, solar, and nocturnal community. Our associations are also communities with those who are dying and who are dead. Evolutionary biology, microbiology, and ecological sciences are constructing representations of the community we form with other species, both with the bacteria, macrophages, viruses—who share the space of our bodies and with whom we live in symbiosis—and with all the other animals and plants with which we form ecosystems.

The technological representations of the possible transformation of the resources of the field within reach but also of the whole planet and of outer space must today shape our images of our powers and skills. The representations of the cultural production of identity, worth, and networks of association with others out of mass-produced consumer commodities must also shape our images of our internal operations. The representation of the storage, processing, and uses of data in information and media technology also redesigns our images of our internal circuitry.

The technological representation of the material environment as resources and instrumentalities, extended ever further—already today using artificial satellites as information-gathering and -disseminating factories—and extended to concepts, images, and desires, recalls and reinforces today the Kantian image of rational man as an end in himself and all things in the universe existing really as means to serve him. But at the same time, understanding further the way manpower and brainpower are employed in technological production, understanding the way postindustrial postindustrious civilization requires citizens as consumers, and understanding the ways information-processing and infotainment eliminate so many of the private, civic, and political spaces where rational deliberation had been conducted, make us denounce that Kantian image as ideological, an idol glorified in technocratic propaganda.

Today alongside of technological representations of our practicable environments, we also have representations of the utility of natural things within their ecosystems and our own vitality within ecosystems we share with nonhumans. We also have the poetics, musical theory, architectural theory, dance theory, and poetics of theater and cinema which represent the functioning of artworks and of the artworks we can make of ourselves. All these too must shape our images of our own powers and skills, our talents and tastes. Representations of the unpracticable spaces of color and sound harmonics and dissonances, of private and public dreams, of the night of the earth and of the cosmic night must shape our images of our patience and our passions, our torments and the exhilarations in which we lose ourselves.

The Ordered Representations and the
Ordinance in the Presentations

Scientific as well as nonscientific, mythical and theological theories, tradition, and literature elaborate representations of our environment first made present to us in perception, action, and association with others. The environment as perceived by our sensory-motor organisms is not a stream of sensations rippling on the surfaces of our bodies. The visual field is not just a patchwork of tints, although that is all that there is on our retinas. Before thought identifies something perceived with a concept, that thing holds together for the sensorial samplings with which our organisms explore it. Before reason formulates relationships with which it connects the terms it has identified, the visible, tangible, audible field extends on levels in contours and reliefs, groupings and dispersions.

The perceived environment is open to the manipulations, isolations, and experimentations by which the theorist selects and observes his data; it is open to the instruments the theorist uses to refine his substances and engineer his verifications. Theoretical practices are but one group among the larger number of initiatives our practical powers take in the perceptual field, to advance into it, to uncover things, to bring them and their possibilities and relationships to light.

The determination of what is, in each discipline, to count as truth—the elaboration of the vocabulary, the identification of the criteria for what is to count as evidence and argument, the setting up of institutions to distribute and certify the results of research, and the training and certification of researchers in the various scientific fields—makes of science a social practice. Before the scientific community is represented by economic and political science, it forms in pledges, pacts, alliances, combats, compromises, and armistices. It is one of the forms of association among humans who face one another, appeal to and contest one another.

The theoretical representation of nature does not disqualify and replace the perceptual exploration of the environment. Geology derives not only from scientifically conducted explorations but from the inhabitation, migrations, journeys, and nomadism of humans in the multiple concerns of their lives. Biology, botany, pharmacology, and astronomy presuppose the natural perception that locates other animals, vegetables, minerals, and celestial bodies and locates for the scientific researcher his laboratory, his implements, and his books. Technological operations still and always require the natural sensory motility of the skillful body of the one who leaves his bed and his home for the laboratory and the workplace. The mathematical calculations with which Claude Lévi-Strauss represents the elementary and composite relations of kinship of gender-based societies presuppose alliances and recognitions of descendence with which those societies form, with which individuals associate without having calculated their forms of association mathematically, and interact with the anthropologist who comes to them.

Every theoretical entity we construct in an empirical science remains but hypothetical, an instrument of calculation, until it enables us to make predictions which are verified by observation, that is, by perceivable events in a practicable field. If we were to doubt that the rocks, trees, birds, and fishes were real, we would revoke into doubt at the same time the theoretical entities constructed by the natural scientists.[3]

The empirical researcher makes his observations and verifies his hypotheses in a field where perceived things have real properties and maintain relations among themselves in a distinctive perceptual space—a field that has a distinctive order—or, more exactly, *ordinance*. For the tasks we see in things, the directives in them that regulate our manipulations and initiatives, and the appeals and demands with which we recognize others do not constitute an order, or multiple orders, that we observe; they are directives we know in responding to them. Ordinances extend about us an environment to perceive, a practicable zone to inhabit and to manipulate, and a constellation of others to respond to and associate with.

The force of the ordinances is the weight of nature inasmuch as it not only presses upon our psychophysical natures with its determinisms but requires our sensory attention and our thought. It is the expanse of practicable fields which not only forces adjustments in our positions and moves with its inertia and resistances but requires that we take initiatives. It is the exteriority of others inasmuch as they do not only interrupt our own imperatives with specific formulations but their approach contests what we are doing and thinking, inasmuch as their surfaces of exposedness are appeals put to and demands put on us.

The forms of order scientific thought puts on its representations of nature, the practicable universe, and society can then not simply be attributed to the logical, psychological, or genetic programming of the scientist's mind or the conventions of culture. The layout of the field of perception functions as an ordinance imperative for perceptual exploration but also for theoretical organization of observations. The paths between manipulable things function as an ordinance imperative for action and also for technological theory. The lines of action-at-a-distance between oneself and the appeals and demands of which others are the loci function as an ordinance imperative for our forms of association and also for the social sciences. To understand not only the form scientific theory gives to nature, to the practicable reality, and to civil society, but also the imperative character of that form, we have to bring forth the ordinance in these first-order presentations. The diverse kinds of laws, paradigms and schemata used to relate observations, the different mathematics and different logics used to formulate observations and laws, the models used to construct theories respond to the ways nature is ordered.

Since the researcher selects and observes her data with manipulations, isolations, and experimentations, and refines her substances and engineers her verifications with instruments, the specific ordinance of instrumentalities in the practicable field is also reflected in the order put on the theoretical representation of nature. And since the determination of what is, in each discipline, to count as truth—the elaboration of the vocabulary, the identification of the criteria for what is to count as evidence and argument, the institutions to distribute and certify the results of research, and the training and certification of researchers in the various scientific fields—are social practices in institutions, the ordinance governing the pledges, pacts, alliances, combats, compromises, and armistices in the scientific community is also reflected in the order put on the theoretical representation of nature. What are taken to be purely rational ideals and imperatives—the universality and necessity of laws that would compose the patterns of sensation into one nature, unity and simplicity in the forms of our representations, logicomathematical calculability, analogy to supported lawlike statements in related areas, fit with other accepted theories, explanatory power, theoretical fruitfulness, and ease of computation—are dictated not only by the ordinance of the perceived environment, but also by the ordinance unfolding a zone of practicable reality, and by the ordinance governing the social field.

Because the perceptual world is not an amorphous sensuous flux, it is open to a phenomenology of perception that would describe the array of things as apprehended by natural perception and the ordinances in the perceived field which perception does not perceive but obeys. Practicable reality is open to a phenomenology that would describe the field of action as discovered by inhabiting it and by our movements, manipulations, and utilizations. The social field is open to a phenomenology that would describe the encounter with others as loci of appeals and demands and the associations formed with them. Part One of this book has endeavored to supply the descriptions of the ordinances that direct us in our daily contact with multiple kinds of realities.

The natural sciences do not only elaborate representations of nature which we contemplate, while we continue to live and act in the sensible environment our natural sense organs illuminate about us. There is now far more electricity and electrically powered and illuminated things to perceive than a century ago. Radio telescopes, scanning electron microscopes, stethoscopes, ultrasounds, CAT-scans, radio-isotope tracers, DNA sequencers, and other prostheses have populated the real world of perception with myriads of new entities. Our perceived environments now contain bacteria, oxygen, and the moons of Jupiter. Our bodies now see themselves moving on a spherical planet in orbit in empty space and see what is behind their opaque skins as they are seen by X-ray machines, feel themselves as the germs on trash and the toxic substances in polluted air feel them. Our bodies seated in automobiles, equipped with contact lenses and cellular phones, perceive themselves as the speedily passing landscape, things on the horizon, and sounds beyond the horizon see and hear them. When not only scientists in their laboratories but we too are equipped with the prostheses that enable us to see like eagles and wasps, perceive with the sonar echolocation of bats and the sixth sense of fish, navigate with the magnetic or cosmic sense of migratory birds and insects, discern infinitesimal vibrations with the sensitivity of single cells or single molecules in those bats and fish, our bodies will produce the body images that will enable them to inhabit the mountain heights of eagles, the coral reefs with the fish, and the corollas of jungle flowers. Phenomenology will have to describe the ways these entities, inasmuch as they are found in the environment we perceive and inhabit and inasmuch as they are available for our use and enjoyment, direct our perception, action, and sensibility.

TWENTY-TWO

— *The Rational and the Required*

*I*t is the intrinsic importance of the rational faculty, and not its use to re-solve specific practical problems, that commands in the theoretical use of reason. In working out the value for *pi*, in seeking to fill in the fossil record of the evolution of reptiles, science acknowledges the intrinsic importance of rational knowledge and the intrinsic importance of the rational faculty.

But Immanuel Kant is wrong to recognize only the intrinsic importance of the rational faculty in what we have to do. In caring for a brain-damaged child, we acknowledge the intrinsic importance of a child who will not accede to the use of reason. In snuffing out a smoldering cigarette, we ac-knowledge the intrinsic importance of the sequoia forests.

Kant believed that all the cases where *what I have to do* is imposed inde-pendently of my wants and needs—is categorically imperative—can be iden-tified with formal characteristics. They require action, but also thought. Conceptual thought recognizes, in what has to be done, traits that recur in an unending series of like situations. Thought then recognizes that situa-tions that show certain general traits make necessary actions that have a certain general form. Practical thought determines "What should I do about this?" by determining "What should anyone do about this?"

Kant holds that sensuous desire attaches us to sensuous beings, which are particulars, and concludes that all sensuous desire must be suspended in order to conceive a rational action, an action for which one could supply the reason, the law. But in doing so, does one not eliminate the motivating force for a decision and the subsequent action? The action to be under-taken will be a sensuous particular, which will have to be desired. John Rawls holds that to come to just or fair decisions, one has to eliminate any consideration of one's own, or anyone else's particular interests. But if what is to be done about environmental pollution does not correspond to the city government's or the industry's desires, the practical deliberation will have to determine how to make them want to do it.

If I, or we, are deliberating about what should be done, we envision the situation about specified agents. What is to be done is read in the layout of the instruments and obstacles in relationship with my, our, or someone else's resources and skills. Deliberation about what is to be done about environmental pollution in a specific region is practical in the measure that it will end up, though it may not begin, by specifying who should undertake this action. Practical thought answers "What should be done about this?" by determining what I, or this other individual or group, should do about this.

What has to be done requires attention to the concrete particularities of this situation, and the thinking that recognizes *what I have to do* is ad hoc. Envisaging the situation in general terms may well suggest that the kind of action, and the kind of implements that resolved a similar situation may work here. It may determine a certain kind of action to be necessary: if this child has cholera, immediate rehydration is required. But ad hoc thinking is required to determine if this child has cholera and how the means of rehydration are to be acquired and administered.

The notion of "rational action" can mean an action for which someone can supply a rational justification, or it can mean an action done for reasons—that is, the agent is driven by a desire to have beliefs he has supplied reasons for, and wants these beliefs to be the cause of his actions.

When we review cases of practical necessity, however, we quickly see that practical necessity, which imposes *what I have to do*, does not require the second kind of rational action, which may indeed be quite obstructive. His passion, not my beliefs, dictates that this lovesick man in Haiti get to Souvenance, and it is my rented jeep he has stopped. The intrinsic importance of this man and his love is what imposes what is to be done and its urgency; it displaces the intrinsic importance I assign to my desire to have beliefs I have supplied reasons for be the cause of my actions. To insert a reasoning between that imperative force and my action is only to dally and hold up the urgency of what I have to do.

Not everything we do, want to do, and praise is done for reasons. A lifeguard who leaps into the sea to save a drowning person does not first formulate beliefs and make these the cause of his action. A mother who nurtures her brain-damaged infant may not even be able to supply reasons for doing so. When we admire the character of the lifeguard and the mother, character is not the possession of a set of rationally justified beliefs in the lifeguard or the mother, but healthy impulses and sound instincts.

The desire to make beliefs for which we have supplied reasons the cause of our actions makes our actions deliberate or self-conscious. It is certainly not true that what we do self-consciously we do more effectively.[1] Conscious attentiveness to our moves can at best be one of the means to eliminate a bad habit. It must vanish when we have learned to swim and swim like a fish, when we have learned to dance, when we have learned to type. Thought itself is not produced by deliberation about how to form concepts and how to connect them; insights come as gifts from a contact with things where we give ourselves completely to them and they to us.

For someone, or myself later, to be able to supply a rational justification too may be pointless and even always falsify the imperative involved. It is the intrinsic importance of what had required action to conserve it, rescue it, or repair it that intruded with the imperative force, the urgency, of *what I had to do*. I come upon a cigarette smoldering in dry leaves in the sequoia forest. Someone, in cramps or panicking, is in danger of drowning, and I am the one who can swim. For someone later, or myself, to recast the situation as an action derived from principles falsifies it. The sequoia forest, this stranger in danger of drowning, are contingent realities and not principles. The sequoias came into existence by random genetic mutation. Behind the birth of this stranger I could not find his existence programmed in the laws of nature, but only extremely improbable accidents. As I do not find reasons for the genetic mutation or the improbable accidents which made these individuals exist, I do not find reasons for my act to save just these.

Why do I deliberate not only about what materials and what means to use, but about what reasons or justification could be supplied? How often is it because I want in advance to be able to answer for my action? I decide to take my son out of school and enlist him as an apprentice farmer. There may well be no question of this case coming up again—I have no other children, and have no interest or reason to argue that other students be taken out of school. But an important part of what I want is to be able to give first him the reasons, and then also to answer for my decision to any question his mother may put. I could not argue with the distraught face of this lovesick man in Haiti who stopped my jeep; on the way I construct an argument to justify my taking him and failing to make the date with my lover or the meeting with my boss.

If, when I act, I wish to act on reasons, it is not simply that I expose, and wish to expose, my action in advance to any witness, and possess reasons such that my action can be justified to just anyone. I do appeal, from the special interests of someone standing before me and judging what I do, to the next one to come along. But I may well act in order to respond to the most needy one. I forget my promise to visit an elderly relative today in order to join the march on the police headquarters. When I deliberate, it is not to ask what just anyone would do in this situation. It is to ask what Malcolm X would do, what subcomandante Marcos would do, what Arnold Schoenberg would say.

For Kant, rational action alone is *my* action. To supply a justification for an action which would be anyone's reasons makes that action rational. The desire to have beliefs I have supplied reasons for and to make these beliefs be the cause of my action is what makes the action mine, a first-person action. In performing such acts, I put myself forth, and do not simply put the act forth.

But the neighbor who joins the search operation for the child lost in the snowstorm does not do it in order to perform an action that is his, that satisfies a desire distinctively his. His joy in finding the child is indeed his, though not distinctively his, and it cannot be the goal but only a side-effect of the search. When he reflects on what he has to do, the I that reflects may be as impersonal as the theoretical I that seeks to determine the truth about a state of affairs: this I seeks to determine what there is to be done. In the measure that he seeks to determine what he specifically has to do, he seeks to identify specific abilities or resources that may be distinctive to him. He does not act in order to distinguish himself, to set himself forth.

What the nurse has to do in this sickroom is what any nurse has to do with any patient suddenly bleeding after an operation. What the mother has to do to rehydrate this child sick with cholera is what anyone coming upon any child sick with cholera has to do. But a nurse who acts responsibly also does not act in order to actualize "the nurse," in order to posit an exemplary act, in order to legislate for everyone. If in doing what I have to do, I do not act to actualize myself, neither do I act in order to actualize the universal agent.

NOTES

Preface

1. "The Mind is made up of innumerable fragments: mouths, breasts, beatings, postures, smells, decorations, tattoos, music, genitals, symbols, humiliation, invasions, anxiety, danger, masquerades, foolishness, disgust, hopes, the dorsal but never the ventral surface of the left (much more than the right) earlobe." Robert Stoller, in Gilbert Herdt and Robert J. Stoller, *Intimate Communications, Erotics and the Study of Culture* (New York: Columbia University Press, 1990), pp. 369–70.

2. "The fact is that we have an *underived*, a *primitive* obligation of some kind to be reasonable, not a 'moral obligation' or an 'ethical obligation', to be sure, but nevertheless a very real obligation to be reasonable, which—contrary to Peirce—is *not* reducible to my expectations about the long run and my interest in the welfare of others or in my own welfare at other times." Hilary Putnam, *The Many Faces of Realism* (LaSalle, IL: Open Court, 1987), p. 84.

3. Bernard Williams shows that the languages with which we speak of our interaction with others use concepts such as *malicious, selfish, brutal, inconsiderate, self-indulgent, lazy, greedy, cowardly, lying, grateful*. The fact-value theorists such as R. M. Hare decompose these concepts into a descriptive element and an attached prescription (a statement of what one ought to do). Yet a life, and a society, which would analyze behavior in value-free terms, and then add the general and abstract notion of obligation to certain forms of behavior would be quite different from a life and a society that understands itself and interacts with the undecomposed terms. Bernard Williams, *Ethics and the Limits of Philosophy* (Cambridge: Harvard University Press, 1985), pp. 128–31.

4. George Lakoff, *Women, Fire, and Dangerous Things* (Chicago: The University of Chicago Press, 1987), pp. 266–68, 269–73.

5. "It is less paradoxical . . . to stick to the classic notion of 'better describing what was already there' for physics. This is not because of deep epistemological or metaphysical considerations, but simply because, when we tell our Whiggish stories about how our ancestors gradually crawled up the mountain on whose (possibly false) summit we stand, we need to keep some things constant throughout the story. . . . Physics is the paradigm of 'finding' simply because it is hard (at least in the West) to tell a story of changing universes against the background of an unchanging Moral law or poetic canon, but very easy to tell the reverse sort of story." Richard Rorty, *Philosophy and the Mirror of Nature* (Princeton: Princeton University Press, 1980), pp. 344–45.

2. The Elements

1. Emmanuel Levinas, *Totality and Infinity*, trans. Alphonso Lingis (The Hague: Martinus Nijhoff, 1979), pp. 109–42.

2. Maurice Blanchot, *The Space of Literature* (Lincoln: University of Nebraska Press, 1982), pp. 264–68.

3. Emmanuel Levinas, *Totality and Infinity*, pp. 109–51.

4. Maurice Merleau-Ponty, *Phenomenology of Perception*, trans. Colin Smith (London: Routledge & Kegan Paul, 1979), pp. 137–42.

3. The Levels

1. Modern epistemology, whose categories go back to the matter-form physics of Aristotle, separated, in the sensible perception of the environment, the sensory content of the sensation—taken as what is by excluding other matter from its here and now—from the structure or organization—taken to be transposable upon other content. The perceptible structure or organization was, consequently, to be explained by an agency external to the matter of sensation; it was taken to be imposed on that matter by the categorizing and relating initiatives of thought. The sensory quale was defined as a positum, a positive fact, a punctual plenum, for which to be is to occupy exclusively and exclusionarily a here and now position. Thought then would be an activity spontaneously moving across spatiotemporal points to relate them. Continental phenomenology had introduced the concept of transcendence or ex-istence to characterize mental or intentional events as opposed to the being of external, or transcendent, facts; a mental event was said to ex-ist by projecting itself beyond the here and now where it is toward a there and a future before it. A mental or intentional event projecting itself beyond the here and now of what is posited before it projects itself beyond its own here and now. This kind of self-transcending ex-istence was identified by existential phenomenology as the inner diagram in all the conscious forces in us, which makes them not just reactions to the impact of mundane forces but comprehensive and comprehending powers. The concept of ex-istence or transcendence was introduced to differentiate decisively mental events from facts, revealing powers from intramundane events, the sensing from the sensible. Merleau-Ponty takes this very concept of ex-istence or transcendence and uses it to characterize the way the sensible is and is given. The sensible is what it is by projecting itself into an elsewhere, by approaching and passing. Maurice Merleau-Ponty, *Eye and Mind*, trans. Carleton Dallery in James M. Edie, ed., *The Primacy of Perception* (Evanston: Northwestern University Press, 1964), pp. 166, 178–88; *The Visible and the Invisible*, trans. Alphonso Lingis (Evanston: Northwestern University Press, 1968), pp. 113, 115, 195, 218, 237.

2. Maurice Merleau-Ponty, *The Visible and the Invisible*, p. 103. Alphonso Lingis, *Phenomenological Explanations* (The Hague: Martinus Nijhoff, 1986), pp. 41–57.

3. Maurice Merleau-Ponty, *Eye and Mind*, p. 182.

4. Goldstein and Rosenthal, "Zur Problem der Wirkung der Farben auf den Organismus," *Schweizer Archiv für Neurologie und Psychiatrie* (1930): 3–9.

5. G. M. Stratton, "Some Preliminary Experiments on Vision without Inversion of the Retinal Image," *Psychological Review* 3 (1896): 611–17; "Vision without Inversion of the Retinal Image," *Psychological Review* 4 (1897): 341–60, 463–81.

6. Irvin Rock argues that the persistence of the up-down axis when one lies prone indicates the persistence of a memory trace in the nervous substrate. (Irvin Rock, *The Nature of Perceptual Adaptation* [New York: Basic Books, 1966], pp. 26, 32–34, 34–39.) But what has privileged this axis in the memory trace? It is not the statistically most frequent position, but the position at which one is practically most effective.

7. The Wertheimer effect: sky and earth will be seen as environmentally up and down wherever their images fall on the retina. Max Wertheimer, "Experimentelle Studien über das Sehen von Bewegung," *Zeitschrift für Psychologie* (1912): 161–265.

8. Maurice Merleau-Ponty, *Phenomenology of Perception*, trans. Colin Smith (London: Routledge & Kegan Paul, 1979), p. 328.

9. "I have known patients almost totally immobilized by Parkinsonism, dystonias, contortions, etc., capable of riding a horse with ease—with ease and grace and intuitive control, forming with the horse a mutually influencing and natural unity; indeed, the mere *sight* of riding, running, walking, swimming, of any natural movement what-

ever—as a purely visual experience on a television screen—can call forth by sympathy, or suggestion, an equal naturalness of movement in Parkinsonian patients. The art of 'handling' Parkinsonian patients, learned by sensitive nurses and friends—assisting them by the merest intimation or touch, or by a wordless, touchless moving-together, in an intuitive kinetic sympathy of attunement—this is a genuine art, which can be exercised by a man or a horse or a dog, but which can *never* be simulated by any mechanical feedback; for it is only an ever-changing, melodic, and *living* play of forces which can recall living beings into their own living being. . . . Thus while severely affected Parkinsonians are particularly dangerous at the controls of motorcars and motorboats (which tend to amplify all their pathological tendencies), they may be able to handle a sailing boat with ease and skill, with an intuitive accuracy and 'feel.' Here, in effect, man-boat-wind-wave come together in a natural, dynamic union or unison; the man feels at one, at home, with the forces of Nature; his own natural melody is evoked by, attuned to, the harmony of Nature. . . ." Oliver Sacks, *Awakenings* (London: Picador, 1991), pp. 348–49.

10. Maurice Merleau-Ponty, *The Visible and the Invisible*, p. 133.

4. The Intimate and the Alien

1. Isabelle Eberhardt, *The Passionate Nomad, the Diary of Isabelle Eberhardt*, trans. Nina de Voogd (Boston: Beacon, 1988).

2. "The pine tree, a hundred and twenty meters high, in the courtyard of the Casa Reisser y Curioni, and which dominates all the horizons of this intense city which is defending itself against the aggression of ugly cement (not against good cement)—this pine ended up being my best friend. These are not simply words. It is the only giant of Arequipa. At two meters from its trunk, its powerful, blackened trunk, one hears a sound, the typical sound that breaks forth at the feet of these solitary beings. The tree had been pruned to a great height, perhaps to eighty meters, and the cut stubs of its branches staggered up to the heights made it look like a being that is probing the air of the world with its thousands of sectioned branches. From close up one cannot see much of its height but can see only its majesty and hear this subterranean sound— which I was apparently the only one to perceive. I spoke to it with respect. It was for me something supremely affectionate and at the same time belonging to another hierarchy, bordering on what in the mountains we call, but very respectfully, 'alien.' But what a tree! I listened to its voice, the deepest and most charged with feeling I have never heard in any other thing or any other place. A tree such as this—and like the eucalyptus of Wayqoalfa in my home country—knows how much there is under the earth and in the heavens. It knows the matter the stars, all types of roots and waters, insects, birds, and worms are made of, and this knowledge is directly transmitted in the sound its trunk puts forth, but very close by; it transmits it in the form of music, wisdom, counsel, and immortality. If you move off a little from these immense solitary ones, then it is its image that contains all these truths—its complete image, stirring with the slowness which the weight of its wisdom and beauty does not require but does impress on it. Never, never, never had I seen a tree like this one, and still less in the midst of an important city. In the Peruvian Andes the trees are solitary. This blackened pine, the tallest my eyes had ever seen, stood in the coutyard of an arisocrat's residence now converted into a commercial building. It received me with benevolence and tenderness. It poured all its shade and its music upon my joyful head. Bach, Vivaldi, and Wagner could not have made a music so intense and transparent with wisdom, love, so oneirically penetrating the matter of which we are all made—and which on contact with this shade is troubled with poignant joy, with totality.

"I spoke to this giant. I can assure you that I listened! In its stumps and fibers and in the semitransparent gum which was ceaselessly flowing from its chopped branches but hardly moving any distance, I put my trust. The reverent and intimate words with which I greeted it told how happy and preoccupied I was, and how surprised I had been to encounter it here. But I did not ask it to transmit to me its forces, that power one feels in looking at its trunk from close up." José María Arguedas, *"El zorro de arriba y el zorro de abajo,"* in *Un mundo de monstruos y de fuego,* ed. Abelardo Oquendo (Lima: Fondo de Cultura Económica, 1993), pp. 176–77.

5. Things

1. The duration of the perceived world also has to be conceived as a level. The time of the world is not a dimension *t+1* projected by a conceptual operation, in which we locate the present moment in which all that is perceivable is presented. The future and the past extend not as horizons we view but levels on which we find ourselves embarked and that sustain the configuration of the present. Our perceiving organism presents itself in the course of the world, and the present moment it determines is not a closed form that reproduces itself along a linear dimension but a relief on a level of futurity and passage. The future extends not as a unit about to displace the present moment but as a directive toward which and with which we turn. The present as it passes does not subsist in the form of a closed moment that has, as Husserl put it, undergone simply the modification of distance; it loses its particularity, veers into generality, is no longer before us as the object of perception or the object of recall but becomes the angle and the momentum with which we now envision what is there.

2. Maurice Merleau-Ponty, *Phenomenology of Perception,* trans. Colin Smith (London: Routledge & Kegan Paul, 1979), pp. 229–30.

3. Ibid., p. 315.

4. The weight of things lifted by any part of the body is retained in memory as a weight felt by the hands. David Katz, *The World of Touch,* trans. Lester E. Krueger (Hillsdale, NJ: Lawrence Erlbaum, 1989), p. 125.

5. Of course some things approached through divergent paths may have several orientations in which they display what they are and how they function.

6. The shed seen in Figure 1 when tilted 45 degrees becomes an arrowhead (Figure 2). But if Figure 2 is now viewed by someone whose head is tilted counter-clockwise 45 degrees, such that the retinal image is oriented just as the retinal image of Figure 1 was a moment ago, the subject continues to see an arrowhead, and may well not recognize the shed of Figure 1. The orientation that makes the figure recognizable is thus its position in the up-down axis of the setting which the look follows, and not the orientation of the retinal image on the surface of the eye. Irvin Rock, "The Orientation of Forms on the Retina and in the Environment," *American Journal of Psychology,* 69 (1956): 513–28; I. Rock and W. Heimer, "The Effect of Retinal and Phenomenal Orientation on the Perception of Form," *American Journal of Psychology,* 70 (1957): 493–511; I. Rock and R. Leaman, "An Experimental Analysis of Visual Symmetry," *Acta Psychologica,* 21 (1963): 171–83.

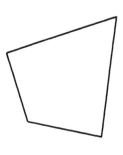

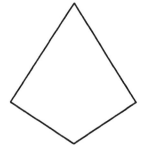

Figure 1   Figure 2

7. The eyes strive to see in line drawings the figure of some thing; the drawing tends to an equilibrium by delving into depth. The poplar on the road which is drawn smaller than the man succeeds in becoming really a tree by retreating toward the horizon. To see the figure as a mosaic pattern on the flat surface of the paper, one has to first concentrate one's eyes on the center, then extend one's gaze equally and simultaneously across the whole figure. The vision is unstable; one tends to see the pattern as a thing, one's eyes are drawn to one of the larger squares and the concentration of the look there brings it forth, while the oblique lines form a second side receding toward the background. The lines acquire the values, some being the edges of a plane parallel to the frontal plane of our eyes, others being those of a plane set horizontally to it, not by a mental act of interpretation but by a usage of the eyes finalized by the intention to see explorable things. The box with square ABCD forward is unstable, since the square EFGH equally solicits our gaze as an equally equilibrated structure to hold it. In the normal visual field the segregation of close-up and receding figures is irresistible; as we walk along the avenue we cannot succeed in seeing the spaces between the trees as things and the trees as sides receding in depth. See Maurice Merleau-Ponty, *Phenomenology of Perception*, p. 263.

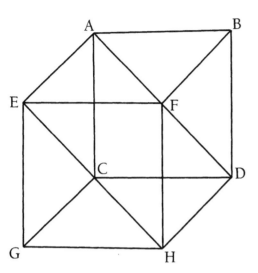

8. Ibid., p. 270.

9. Ibid., p. 317.

10. Kurt Goldstein, *The Organism* (Boston: Beacon, 1963), pp. 222–23.

11. "When I awoke like this, and my mind struggled in an unsuccessful attempt to discover where I was, everything would be moving round me through the darkness: things, places, years. My body, still too heavy with sleep to move, would endeavour to construe from the pattern of its tiredness the position of its various limbs, in order to deduce therefrom the direction of the wall, the location of the furniture, to piece together and give a name to the house in which it lay. Its memory, the composite memory of its ribs, its knees, its shoulder-blades, offered it a whole series of rooms in which it had at one time or another slept; while the unseen walls, shifting and adapting themselves to the shape of each successive room that it remembered, whirled around it in the dark. . . . My body, the side upon which I was lying, faithful guardian of a past which my mind should never have forgotten, brought back before my eyes the glimmering flame of the night-light in its urn-shaped bowl of Bohemian glass that hung by chains from the ceiling, and the chimney-piece of Siena marble in my bedroom at Combray, in my grandparents' house, in those far distant days which at this moment I imagined to be in the present without being able to picture them exactly." Marcel Proust, *Swann's Way*, trans. C. K. Moncrieff and Terence Kilmartin (New York: Random House, 1981), pp. 6–7.

12. "If I dared to be a metaphysician, I think I would create a system in which there were nothing but obligations. What would be metaphysically ultimate, in the picture I would create, would be what we *ought* to do (ought to say, ought to think). In my fantasy of myself as a metaphysical super-hero, all 'facts' would dissolve into 'values.' That there is a chair in this room would be analyzed (metaphysically, not conceptu-

ally—there is no 'language analysis' in this fantasy) into a set of obligations: the obligation to think that there is a chair in this room if epistemic conditions are (were) 'good'
enough, for example. (In Chomskian language, one might speak of 'competence' instead of 'obligation': there is the fact that an ideally 'competent' speaker would say
[think] *there is a chair in this room* if conditions were sufficiently 'ideal.') Instead of
saying with Mill that the chair is a 'permanent possibility of sensations,' I would say
that it is a *permanent possibility of obligations.* I would even go so far as to say that my
'sense-data,' so beloved of generations of empiricists, are nothing but permanent possibilities of obligations, in the same sense.

"The reverse tendency—the tendency to eliminate or reduce everything to description—seems to me simply perverse. What I do think, even outside my fantasies, is that
fact and obligations are thoroughly interdependent; there are no facts without obligations, just as there are no obligations without facts." Hilary Putnam, *Realism with
a Human Face,* ed. James Conant (Cambridge: Harvard University Press, 1990), pp.
115–17.

13. Maurice Merleau-Ponty, *Phenomenology of Perception,* p. 327.
14. Ibid., pp. 280–98.

6. Intimate and Alien Things

1. Emmanuel Levinas, *Totality and Infinity,* trans. Alphonso Lingis (The Hague:
Martinus Nijhoff, 1979), pp. 160–61.
2. Henri Wallon, *Les origines de la pensée chez l'enfant,* vol. 2 (Paris: Presses Univer-
sitaires de France, 1945), pp. 382–402.
3. Emmanuel Levinas, *Existence and Existents,* trans. Alphonso Lingis (The Hague:
Martinus Nijhoff, 1978), p. 38.
4. Emmanuel Levinas, *Totality and Infinity,* p. 162.
5. Ibid., p. 131.
6. J. M. G. Le Clézio, *Exstase matérielle* (Paris: Gallimard, 1967).

7. Action with Things

1. Friedrich Nietzsche, *Thus Spoke Zarathustra,* in *The Portable Nietzsche,* trans.
Walter Kaufmann (New York: Viking, 1971), III, 30, 2.
2. *Birdy,* a film directed by Alan Parker, starring Matthew Modine and Nicolas Cage
(1984).
3. Emmanuel Levinas, *Totality and Infinity,* trans. Alphonso Lingis (The Hague:
Martinus Nijhoff, 1979), p. 167.

8. The Production of Purposes

1. "Scarcely an object, [the glassy plastic drinking cup] is so superbly universal
Hegel might have halloed at it. Made of a substance found nowhere in nature, manufactured by processes equally unnatural and strange, it is the complete and expert arti-
fact. Then packaged in sterilized stacks as though it weren't a thing at all by itself, this
light, translucent emptiness is so utterly identical to the other items in its package, the
other members of its class, it might almost be space. Sloganless—it has no message—
often not even the indented hallmark of its maker. It is an abstraction acting as a glass,
and resists individuation perfectly, because you can't crimp its rim or write on it or
poke it full of pencil holes—it will shatter first, rather than submit—so there is no way,
after a committee meeting, a church sup or reception (its ideal locales), to know one
from the other, as it won't discolor, stain, craze, chip, but simply safeguards the world
from its contents until both the flat Coke or cold coffee and their cup are disposed of.
It is a decendental object. It cannot have a history. It has disappeared entirely into its

function. It is completely what it does, except that what it does, it does as a species. Of itself it provides no experience, and scarcely of its kind. Even a bullet gets uniquely scarred. Still, this *shotte*, this *nebech*, is just as much a cultural object, and just as crystalline in its way, as our golden bowl, and is without flaws, and costs nothing, and demands nothing, and is one of the ultimate wonders of the universe of *dreck*—the world of neutered things. It *is* perfect. That is Arnold's word.

"Nevertheless, the perfections of this plain clear plastic cup perversely deny it perfection. Since it is nothing but its use, its existence is otherwise ignored. It is not worth a rewash. It is not worth another look, a feel, a heft. It has been desexed. Thus indifference is encouraged. Consumption is encouraged. Convenience is encouraged. Castoffs are multiplied, and our world is already full of the unwanted and used up. Its rim lies along the lip like the edge of a knife. That quality is also ignored and insensitivity encouraged. It is a servant, but it has none of the receptivity of artistic material, and in that sense it does not serve; its absences are everywhere. Since, like an overblown balloon, it has as much emptiness as it can take, it is completely its shape, and because it totally contains, it is estranged from what it holds. Thus dissociation is encouraged. Poured into such a vessel, wine moans for a certain moment, and then is silent; its color pales, its bouquet fades, it becomes pop; yet there is a pallid sadness in its modest mimicry of the greater goblets, in its pretense to perfect nothingness, in its ordinary evil, since it is no Genghis Khan, or Coriolanus, but a discreet and humble functionary, simply doing its job as it has been designed and directed to do, like the other members of the masses, and disappearing with less flutter than leaves." William H. Gass, *Habitations of the Word* (New York: Simon & Schuster, 1985), pp. 204–205.

9. The Pageantry of Things

1. "The most lucid writer finds himself in the world bewitched by its images. He speaks in enigmas, by allusions, by suggestion, in equivocations, as though he moved in a world of shadows, as though he lacked the force to arouse realities, as though he could not go to them without wavering, as though, bloodless and awkward, he always committed himself further than he had decided to do, as though he is spilling half the water he is bringing us." Emmanuel Levinas, *Collected Philosophical Papers*, trans. Alphonso Lingis (Dordrecht, The Netherlands: Martinus Nijhoff, 1987), p. 13.

10. Phantom Equator

1. Jean-François Lyotard, "L'obédience," in *L'inhumain* (Paris: Galilée, 1988), pp. 177–92.

2. "I can at night retain the general setting of the daytime, as when I grope about in my flat, and in any case night is included in the general framework of nature, and there is something reassuring and earthly even in pitch black space." Maurice Merleau-Ponty, *Phenomenology of Perception*, trans. Colin Smith (London: Routledge & Kegan Paul, 1979), p. 284.

3. Ibid., p. 285.

4. Jean-Paul Sartre, *Imagination*, trans. Forrest Williams (Ann Arbor: University of Michigan Press, 1962), pp. 85–104.

5. "Illuminated things can appear to us as though in twilight shapes. Like the unreal, inverted city we find after an exhausting trip, things and beings strike us as though they no longer composed a world, and were swimming in the chaos of their existence. Such is also the case with 'fantastic,' 'hallucinatory' reality in poets like Rimbaud, even when they name the most familiar things and the most accustomed beings. The misunderstood art of certain realist and naturalist novelists, their prefaces and professions of faith notwithstanding, produces the same effect: beings and things that collapse into their 'materiality' are terrifyingly present in their density, weight, and shape. Certain

passages of Huysmans or Zola, the calm and smiling horror of de Maupassant's tales do not only give, as is sometimes thought, a representation 'faithful to' or exceeding reality, but penetrates behind the form which light reveals into that materiality which, far from corresponding to the philosophical materialism of the authors, constitutes the dark background of existence. It makes things appear to us in a night, like the monotonous presence that bears down on us in insomnia." Emmanuel Levinas, *Existence and Existents*, trans. Alphonso Lingis (The Hague: Martinus Nijhoff, 1978), pp. 59–60.

6. Isabelle Eberhardt, *The Oblivion Seekers*, trans. Paul Bowles (San Francisco: City Lights, 1972).

7. Maurice Merleau-Ponty, *Phenomenology of Perception*, p. 287.

8. It is from the order of perceived creation that theodicy ascends to a creator; it is from perceived texts or voices that revealed religion derives its interpretations.

9. Maurice Merleau-Ponty, *Phenomenology of Perception*, p. 343.

10. Ibid., p. 293.

11. Ibid.

12. Ibid.

13. Ibid., p. 294.

14. Ibid., p. 344.

15. Ibid., p. 293. This quite ignores the ways that dreams, though not recollected in diurnal consciousness, recur to elaborate their problems in a succession of reiterated and divergent dreams and also haunt and accent the paths and hollows of the perceived world. For Freud the daytime recollection does not give the dream its existence, but effects its cathexis and neutralizes its powers; dreams not recollected extend their forces into the unavowed but active passions of men of action who "have no time for dreaming" and into the work-absorbed trances of artists.

16. Ibid., p. 293.

17. Ibid., p. 329.

18. Ibid., p. 321.

19. Ibid., pp. 327–28.

20. Ibid., pp. 283–84.

11. The Reasons of the Heart

1. Emmanuel Levinas, *Existence and Existents*, trans. Alphonso Lingis (The Hague: Martinus Nijhoff, 1978), p. 9.

12. Other Passions

1. "We see in another's eyes that they are troubled or unconcerned, caring or uncaring, certain or uncertain, reflective or unreflective, serious or playful, sad or happy, near-focused or far-away focused, noticing us or not, dominant or submissive, friendly or hostile, interested or not, desiring or hating, trusting or distrusting, alert or fatigued, scheming or sincere, surprised or knowing, angry or forgiving." Simon Baron-Cohen, *Mindblindness* (Cambridge, MIT Press, 1995), p. 114.

"Variants of to look include stare, watch, peer, glance, peep, glare, glower, contemplate, and scan. Adverbial modifiers of the verb are frequent. A person can be said to look directly, or askance, overtly, or covertly, boldly, or bashfully, sternly, or mildly, critically, or kindly, or even unseeingly. Among the many idiomatic expressions of metaphors are: he caught my eye, or held my eye, or looked me up and down, or his eyes dropped, or flickered, or his gaze wandered. A person may either cast an eye on, or fasten his eyes on, or look down his nose at. He may steal a glance, give a sidelong glance, or a guarded glance, or have a discerning glance, a piercing glance, or a fixed stare. He may also give a sly look, an open look, or a black look." J. Gibson and A. Pick,

"Perception of another person's looking behavior," *American Journal of Psychology* (1976): 386–87.

2. Georges Bataille, *Inner Experience*, trans. Leslie Anne Boldt (New York: State University of New York Press, 1988), pp. 95–96.

3. Georges Rey, "Functionalism and the Emotions," in Amélie Oksenberg Rorty, ed., *Explaining Emotions* (Berkeley: University of California Press, 1980), pp. 174–75.

13. Face to Face

1. Humans are not hunted by any other beast of prey. The great white, tiger, and mako sharks feed on seals and sea lions, and sometimes mistake surfboard riders for them. They most often lose interest in a human victim after the initial bite. There have been only 100 shark fatalities in Australia during the past 150 years.

15. Erotic Demands

1. "Noble and Bradley (1933) in their study of mating procedures in lizards . . . revealed the astonishing facts that in the species investigated the females have no sexual 'drive' (so that the frequent statement that the male's display 'attracts females' is without foundation), and the male will subject weaker males to his sexual passion as often as females; so it is only because of the constant activity of the males that probably all females become impregnated sooner or later." Susanne K. Langer, *Mind: An Essay on Human Feeling*, abridged ed. (Baltimore: The Johns Hopkins University Press, 1988), p. 192; K. S. Noble and H.T. Bradley, "The mating behaviour of lizards; its bearing on the theory of sexual selection," *Annals of the New York Academy of Sciences* 35 (1933): 25–100.

2. "Obscenity is our name for the uneasiness which upsets the physical state associated with self-possession, with the possession of a recognized and stable individuality." Georges Bataille, *Erotism: Death and Sensuality*, trans. Mary Dalwood (San Francisco: City Lights, 1986), pp. 17–18.

3. Ibid., p. 86.

16. The Summons of Death

1. "I believe in resurrection; better, I see, I know, I experience death as a commencement and not as an end. Far from destroying us, it produces us; behind us, in us, it pushes us on into culture, usages, speech, thought, hominity, humanity; behind me, in me, it pushes me to a work at all hours of the day and night. . . . Everything comes from it while we seem to go to it. History has changed its orientation and time has changed the direction of its flow. It no longer flows toward us but flows from death." Michel Serres, *L'hermaphrodite* (Paris: Flammarion, 1987), p. 113.

2. Michel Tournier, *Friday, or The Other Island*, trans. Norman Denny (Middlesex, England: Penguin, 1974), p. 162.

3. Omar Cabezas, *Canción de Amor para los Hombres* (Managua: Editorial Neuva Nicaragua, 1988).

4. Friedrich Nietzsche, *The Gay Science*, trans. Walter Kaufmann (New York: Viking, 1974), 326.

17. The Death of Strangers

1. "Odd to think that the piece of you I know best is already dead. The cells on the surface of your skin are thin and flat without blood-vessels or nerve-endings. Dead cells, thickest on the palms of your hands and the soles of your feet. Your sepulchral

body, offered to me in the past tense, protects your soft centre from the intrusions of the outside world. I am one such intrusion, stroking you with necrophiliac obsession, loving the shell laid out before me.

"The dead you is constantly being rubbed away by the dead me. Your cells fall and flake away, fodder to dust mites and bed bugs. Your droppings support colonies of life that graze on skin and hair no longer wanted." Jeanette Winterson, *Written on the Body* (New York: Knopf, 1993), p. 123.

2. Maurice Blanchot told us recently of a Nazi commando, during the bitterest days of the battle for France, arriving at a chateau and ordering all those inside to come out and lining up his men to fire upon them. In the chateau was the young heir, who had been spared recruitment when the war broke out and had not gone to join the underground resistance when France had been defeated. Now he acts; he stands ready to die and asks that the women be sent back inside. The Nazi lieutenant assents. The young heir now knows the extraordinary lightness with which he rejoins his country-men falling under Nazi bullets. But just then gunfire breaks out of a guerrilla assault nearby. The Nazi lieutenant officer departs to reconnoitre, and his men holding their rifles signal that the young heir make his escape. Hidden in the woods, he watches all night the combat on all sides, on all sides the farmhouses go up in flames. Later he learns that three young men, farmers' sons whose only fault was their youth, had been shot. Although the Nazi lieutenant officer was enraged when he came back to find the young heir escaped, he did not set fire to the chateau.

It was then no doubt, Blanchot writes, that began for the young heir the torment of injustice. The ecstasy he had known before the firing squad was no more, giving way to the realization that he was alive because he belonged to the aristocratic class. Maurice Blanchot, *L'instant de ma mort* (Paris: Fata Morgana, 1994).

18. Walkabout

1. "I arrive in a village for my holidays, happy to leave my work and my everyday surroundings. I settle in the village, and it becomes the centre of my life. The low level of the river, gathering in the maize crop or nutting are events for me. But if a friend comes to me bringing news from Paris, or if the press and radio tell me that war threat-ens, I feel an exile in the village, shut off from real life, pushed far away from every-thing. Our body and our perception always summon us to take as the centre of the world that environment which they present us. But this environment is not necessarily that of our own life. I can 'be somewhere else' while staying here, and if I am kept far away from what I love, I feel out of touch with real life. The Bovary mentality and certain forms of home-sickness are examples of life which has become decentred." Maurice Merleau-Ponty, *Phenomenology of Perception*, trans. Colin Smith (London: Rout-ledge & Kegan Paul, 1979), pp. 285–86.

2. The psychoanalysis of dreams and of wit, acts manqués, déjà vu, premonitions, etc., and of psychedelic visions, the syntactic, semantic, rhetorical analyses of myths, the economic-political analysis of ritual are representations whose order is commanded by the ordinance in these unpracticable fields. They, no more than physics, do not impose a simply conceptual order upon a medley of nonperceptual sensations. But they also insert the ordinances of these unpracticable spaces into the coordinates of the practicable world, and thus occult the imperative force of their ordinances which de-part from the practicable world. Thus while our aesthetics is often concerned with delineating the specifically musical imperatives that command classical and baroque and Balinese music, our cultural anthropology does not represent the specific impera-tives that lead the Zen adept beyond the ordinances of the civil society. It would be in an aesthetic practice that our culture forms representations of the ordinances that gov-ern dreams, the imperative destiny that conducts an individual into the practicable and

unpracticable vistas of his nomadic vital space. We are thinking now of Faulkner, in *The Wild Palms* and *The Old Man.*

19. Importance, Urgency, Immediacy

1. "In the ethical case, I do think, and I think it is warranted to think, that a person who has a sense of human brotherhood is better than a person who lacks a sense of human brotherhood. A person who is capable of thinking for himself about how to live is better than a person who has lost or never developed the capacity to think for himself about how to live; but, whether the question be about single-case probability or about ethics, I don't *know how I know* these things. These are cases in which I find that I have to say: 'I have reached bedrock and this is where my spade is turned.'" Hilary Putnam, *The Many Faces of Realism* (LaSalle, IL: Open Court, 1987), p. 85.

20. Images of the Imperative

1. Immanuel Kant, *Kritik der praktischen Vernunft, Kant's gesammelte Schriften,* Königlich Preussischen Akademie der Wissenschaften, Bd. V (Berlin: G. Reimer, 1913), p. 75; trans. Lewis White Beck, *Critique of Practical Reason* (Indianapolis: Bobbs-Merrill, 1956), p. 78.

2. Ibid., p. 23; trans., p. 21.

3. " . . . the man who has a moral motivation for doing things of the non-self-regarding sort, has a disposition or general motive for doing things of that sort; whereas the self-interested man has no such steady motive, for it will always only be luck if what benefits others happens to coincide with what, by the limited criteria of simple self-interest, happens to benefit him." Bernard Williams, *Morality: An Introduction to Ethics* (New York: Harper Torchbooks, 1972), pp. 73–74.

4. "It is in fact absolutely impossible by experience to discern with complete certainty a single case in which the maxim of an action, however much it may conform to duty, rested solely on moral grounds and on the conception of one's duty." *Grundlegung zur Metaphysik der Sitten, Kant's gesammelte Schriften,* Königlich Preussischen Akademie der Wissenschaften, Bd. IV (Berlin: G. Reimer, 1911), pp. 406–407; trans. Lewis White Beck, *Foundations of the Metaphysics of Morals* (New York: Macmillan, 1985), p. 23.

5. *Die Metaphysik der Sitten, I. Metaphysische Anfangsgrunde der Rechtslehre, Kant's gesammelte Schriften,* Königlich Preussischen Akademie der Wissenschaften, Bd. VI (Berlin: G. Reimer, 1914), p. 246; trans. John Ladd, *The Metaphysical Elements of Justice* (Indianapolis: Bobbs-Merrill, 1965), pp. 52, 53.

6. Immanuel Kant, *Kritik der Urtheilskraft, Kant's gesammelte Schriften,* Königlich Preussischen Akademie der Wissenschaften, Bd. V (Berlin: G. Reimer, 1913), p. 431; trans. Werner S. Pluhar, *Critique of Judgment* (Indianapolis: Hackett, 1987), p. 318.

7. Immanuel Kant, *Metaphysik der Sitten,* p. 246; *The Metaphysical Elements of Justice,* p. 52.

8. *Grundlegung,* p. 431; *Foundations of the Metaphysics of Morals,* p. 49.

9. "The same subject, which, on the other hand, is conscious also of his own existence as a thing-in-itself, also views his existence . . . as determinable only by laws which he gives to himself through reason." *Kritik der praktischen Vernunft,* p. 97; *Critique of Practical Reason,* p. 101.

10. Immanuel Kant, *Kritik der Urtheilskraft; Critique of Judgment,* ¶ 59.

11. "All actions relating to the right of other men are unjust if their maxim is not consistent with publicity." Immanuel Kant, *Zum ewigen Frieden, Kant's gesammelte Schriften,* Königlich Preussischen Akademie der Wissenschaften, Bd. VIII (Berlin: G. Reimer, 1912), p. 381; trans. Lewis White Beck, *On Perpetual Peace* (Indianapolis: Bobbs-Merrill, 1957), p. 47.

12. Immanuel Kant, *Kritik der praktischen Vernunft*, p. 88; *Critique of Practical Reason*, p. 91.

13. Ibid.

14. Immanuel Kant, *Die Metaphysik der Sitten, Kant's gesammelte Schriften*, Bd. VI (Berlin: Königlich Preussischen Akademie der Wissenschaften, 1911), p. 440; trans. James Ellington, *The Metaphysical Principles of Virtue* (Indianapolis: Bobbs-Merrill, 1964), p. 103.

21. The Theoretical and Practical Uses of Reason

1. "Many aspects of tanning, dyeing, and the production of adhesives, rubber, and explosives do not correspond to the laws of classical chemistry. Furthermore, special laws must be assumed to explain how agricultural soil can retain nutrient salts, which according to classical chemical and physical laws should be washed away freely by the groundwater." Ludwik Fleck, *Genesis and Development of a Scientific Fact*, trans. Fred Bradley and Thaddeus J. Trenn (Chicago: University of Chicago Press, 1979), p. 29.

2. Kant, on the contrary, finds that "when we discover that two or more heterogeneous empirical laws of nature can be unified under one principle that comprises them both, the discovery does give rise to a quite noticeable pleasure. . . . [W]e would certainly dislike it if nature were presented in a way that told us in advance that if we investigated nature slightly beyond the commonest experience we would find its laws so heterogeneous that our understanding could not unify nature's particular laws under universal empirical laws." *Kritik der Urtheilskraft, Kant's gesammelte Schriften*, Königlich Preussischen Akademie der Wissenschaften, Bd. V (Berlin: G. Reimer, 1913), pp. 187–88; trans. Werner S. Pluhar, *Critique of Judgment* (Indianapolis: Hackett, 1987), pp. 27–28. Paul Feyerabend sees here a base intent "to please their lower instincts, their craving for intellectual security in the form of clarity, precision, 'objectivity', 'truth' . . . ," *Against Method* (London: Verso: 1978), pp. 27–28.

3. "Hence the commonsense realist can plausibly argue that our natural prior commitment to the view of physical things as sensibly or phenomenally propertied is a necessary precondition of our even entertaining the view of scientific realism which would deny them such properties. . . ." P. F. Strawson, *Skepticism and Naturalism: Some Varieties* (New York: Columbia University Press, 1985), p. 44.

22. The Rational and the Required

1. Friedrich Nietzsche, *The Gay Science*, trans. Walter Kaufmann (New York: Random House, 1974), sec. 354.

ALPHONSO LINGIS is Professor of Philosophy at Pennsylvania State University. His publications include *The Community of Those Who Have Nothing in Common*; *Abuses*; and *Foreign Bodies*.